Date Due

YALE PUBLICATIONS IN ECONOMICS
SOCIAL SCIENCE AND GOVERNMENT

———————

III
UNION-MANAGEMENT COÖPERATION
ON THE RAILROADS

# Union-Management Coöperation on the Railroads

By Louis Aubrey Wood

Associate Professor of Economics in the University of Oregon

New Haven · Yale University Press
London · Humphrey Milford · Oxford University Press
1931

## THE WILLIAM McKEAN BROWN
## MEMORIAL PUBLICATION FUND

THE present volume is the seventh work published by the Yale University Press on the William McKean Brown Memorial Publication Fund. This Foundation was established by gifts from members of his family to Yale University in memory of William McKean Brown, of Newcastle, Pennsylvania, who was not only a leader in the development of his community, but who also served the commonwealth as state senator and later as lieutenant-governor of Pennsylvania.

To Lenore Aileen

# Preface

PREPARATION of this book has been rendered possible by the fact that the author was the holder of a Sterling Research Fellowship in Yale University for the academic year, 1928–29. The task of investigation necessary to its compilation was performed under the direction of the Faculty of the Graduate School of Yale University. Between forty and fifty maintenance of equipment stations on the railroads committed to union-management coöperation were visited, in order that the picture presented and conclusions arrived at in the book might be more nearly representative of actual conditions. Many data were also gathered at the central, regional, and divisional headquarters of the railroads upon which the study was conducted, and, by means of personal interviews, from the general and local officers of the trade unions subscribing to the coöperative plan.

While the use of a considerable amount of technical terminology has been unavoidable in the text, a steady endeavor has been made properly to interpret this for the benefit of readers with no widely expanded knowledge of railroad policies and practices. At the same time, it is hoped that the work may have been written in a manner scientifically detailed and definitive enough to meet the requirements of transportation experts, leaders of labor, and students who may have a particular interest in the field of industrial relations.

Acknowledgment is made of heavy obligations to Winthrop More Daniels, Professor of Transportation in Yale University, and former member of the Interstate Commerce Commission, who assisted in planning the investigation, placed a rich store of information generously at the author's disposal, and critically read large portions of the manuscript. A debt of gratitude is also expressed to Edgar Stevenson Furniss, Dean of the Graduate School of Yale University, for valuable guidance when questions relating to the book's form and substance were under discussion, and to Kent Tenney Healy, Assistant Professor of Transportation in Yale University, for advice of a technical character.

It is deeply regretted that the individual contributions of many others who have helped forward the investigation cannot be here set down as a matter of record. A special tribute of thanks, however, is due to the following persons for data supplied and courtesies extended: Otto S. Beyer, Jr., consulting engineer, Railway Employees' Department, American Federation of Labor; A. G. Walther, assistant supervisor of shops, Baltimore & Ohio Railroad; A. J. Thomas, assistant to the general supervisor of shop methods, Canadian National Railway System; William Walliser, vice-president in charge of personnel, Chicago & North Western Railway; J. T. Gillick, vice-president of the operating department, Chicago, Milwaukee, St. Paul & Pacific Railroad; Florence C. Thorne, secretary to the president of the American Federation of Labor; Martin F. Ryan, general president, Brotherhood Railway Carmen of America; Peter J. Conlon, general vice-president, International Association of Machinists; William F. Kramer, general secretary-treasurer, International Brotherhood of Blacksmiths, Drop Forgers, and Helpers; James M. Burns, secretary-treasurer, Railway Employees' Department, American Federation of Labor; Laura A. Thompson, librarian, United States Department of Labor; and Harlow S. Person, managing director, the Taylor Society.

L. A. W.

University of Oregon,
    December, 1930.

# Contents

# Chapter I

## Scope of the Coöperative Movement on the Railroads

QUITE a leading feature of economic development in more recent years has been the higher estimate placed in many quarters upon the value of wageworkers' ideas in relation to the conduct of industry. This has brought an important change in the status of the workers affected. With the onset of the machine age and the introduction of capitalistic forms of production, it became traditional that management alone should plan the methods by which work should be accomplished, and that those who hired for wages should, within the sphere allotted to them, concern themselves unquestioningly with its performance. To be consulted, therefore, at least in a systematized manner, when machines were being secured and lined up, processes coördinated, materials bought, or additional services projected, was foreign to the workers' experience. Nowhere in these days was management, perhaps, functionally more self-sufficient than on the average American railroad.

Daniel Willard, president of the Baltimore & Ohio Railroad, has recounted an incident of his early career which casts some light on the separation of interest existing between management and men on the common carriers of America a little over a generation ago.[1] He had been taken on the pay roll as a helper at the Lyndonville, Vermont, repair shop of what was then the short-line Connecticut & Passumpsic River Railroad. Hardly had he accustomed himself to working in the shop before he discovered something that he thought should be done but apparently was being neglected. Youthful and uninitiated into the conventions prevailing in railroad shops at the time, he was ready to express

[1] Briefly referred to in an address by Daniel Willard before the National Civic Federation at New York City on February 17, 1927, and reported in *Industrial Management*, May, 1927, p. 263.

his views to a representative of management on the subject, when checked by the friendly counsel of an older associate. "Sonny," said the older man, "you had better keep still. When they want your advice they will ask you for it, and I wouldn't volunteer any advice." From that moment Daniel Willard began to realize that the workers in the shop were expected to serve in obedience to orders and practically never to advance suggestions. They had learned, as had workers elsewhere on American railroads and in other employments, that, if they desired to get along well with management, they had best keep silent on matters of industrial control.

## Meaning and Extent of the Problem for Study.

THE movement to give wageworkers in America a responsible share in the management of industry first took definite shape about 1910–11, and spread with considerable rapidity during the period of the European War. A like movement which had begun a few years previously in Great Britain received a marked impetus when, in October, 1917, the government of that country accepted a report of its so-called Whitley Committee for incorporation into its program for post-war reconstruction.[2] The recommendations of this committee, it has generally been acknowledged, had an important influence in molding opinion in America with respect to the technique for joint dealing between management and workers that might advisedly be adopted to bring about a more democratic control of industry. The Whitley Committee urged that a national council be established for the whole of an industry, a district council for each of its territorial divisions, and a works committee for each of its individual plants. Management and men should have equal representation on these bodies, before one or another of which it was hoped that all matters of common, industrial interest would eventually arise for discussion. The Whitley plan was formulated for application only where trade-

[2] Cf. Earl J. Miller, *Workmen's Representation in Industrial Government*, pp. 9–36; W. Jett Lauck, *Political and Industrial Democracy*, pp. 132–134.

unions were organized in British industries. Works council movements, it may be pointed out, which sprang up in Germany, Czechoslovakia, and other European countries after the war have also functioned mainly on a trade-union basis.

In America, on the contrary, hundreds of employing companies, having but partial or, more often, no contractual relations with organized labor, have within the past ten to twenty years signified a willingness to devise means whereby their workers might be given a share of managerial authority.[3] The title, "plans of employee representation," has been selected to describe the diversity of arrangements for mutual benefit made by these companies with their respective groups of workers. Such plans have operated almost entirely in the single plant or limited number of plants belonging to each company, where a works committee or council has been the basic unit of organization, with which in some instances may be allied departmental or shop committees for sections of a plant. A general joint council may be set up embracing representatives from the works councils in different plants. A few companies have adopted instead a "senate-house" system of representation which calls for a type of industrial government according to a legislative model.

Details will be furnished in chapter xx of the way in which, by mutual consent of manufacturers and trade-unions, forms of coöperative control were instituted in the American garment industries during 1910–11. In 1918, the executive council of the American Federation of Labor declared itself in favor of the principles of democratic, industrial management already enunciated by the Whitley Committee.[4] Thereafter, as further types of joint arrangement were consummated in the United States and Canada, permitting to organized workers a share of managerial responsibility, the term, union-management coöperation, was coined to apply to all plans with which the trade-unions were

[3] Cf. Ernest Richmond Burton, *Employee Representation*, pp. 25 ff.
[4] Cf. *Report of the Proceedings of the Thirty-eighth Annual Convention of the American Federation*, pp. 83–85.

identified. One of these plans, as it has become effective on a number of American railroad systems will be the chief topic for study in the following pages. National councils, works councils, and shop committees have each been employed under varying circumstances where union-management coöperation has been practiced.

In whatever industry it has been introduced, union-management coöperation has depended for its outworking upon some form of joint agreement between management, representing a business corporation on the one hand, and one or more trade-unions on the other, for the observance of certain coöperative practices. In general, through these practices and the spirit which they engender, it is expected that more harmonious relations will subsist between the parties to the agreement, that economic benefits will accrue to the industry, and more satisfactory employment conditions prevail. As established on the railroads, no claim is made that coöperation can ever be a panacea for all existing industrial evils. Wages and working conditions on the railroads concerned are still determined by the regular trade agreement or agreements, negotiated by the employing company with its workers' representatives, and coöperation is only intended to enter in the rôle of a corrective agency to make industrial relations more effective and wholesome. The will to coöperate, it is stated, is due to an inclination on the part of management and men to act in concert. So long as that will is present, it is believed that industrial relations should be better, and in a measure economic ills should be righted. An urge to the acceptance of coöperation and a guaranty of its successful continuance on the railroads have been provided, it is admitted, by the fact that both the employing companies and their workers have been confident that material gains will accrue as a result of their participation.

The maintenance of equipment department, also commonly known as the mechanical department, was the place of origin and until now has remained the chief place of development of union-management coöperation on the railroads. This department is that important section of a railroad's operating department which is constantly engaged in keeping its locomotives, train cars, and other moving units of equipment in a proper state of repair. It is proposed to devote by far the larger portion of this volume to a consideration of the plan of coöperation as it has come into existence and at present functions in the mechanical department of the various carriers that have adopted it. But, since the movement has been officially established in two other sections of the operating department on the Baltimore & Ohio Railroad, namely, in its transportation department and in the department of maintenance of way and structures, and has also been set up in the last-named department on the Canadian National Railway System, some account of these developments will be reserved for special treatment in chapter xix. A general summary will be offered in chapter xx of types of union-management coöperation that have developed elsewhere in the field of transportation and in the non-transportation industries.

At this writing, a plan of union-management coöperation has been officially authorized, and, with the concurrence of accredited labor organizations, is actively in effect on four major systems of rail transportation in the United States and Canada, having together about one-sixth of the total combined railroad mileage of the two countries. First of these systems to be mentioned should be that controlled by the Baltimore & Ohio Railroad Company, America's oldest common carrier, which began to test out a coöperative plan in its mechanical department in 1923, and accepted it for this and two other sections of its operating department the following year. It has also brought its subsidiary, the Baltimore & Ohio Chicago Terminal Railroad Company, within the scope of the movement. In 1925, the Canadian National Railway Company introduced a form of union-management coöperation in its mechanical department which is effective now on all the lines that it owns and operates except those of the Central Vermont Railway Incorporated, a subsidiary under independent management with mileage in the New England States, and those of the Duluth, Winnipeg & Pacific Railway Company, a directly managed subsidiary in Minnesota. In other words co-operation is practiced in Canadian National Railway Company's mechanical department everywhere in the Dominion of Canada, on the short strip of mileage which it directly operates in New Hampshire and Maine terminating at Portland, and on the lines of its directly managed subsidiary, the Grand Trunk Western Railroad Company, with mileage west of the Detroit River. Extension of coöperation to its department of maintenance of way and structures was begun by the Canadian National Railway Company in 1929. A plan of systematized coöperation was adopted for its mechanical department by the Chicago & North Western Railway Company in 1925 which at present functions on all its directly operated lines, although not on its subsidiary, the Chicago, St. Paul, Minneapolis & Omaha Railway Company. The latest carrier to indorse the movement has been the Chicago, Milwaukee, St. Paul & Pacific Railroad Company which officially established a plan of coöperation in its mechanical department in 1926.

*Relationship of the Coöperation Plan to Scientific Management.*

In assuming the obligations required of them under the plan of union-management coöperation, the railroad labor organizations participating have taken up a new position with respect to the tenets of what has been known as scientific management in industry. This fact may be considered a matter of prime importance in view of the past attitudes of organized labor toward scientific management. During a period of from 30 to 40 years or more, groups of industrial engineers have been seeking by allegedly scientific methods of analysis and classification to set up a body of principles for the more efficient conduct of business. These have been applied in multifarious ways by business executives, each having in mind the needs of his particular enterprise, sometimes with expert knowledge but oftener perhaps with a limited idea of what scientific management really has meant. In its milder phases, scientific management, among other things, has implied a standardization of the productive agencies of industrial plants and of their methods of procuring and handling materials. Its advocates have stood for: careful attention to machine performance; elimination of waste motion in industrial processing; the introduction of labor-saving devices; arrangement of equipment in sequence in order to economize in time; the development of systems of planning, routing, and scheduling of work; efficient buying of materials; and improvement in means of storing and delivering materials. The more radical innovations of scientific management have been: time study, or the determination (it may be by stop watch observation) of the time that an operation or set of operations should take; task setting, or an assignment of the amount of work that should be done in a given time; modes of wage payment based on time study, whereby piecework rates, bonuses, or premiums are paid; and the functionalization of business which for the workers has implied a minute specialization of operations.

At times organized labor has been bitter in its denunciation of scientific management, especially in the days immediately antecedent to the European War. Labor's attack, however, has been mainly leveled against what it has considered to be the extremer tenets of scientific management, which labor claims has tended to make each industrial worker "a mere instrument of production," forcing him as a reward for his effort to depend upon the employer's conception of fairness.[5] The time study, task setting, wage fixing methods of scientific management have been labeled "a cunningly devised speeding up and sweating system." It has aimed a blow, has been labor's assertion, at the foundations of mechanical education, transferring the workers' traditional craft knowledge to management, and in the meantime augmenting the ranks of the unskilled.[6] Its much-heralded incentives in industry

[5] Robert Franklin Hoxie, *Scientific Management and Labor,* pp. 169–170.
[6] *Ibid.,* pp. 16–17.

have only in the long run brought more work for the same or lower pay.

But more recently the gap in opinion between organized labor and the exponents of scientific management has perceptibly lessened. Industrial engineers have been slowly revising certain of the original doctrines of scientific management after proof of their fallibility has been rendered in actual practice. They have learned that an essential quality of flexibility may be lost in any industry when it becomes too highly standardized and function-alized. They have agreed to a more reasonable application of the standards governing time study, task setting, and other formulae of scientific management, than would orthodox believers of an earlier period. Most important, they have rediscovered the value of personality in industry, admitting that its effectiveness may suffer if too rigidly confined in a mechanical system. They have, therefore, concluded that if engineering standards are to be pro-gressively of service in business, they must recognize the existence of dynamic conditions and the constant play of human factors.

On the other hand, signs have not been wanting that organized labor has been modifying its opinions of scientific management. This change in viewpoint began when trade-union leaders during the war period sat on committees with men holding the principles of scientific management and gained a new idea of their motives.[7] In 1920, Samuel Gompers, president of the American Federation of Labor, joined with two advocates of scientific management in editing a book entitled *Labor Management and Production.* Ar-ticles commending features in the program of scientific manage-ment have been given space in trade-union journals. Passages in the speeches of union officials would indicate the burial of much of labor's former antipathy to the work of the industrial engi-neer.[8] In April, 1927, a trade-union conference on elimination of

[7] For a discussion of labor's changing attitude toward scientific manage-ment, read various chapters in *Scientific Management in American Industry,* published under authority of the Taylor Society.

[8] See reports of addresses delivered by President William Green, of the American Federation of Labor, as follows: "Labor's Ideals concerning Man-

waste in industry was convened at Philadelphia, Pennsylvania, under the auspices of the Central Labor Union and the Labor College of that city. It was attended by specially invited business executives and industrial engineers who shared the field with representatives of labor in the discussions.[9] It is evident that the rank and file of trade-unionists are being slowly instructed that, even as it was folly for labor in the past to oppose the introduction of machinery, so it would be equally a mistake for them to withstand a reasonable standardization of productive processing and coördination of functions in industry. Rather the policy should be for them to help control, in so far as they may, the application of scientific changes which are inevitable. Naturally, organized labor has put the stamp of its approval more readily upon the milder proposals of scientific management. In large measure it still looks upon time study with distrust, particularly when the stop watch is employed, and is inclined to regard systems of incentive wage payment as unfair.

As procedure has developed under the plan of union-management coöperation, the railroad organizations indorsing it have unofficially, but very definitely, acknowledged that the tenets of scientific management contain much that is worthy of their approbation. Their representatives have not been able to treat with railroad administrators on a coöperative basis, as will presently appear in this volume, unless they have been prepared to discuss

agement," before a joint meeting of the Taylor Society and the Management Section of the American Society of Mechanical Engineers: *Bulletin of the Taylor Society,* December, 1925, pp. 241–246; "The New and Advanced Position of Organized Labor," before the Chicago Forum Council, *Industrial Management,* April, 1926, pp. 221–224; and "The Problems which Modern Trade Unionism Confronts," before the Harvard Union, Harvard University, *American Federationist,* April, 1925, pp. 225–232. Also see address by Matthew Woll, "Educational Training for Industry," before the annual meeting of the American Society of Mechanical Engineers, 1926, reported in *American Photo-engraver,* February, 1927, pp. 195–198.

[9] The papers read at this conference have been published by the American Federation of Labor in a pamphlet entitled *Trade Union Conference on Elimination of Waste in Industry,* 1927. Four of the papers presented may be found in the *Bulletin of the Taylor Society,* June, 1927.

issues in which the principles of scientific management have been involved. Economies, traceable to coöperative effort, have in a great many instances been only possible of achievement through dependence upon those principles. In fact, one craft union, as will be further explained in chapter vii, accepted the leadership of a trained engineer when it began to foster the coöperative movement, and subsequently, in alliance with other crafts represented in a system federation, gave him extensive supervisory powers when the movement was first put on trial at a local railroad repair point. This engineer was in 1924 taken into the employ of the Railway Employees' Department of the American Federation of Labor when it sanctioned the venture into coöperation on behalf of all the mechanical craft unions affiliated with it. So far in their experiences with coöperation, the unions have had no occasion to state what reservations they might be inclined to make if asked to accept the program of scientific management in its entirety. It is probable that, were the whole program submitted to them, a debatable issue that would arise between them and advocates of scientific management would be with reference to the systems of incentive wage payment which the latter prefer. One carrier had a task and bonus plan of wage payment in effect on a portion of its lines when it embraced coöperation. This plan and the manner in which coöperation might function together with systems of incentive wage payment will be discussed in chapter xviii.

### *Economic Compulsion to Maintain Equipment.*

WHILE the general reader may know that a railroad keeps its locomotives and train cars in condition by repair operations performed at shops, enginehouses, and other points on its lines, he may be pardoned if he has only a limited idea of how such work is actually carried on. Apart from what has been written on the subject in technical dissertations, the literature of transportation has been rather barren in its treatment of the activities of the maintenance of equipment department of American railroads. Yet the reader would hardly be competent to pass judgment upon the accomplishments of union-management coöperation in the maintenance of equipment department unless he should have a fairly detailed knowledge of the way in which it conducts its industrial operations. For the benefit, therefore, of those who would gain this desired information several preparatory chapters have been introduced,[10] in which, among other matters relating to the maintenance of equipment department will be discussed: its amenability to federal government regulations; the distribution of its plant and other facilities and its main industrial processes; its system of administrative control and worker classification; and the structure and policies of the labor organizations that have established themselves within its bounds.

A railroad company contracts to receive goods or passengers at a starting point, to haul them a specified distance, and to deliver them in reasonable security at the point of destination. In the performance of these services it must employ moving units of equipment to complete the haul agreed upon over fixed rails laid on a permanent roadbed. As a matter of wisdom it must give continuous attention to the state of repair of the rails and roadbed over which it operates its equipment and of the buildings that for one purpose or another have been located along its right of way. It is equally important that it should adequately maintain all its train cars, locomotives, and other moving units of equipment that provide means of carriage or motive power. Technically, maintenance of equipment connotes a restoration to form either by repairs when steps are taken to correct breakages or wear, or by renewals when complete and entirely new equipment parts are substituted for old. For the sake of simplicity, however, in this volume, as labor is mainly employed at repairs, all work done in the mechanical department will be classified indiscriminately under that heading.

Economic compulsion is the main factor which determines the

10 Viz., ii–v inclusive.

practices of railroads in maintaining their equipment. No carrier can long retain its patrons' business under competitive conditions unless it meets their current needs. It must be prompt in supplying adequate facilities for its shippers, and afford safe and comfortable, and it may be, luxurious, accommodation for its passenger traffic. To complete its hauls without detentions it must keep its motive power in a proper state of efficiency. In other words, a carrier is being constantly forced to recondition its moving units of equipment by the demands of traffic. When earnings are low it may successfully defer its maintenance for a time, yet will eventually have to catch up with the situation or else lose valuable patronage. Some roads are in the habit of allowing their equipment to travel in a chronic state of undermaintenance on sections of their lines where they possess more or less of a business monopoly, but this cannot be regarded as a sound economic policy. Because of the peculiarities of rail traffic, maintenance of equipment expenses are regularly high. The average locomotive has from 300 to 400 different parts, chiefly of metal composition. Of enormous weight, and often moving at great speed, it is borne with unceasing jar, impact, and friction on cast-iron wheels along a steel highway. Seldom is a locomotive housed at the end of a journey without requiring some repairs, and periodically it must be brought in for overhauling. Train cars, which are roofed or unroofed vehicles also consisting of several hundred parts, are subjected, as they move in traffic, to all the rough jolting and strains and stresses of the haul. Outlay for maintenance of equipment on Class I carriers in the United States, that is, on all roads having an operating revenue of $1,000,000 or more, comprised, in 1928, 26.4 per cent of their total operating expenses.

Still, there would be much wider divergences in policy between carriers relative to the maintenance of their equipment than at present exist, if policy in that respect were solely shaped by economic compulsion. Additional influences have been at work making for greater uniformity and efficiency in the maintenance of locomotives and train cars on the railroads of the United States and Canada. Train cars are not only used by the company which owns them, but may be delivered for service to the lines of other carriers. Precise rules for the interchange of traffic have been drawn up by the American Railway Association governing the condition of, and repairs to, train cars that leave their home lines. These have been of consequence in helping to systematize practices of repair to train cars on all carriers. Then the United States Government has enacted a series of laws, which, through the codes for inspection and equipment standards that they have allowed the Interstate Commerce Commission to authorize, have exercised a very compelling effect upon the methods employed by carriers in keeping their locomotives and train cars in repair. Regulations largely identical have also been enforced by sanction of commission in the Dominion of Canada. As the importance of these forms of legal compulsion have been given ample recognition under the coöperative movement, they will be treated at length in the following chapter.

## Chapter II

## Legal Compulsion to Maintain Equipment

IN its enactment of legislation affecting the mechanical department on common carriers, the Government of the United States was prompted in the main by humanitarian considerations. It took action, according to its own declaration, "to promote the safety of employees and travelers upon railroads." There was a time when all train cars on the railroads of America were equipped with only hand brakes, operated by a wheel, and brakemen might be seen hurrying from top to top of box cars, releasing or applying these, to govern the speed of a train. A hand-manipulated, link-and-pin device was used for coupling and uncoupling train cars, to attend to which brakemen had to go between moving cars, in constant danger to life or limb. In the early eighties of last century serviceable power brakes and automatic couplers came on the market for railroad equipment, but, on account of the cost of their introduction, were received with some apathy by the carriers. Eventually the question of forcing the adoption of these upon the railroads was broached in Congress, and precipitated a bitter controversy, which was ended in March, 1893, in favor of the advocates of compulsion, when the first safety appliance act was put on the statute books.

Ten years later, the risks of industrial employment on the railroads due to boiler explosions had begun seriously to engage public attention. This was not a new problem, but locomotives were getting larger and their heating surfaces increasing, so that when a boiler in railroad parlance "went out," it took a greater toll of death and human wreckage than heretofore. While a percentage of accidents were no doubt traceable to workers' negligence, the majority of them, it was believed, were occasioned by imperfections in boiler construction, and insufficient repair. The federal government was earnestly solicited, especially by the organized transportation brotherhoods, to lessen this occupational hazard by means of a rigorous system of inspection. The outcome was the approval on February 17, 1911, of an Act of Congress which bade all carriers engaged in interstate commerce to "equip their locomotives with safe and suitable boilers and appurtenances thereto," and which created a federal inspection bureau for its enforcement. By an amendment of March 4, 1915, the machinery and auxiliary parts of the locomotive, and its tender, were brought within the purview of the law. Finally, as the original measure had applied only to steam power, and as electric and internal combustion engines were coming more extensively into use, these were included under its terms by an amendment of 1924. The locomotive inspection system is more meaningful for this study than the safety appliance regulations and, therefore, will be given prior consideration.

### The Plan of Locomotive Inspection.

To administer the act of 1911 a Bureau of Locomotive Inspection was formed with headquarters at Washington, D. C., in charge of a chief inspector and two assistant chief inspectors, appointed by the President of the United States with the advice and consent of the Senate. The country was divided into fifty transportation areas, in each of which was placed a district inspector acting under the superintendence of the bureau. Under authority of the 1924 amendment fifteen additional district inspectors have since been chosen, and assigned to areas where the work is heaviest. Familiarity, so far as is possible, with the exact condition of all locomotives housed or repaired within his territory is expected of a district inspector, whose main duty is to observe whether or not the carriers are maintaining their equipment in keeping with the regulations. He is required at intervals of his own choosing to visit locomotive repair shops, back shops and enginehouses within his jurisdiction, and personally to examine locomotives for defects. As a matter of policy a district inspector will walk in at a repair point unannounced, trusting that the me-

chanical officer in responsible authority has not been forewarned
of his coming. In this way he hopes to find work proceeding under
normal circumstances, and can conduct a fairer investigation.

Each district inspector compiles a tabulated list of all defects
noted at any shop or enginehouse in his territory, on what, for
purposes of record, is known as Form No. 9, which he sends to
the Bureau of Locomotive Inspection. Should he, however, discover a locomotive in an unwarranted state of disrepair, he may
decide to exercise his right to take it out of service. To accomplish this, he submits to the local officer of the carrier a special
notice for repairs, made out on Form No. 5, ordering the locomotive from use until it has been put in a serviceable condition.
Such a locomotive cannot again be dispatched on the line, unless
necessary repairs have been performed upon it, and the chief
mechanical officer of the railroad has certified to its condition
before a notary public. Local officers sincerely dislike to receive
Form No. 5, as it may lead to a reprimand, or ultimately to loss
of rank or position. Nor do railroad companies care to acquire
too many of them, since it will be ruinous in time to their reputation as common carriers.

According to the law of 1911 carriers had three months in
which to file a set of rules and instructions for the inspection of
locomotive boilers on their lines, but at the end of that time many
of them had failed to take action. The Interstate Commerce Commission thereupon ratified a code of rules and instructions drafted
by the Chief Inspector and ordered that it should be the minimum
standard requirement for all carriers in the United States. Upon
the passage of the amendment of 1915, the railroads asked for
another code governing the machinery and auxiliary parts of the
locomotive and its tender, and the commission therefore promulgated this code to become effective on January 1, 1916. Six
months later the rules and instructions of the second code were
renumbered, making it supplementary to the first, so that in
practice officers in the mechanical department of railroads look
upon the two codes as constituting one document. When locomo-

tives propelled by other than steam power were included for inspection by the amendment of 1924, it was deemed necessary that a special code of rules and instructions be framed to cover such types of power. This code, which was published by the Interstate Commerce Commission under order of December 14, 1925, is identical in many points with those employed for steam locomotives, but contains more elaborate rules for the inspection of brake equipment, and introduces explicit regulations concerning electrical devices and internal combustion engines.

Since the above-mentioned codes incorporate only minimum requirements, carriers of their own volition may enforce additional rules and instructions, if it should appear that these will serve as a precaution against accident. Such has been the regular policy of a limited number of railroads. But undoubtedly the workability and effectiveness of the inspection system can best be judged on those roads that are merely satisfied to observe the federal regulations. In order that the condition of their power may be watched from day to day, carriers designate from the ranks of their mechanics at repair points, a certain group who are known as company inspectors. These men who receive a slight addition in pay, but are still rated in working agreements as mechanics, are mainly assigned for motive power inspection from the crafts of machinists, boiler makers, and electricians. Part of the work of company inspectors, as will be noted, consists of attesting to reports demanded by the federal bureau.

## Requirements under the Inspection Codes.

So packed with mechanical details, and so highly specialized in their application are the several codes for motive power inspection, that few beyond experienced railroad men can really understand them. As a matter of fact, even railroad men have sought an interpretation of their meaning. Questions began to accumulate soon after the first code was issued, and became so numerous that in 1921, the Interstate Commerce Commission authorized the pub-

lication of an explanatory handbook "to clarify and render uniform" for the carriers the rules and instructions governing the
inspection and testing of steam locomotives. It is impossible
within the scope of this volume to furnish a complete account of
the inspection codes. Through a few citations, however, from
those affecting steam locomotives, which comprise over 98 per
cent of the motive power operated in the United States, and
through a brief statement of their provisions rendering necessary
the compilation of regular reports of inspection, some idea may
be gained of the extent and significance of inspection practice.[1]

One rule in the codes demands that each locomotive boiler shall
be washed out thoroughly once a month; another, that it shall be
given an annual test under hydrostatic pressure, witnessed by an
official of the company technically conversant with boiler construction; and another, that its interior and bracing shall be
subjected to a minute examination at least once in every four
years. The lagging and jacket shall be removed from a boiler at
least once in five years, and its exterior inspected under hydrostatic pressure. Intricate rules are enforced to discover by ham-
mer-tapping, breakages in the rigid or flexible stay bolts which
hold sheets of the boiler together, and to prevent the clogging of
telltale holes with which flexible stay bolts may be equipped. A
boiler cannot remain in service when two or more stay bolts ad-
jacent to each other in the fire box or combustion chamber are
clogged or broken, or when in the entire boiler three or more in
a circle four feet in diameter or five or more all told are in a
similar condition. Before each trip the water glass and gauge
cocks on a locomotive shall be tested for irregularities; safety
valves shall be investigated under steam at least once in every
three months; while all steam leaks from valves, joints, studs,
etc., that obscure the enginemen's vision, shall be attended to
immediately.

[1] See *Laws, Rules, and Instructions for Inspection and Testing of Steam
Locomotives and Tenders and Their Appurtenances*, Interstate Commerce
Commission, Bureau of Locomotive Inspection, 1927.

Many rules have been placed in the codes with reference to the driving and running gear of locomotives. Constant observation of piston rods and of main and side rods is required lest they develop cracks or other defects. Inspection shall disclose whether all wheels are pressed securely on their axles; whether they have developed flat spots on their treads, worn flanges or other imperfections; and whether bent truck axles or journals have become so dangerously cut or seamed that they cannot be made to run cool without turning. Springs and equalizers shall be so leveled and adjusted that each wheel of the locomotive will bear its scientifically estimated distribution of weight. The brake equipment on locomotives and their tenders shall be examined for fitness before each trip. Main air reservoirs shall receive a hydrostatic test once a year and their surface in each case be hammertapped once in every eighteen months, or whenever a locomotive is shopped for heavy repairs. Adequate maintenance of brake beams, hangers, levers, and other portions of the foundation gear is demanded, and instructions given that brake shoes shall always be kept in true alignment with the wheel. The draw gear between each locomotive and its tender shall be inspected for defects once in every three months. Practically all engine accessories, moreover, such as cab lamps, headlights, warning whistles, sanders, and ash pans are dealt with by explicit regulations.

Indispensable to the success of the work performed by district inspectors are provisions, embodied in the codes, to the effect that daily, monthly, and yearly reports on inspection and repair shall be drawn up by persons in the employ of the railroads at local points. The carriers are thereby forced to keep a continuous record of their activities under the law, and the district inspectors come into possession of data of unquestioned value. Upon the completion of a trip or the operations of a day, each locomotive and its tender shall be inspected by an employee of the railroad company who fills in and signs a printed form relating to their condition. For the purposes of this report what, as applicable to steam power, is known as Form No. 2 has been approved by the

Interstate Commerce Commission. Space in the form is given for the enumeration of repairs, if any, that have been found necessary, and the inclusion of required information concerning parts that are subject to frequent test. The foreman in charge shall countersign the report, but he cannot do this until explanatory notations have been entered, should defects have not been remedied before the locomotive has been dispatched for service.

The monthly report of inspection and repair is made on Form No. 1, having a list of eighteen items upon which information is desired. At larger repair points two or more inspectors as a rule sign this report, each subscribing for those items about which he is believed to have personal knowledge. One copy of the report shall be filed with the district inspector, another with the mechanical officer at the repair point, and a third be placed under glass in the cab of the locomotive. The procedure which must be followed in compiling the annual report, made out on Form No. 3, is almost identical. In this case thirty-two items are listed in the form with respect to which information is sought, and the date of the submission of the report timed to synchronize with the completion of the regular hydrostatic tests. Also, whenever an accident takes place on a carrier's property as the result of the failure of any part of a locomotive or tender, causing serious injury or death, it is necessary that the Chief Inspector be notified at once by wire. A lengthier account of the occurrence must then be drawn up and sent forward by letter. The Bureau of Locomotive Inspection is compelled by law to investigate all accidents reported, and the Interstate Commerce Commission, if it thinks it advisable, may call for a special probe of any accident which may lead to published findings and recommendations. Provision has been made whereby United States attorneys acting on behalf of the bureau may bring suits against the carriers in district courts having jurisdiction in order to penalize them for violations of the inspection acts or the regulations authorized thereunder.

*Results of Inspection.*

STATISTICS show an appreciable reduction of hazards in the railroad industry since the introduction of the federal plan of locomotive inspection. According to the bureau's first report, presented to cover the year ending on June 30, 1912, accidents due to boiler failures had numbered 856 on the carriers of the United States, causing the death of 91 persons and injury to 1,005. The accident rate then dropped steadily until 1914–15, when the list of deaths was reported as only 13 and of injured persons as 467. During the next five years the totals were higher, which may be accounted for in the main by the widening in the scope of the law, by the derangements incidental to the war, and by the constantly increasing power. In this period accidents averaged 600 a year, deaths 54, and persons injured, 728. A down trend was once more discernible, but the shopmen's strike of 1922 brought a serious interruption; qualified inspectors went out with the strikers and the railroads were handicapped in complying with the law. The accident total for 1922–23 mounted to 1,348, resulting in 72 deaths and injury to 1,560. District inspectors ordered 7,075 locomotives out of service during this year. More recently a marked decline of hazards has taken place which, as well as the extent of inspection practice, will be disclosed in the appended figures, covering the last four years:

|  | 1926–27 | 1927–28 | 1928–29 | 1929–30 |
|---|---|---|---|---|
| Number of locomotives inspected | 97,831 | 101,534 | 97,564 | 102,100 |
| Total number of defects found | 112,431 | 85,941 | 77,597 | 60,581 |
| Number ordered out of service | 2,548 | 1,734 | 1,494 | 1,206 |
| Number of accidents | 493 | 423 | 357 | 298 |
| Number of persons killed | 28 | 31 | 19 | 13 |
| Number of persons injured | 522 | 466 | 391 | 323 |

*Safety Appliance Regulations.*

THE safety appliance act of 1893 made it essential that carriers should have all their locomotives equipped with power brakes by January 1, 1898, and enough cars in every train similarly

equipped to insure an adequate degree of train control. By the
same date they should have installed an automatic coupling device on every train car in service. Within two years they should
have placed handholds, otherwise known as grab irons, at the
ends and sides of each train car as a guaranty of additional
safety to men engaged in coupling and uncoupling operations.
Under an amendment, enacted in 1903, it was provided that at
least 50 per cent of all cars in a train should be equipped with
power brakes, a minimum requirement which the Interstate Commerce Commission some years later raised to 85 per cent. Another important amendment of 1910 enumerated a further list of
appliances to be installed by the railroads, and committed to the
Interstate Commerce Commission the responsibility of drawing
up standards of equipment for all appliances adopted to date.
Under order of March 13, 1911, the commission then issued a
lengthy text of standards for safety appliance equipment[2] which
has been binding on the railroads in unmodified form ever since.
An elaborate system of inspection has been devised under a federal Bureau of Safety to observe all defects in steam locomotives
and train cars under these standards. To safeguard their interests, the carriers maintain a qualified staff of car inspectors
at repair points whose duty it is to see that all train cars moving
in traffic are equipped according to specifications.

In indicating the standards of safety appliance equipment for
freight-train cars, the commission took the house car as a basic
type and related other classes of freight-train car to it. Minute
and very definite instructions, which will be referred to briefly,
were given with respect to the number, dimensions, location, and
manner of application of all safety devices, from which even
slight departures leave the offending carrier open to prosecution.
Each house car shall be equipped with: an efficient hand brake
operating in harmony with its power brake; two uncoupling
levers; a running board; four sill steps; four ladders; a roof

2 Before the Interstate Commerce Commission. *United States Safety-Appliance Standards,* 1911.

handhold at the end of each ladder; and eight horizontal, two
vertical, and four side handholds. Tank cars, which show the
greatest variance under the standards from the house car type,
must also be supplied with safety railings. The appliances requisite for passenger coaches and cabooses, while less numerous, are
regarded as of equal importance. Steam locomotives in road service shall have sill steps and handholds on the pilot, and yard
engines shall be equipped with sill steps and footboards. All
classes of steam locomotives must have running boards, couplers
front and rear, handrails and steps leading to headlights.

### Regulations in Canada.

GROWING interest among the people of Canada in transportation
problems led the Parliament of that country to pass a comprehensive Railway Act in 1903 which authorized the erection of a
Board of Railway Commissioners for Canada with powers, less
far-reaching, but in the main the equivalent of those belonging
to the Interstate Commerce Commission in the United States. As
locomotives, unless under exceptional circumstances, do not move
in traffic between the United States and Canada, the question of
their regulation by either government has been essentially a matter of domestic concern. Nevertheless the Canadian board noted
the steps which were taken in 1911 looking toward the establishment of a system of boiler inspection in the United States, and
during the summer of that year held sittings to determine whether
action along similar lines might not be advisable in Canada.
Finally a series of regulations for boiler inspection were legalized
by the board on July 14, 1911, under General Order No. 14115,[3]
based upon the code of rules and instructions issued in the United
States and embodying most of its provisions. Administration of
the Canadian plan of inspection was left with a civil service division under the board's jurisdiction, known as its Operating Department. However, the extension of inspection to the machinery

[3] See Board of Railway Commissioners for Canada, *Judgments, Orders,
Regulations and Rulings,* I, 283.

and auxiliary parts of the locomotive and tender has progressed by slow stages in Canada, though strongly favored by the railroad labor organizations.

The free interchange of train cars over the border between the United States and Canada has placed that type of equipment in a different category. A few piecemeal rulings with respect to the introduction of safety appliances on Canadian lines were made by the Canadian board during the earlier period of its existence, but these were acknowledged to be wholly inadequate when standards of safety appliance equipment were first promulgated for the railroads of the United States. A close correspondence in the two countries' regulations would be imperative, if smooth relations were to be maintained between their carriers. Accordingly sittings of the Board of Railway Commissioners for Canada were specially devoted to a consideration of this problem from the Canadian angle. A decision was reached to adopt the standards in force in the United States in their entirety, which was sanctioned by General Order No. 102[4] of the board, on February 17, 1913. The new work of inspection thus entailed was again put under the jurisdiction of the board's Operating Department. A strict adherence to safety appliance standards is enforced in Canada, but it would appear that the examination of motive power under inspection requirements in that country is somewhat milder than in the United States.

[4] See Board of Railway Commissioners for Canada, *Railway Safety-Appliance Standards*, Pamphlet No. 24.

# Chapter III

# Industrial Processes Involved in Maintaining Equipment

In order that moving units of equipment on the railroads may be adequately maintained it is necessary that they be more or less frequently suspended from use. As the companies which employ them cannot as a rule spare these units very long from service, they have customarily provided facilities for their prompt repair at stations on their own property. Sometimes, however, they may accept the bid of an outside concern, and send a part or all of their heavier maintenance work to a so-called "contract" shop. In the past the policy of carriers was to multiply the number of their repair stations so that no train car or locomotive need proceed far before receiving attention. Rarely indeed were any repair stations closed when companies amalgamated to form larger systems, which may often explain why carriers today have such an assortment of them at important traffic centers. The extent to which decentralization of maintenance of equipment work has been carried, is revealed in statistical data provided by the Bureau of Locomotive Inspection. The bureau's records show the existence in May, 1929, of approximately 5,600 motive power repair points on the Class I railroads of the United States, which meant that on the average there was one motive power repair point for every 45 miles of first main track. More recently, as will be further noted, because of changes in transportation policy and a desire for greater economy, a tendency has been manifest among carriers to eliminate superfluous repair points and to concentrate both shop equipment and working forces at selected centers.

*Running and Light Repairs to Train Cars.*

From the operating standpoint, railroads in the United States and Canada keep the train car and motive power sections of their mechanical department sedulously apart. The two sections, though, may lie contiguous to one another on a single strip of railroad property where certain plant facilities may be used in common. If both are combined for administrative purposes, it is usual railroad practice to allow precedence to the motive power section. The labor force of each section is always considered as a separate entity, and should workers of one be employed by the other, it becomes a matter of entry in the bookkeeping records. Carriers nowadays, in rearranging old plants or building new ones, are disposed to give even more positive acknowledgment in the plans which they follow to this distinction between the train car and motive power sections.

Maintenance of train car equipment on the railroads involves a recognition of three classes of repairs: running or inspection, light, and heavy. Running or inspection repairs are mostly performed when trains are halted under schedule, thereby avoiding car detention. But in the case of light and heavy repairs cars are cut from the trains, and held out of service. In the various train yards of any railroad system may be seen a gang of men who move among the cars of an inbound or outbound train, and give them attention while in transit. This gang, ranging in size from a mere handful at smaller points to several score at terminals, will consist in the main of car inspectors and of car repairmen and their helpers. Specially appointed brake and safety appliance inspectors, as well as a few oilers, may be included at larger stations. It is not usual for a gang operating in a freight-train yard to be detailed for work in a passenger-train yard except in emergency. All these workers are employed in eight-hour shifts. The car inspector's duty is to examine train cars passing through, or starting from a certain train yard, and to decide what will be done with any that are found defective. Work which the inspectors believe can be quickly accomplished will be done by repairmen and helpers right on the track. Otherwise the car is ordered to be cut from the train and is sent on for light or heavy repairs. In this case a "bad order" card may be attached to the car indicating the nature of its defects. It is anticipated that inspectors will employ judgment in exercising their powers, since the suspension from use of a car may result in a traffic hardship. For example, when a freight-train car is running manifest, laden with a perishable commodity, it may be found possible to fix it up temporarily so that it may continue through to its destination. Repairs to knuckle pins, brake shoes, cotter keys, door hasps, handholds, air hose, and train line are among the miscellaneous forms of work that are done in the train yard. Running repairs may be considered to occupy up to one man hour on the average American railroad.

Maintenance operations on cars cut from trains lasting from approximately one to twenty man hours[1] are ordinarily classified as light repairs. Rip or repair tracks, varying in number with the comparative importance of the station, are placed at the disposal of these cars, and a force of experienced carmen and helpers begin to repair them. Employment here is on the straight eight-hour basis. Occasionally all or a portion of the day shift of a yard gang, if near at hand and unoccupied, may be requisitioned for work on the rip tracks. A blue flag, wedged in the end handhold of the first in a string of cars, is always evidence that carmen are working about or beneath them and that to move them may imperil life. For the purpose of transporting materials and supplies to the place needed, a system of narrow-gauge service tracks are frequently laid crosswise of or parallel to the rip tracks. Under a light repair schedule, time is permitted among other things for the jacking up of cars, the removal of trucks, and, if necessary, the mounting of new wheels; for the straightening of parts of steel structure by means of the blowtorch; for the application of draft timbers, sill splices, and roof boards to wooden cars; and for important repairs to be made to air brakes and other safety appliances.

[1] See instructions given in the form used by the railroads in submitting their semimonthly report of revenue freight cars to the Car Service Division of the American Railway Association.

*Heavy Train Car Repairs and Car Shop Facilities.*

HEAVY repairs to train cars are rated as consuming more than twenty man hours of applied labor. Carriers are wont to refer to an intermediate class which is designated as medium, or light-heavy, repairs, occupying from twenty to sixty hours and to reserve the full title of heavy for times when the car is given a more extensive overhauling. Although some heavy repairs are done on rip tracks, the major proportion are completed within shops or on nearby shop tracks, equipped with facilities for the purpose. Each railroad has a plan of its own for the shopping of its train cars. The more systematic and efficient its handling of light and running repairs, the less often need its train cars be sent to the shop. A number of railroads are now endeavoring to adhere to a definite program of future maintenance which causes them to order in for general repairs quotas of train cars in succession, based on similarity in design and other characteristics.

A railroad car shop is in reality a group of shops, the arrangement of which from point to point in the United States and Canada varies in every conceivable manner. A central shop may have a dozen or more buildings spread out over a wide area, while a small local shop may have but three or four. Passenger coaches and freight-train cars, if repaired at the same station, are regularly provided with separate housing facilities. In addition to its main structure or structures, into which cars are taken for repairs, a larger shop will have accommodation for individual machine, blacksmith, sheet metal, and wheel shops, a wood mill, a paint shop, a storeroom, a reclamation shop, and storages for lumber, castings, and other material. Cabinet and upholstery shops are also required where work is performed on passenger coaches. Vivid contrasts may be noted in the degree of modernity in equipment displayed by these shops. Many are yet performing their functions with machine and hand tools that are decidedly antiquated. Others have a certain percentage of new equipment mixed with the old. Still others, more recently erected, or favored by liberal appropriations, are supplied with the latest air and hydraulic hoists, overhead and portable cranes, welding outfits, punches and shear machines, forms, and presses. The introduction of the unit system of making heavy repairs by a majority of the carriers has been of remarkable consequence for train car maintenance, and will be afforded special treatment at the end of this chapter.

### Methods of Maintaining Locomotives.

SINCE the war-time period of government control of railroads repairs to motive power have been designated as either classified or unclassified. Previously each carrier had had its own method of assessing the relative importance of repairs, and the United States Railroad Administration upon its formation found it impossible to check the output of one shop against another. Accordingly the Locomotive Section of the administration prepared a set of classification rules, applicable to maintenance of a heavier sort, which were to become standard for all railroads from June 1, 1918. These rules inaugurated a division of heavier repairs into five classes, based upon the amount and kind of work to be performed upon an engine. Of the five, Class 3 is accepted by the railroads as the standard to be followed when the time arrives for the general overhauling of a locomotive. It involves. the making of necessary repairs to the boiler and fire box; an installation of new flues or a resetting of those already applied; a turning of the wheel tires, or an application of new tires; and a completion of general repairs to the machinery and tender. Repairs performed under Classes 1 and 2 are relatively more exacting in character in that an entirely new boiler or the back end of one is demanded under the former, and a new fire box or important sections of one is required under the latter. Class 4 on the contrary involves only light repairs to the boiler and fire box and necessary, not general repairs to machinery and tender. Class 5 is almost identical with Class 4 except that it omits any reference to the flues. Maintenance operations which may be graded below these standards are generally spoken of as running or unclassified repairs.

Locomotives are repaired at power terminals, known as enginehouses or roundhouses, where they are taken after they have finished a trip or day's work, or they are repaired at special shops of one description or another. When a locomotive is brought in from a run, its condition is reported by the engineer in charge who has noted any faults in performance, and it is then placed on a pit for regular inspection. All minor defects that may be remedied quickly are attended to before the locomotive is dispatched on its next run. Should something more serious be disclosed in its condition, it may be detained for repairs beyond the scheduled hour for departure. Repairs may be made to a locomotive with its fire still burning, when it is called a "live" engine, but, if the fire is out, it is said to be "dead." Enginehouse workers have been traditionally disinclined to handle "dead" engines, if accustomed to "live" ones, although this is becoming an outworn prejudice.

Two viewpoints have grown up among mechanical department officials respecting the interval that should be allowed to elapse between shoppings of an engine for general repairs. One school, favoring a low frequency of shopping, thinks that the locomotive should be retained in service as long as is warrantable by means of an excellent standard of enginehouse maintenance. Another group advocates the shopping of the locomotive as often as once a year or year and a half, and a minimum of attention in the enginehouse. Where low-frequency doctrines have prevailed, the terminal has been supplied with increased facilities, and usually has been allowed to do some classified repairs. By the same token the adoption of high-frequency policies has encouraged the development of larger, central shops, and the expenditure of less money on enginehouses, which are relegated to the performance of necessary running repairs.

### Back Shops and Locomotive Repair Shops.

An earlier generation of railroad men employed the title, "back shop," to describe the little plant which they saw arise behind or near the enginehouse to take care of heavier repairs. In transportation circles the "back shop" still passes currency, but is waning in significance as large-scale locomotive repair shops, often quite apart from an enginehouse, have been making their appearance on many carriers. Instead of depending only upon engines tributary to them coming in for repairs, these shops may receive consignments of power from a distance. As a rule their layout comprises one main shop structure, with a great erecting bay at its center in which engines are rebuilt, and it may be, other subsidiary bays. Heavy-duty machine tools are always essential for erecting operations and for that reason are invariably located in the main shop. An array of lighter machine tools will be assembled elsewhere, possibly in another shop. Blacksmith and boiler shops, so important in locomotive maintenance, will probably be in separate buildings, while electrical, sheet metal, paint and wheel shops, and tool, store, and engine rooms will be distributed throughout the plant. Tracks lead into the erecting bay of the main shop either on a longitudinal or transverse plan. Where the longitudinal method is used, opportunity is given to move engines from end to end of the shop without lifting. Under the transverse system a number of cross-shop tracks are run in, and engine bodies, slung on huge cables, carried from one to the other by 150–200 ton electric traveling cranes. It is contended that the transverse method makes easier the spacing of machine tools. In addition to a variety of cranes, hoists, and tractors, a locomotive repair shop is equipped with: wheel, turret, axle-turning, and other kinds of lathes; an assortment of drills and grinders; wheel and flanging presses; boring mills; planers; shapers; slotters; pipe machines; steam hammers; forging machines; annealing furnaces; and all devices needed for welding.

## The Spot System as Applied to Train Car Repairs.

OVER half the railroads of the United States and Canada have adopted, in one form or another, what is known as the spot system of handling through work in their mechanical department.

This system which is actually an attempt to relate certain of the basic principles of mass production in industry to the maintenance of railroad equipment, was introduced by J. J. Tatum, Superintendent of the Car Department of the Baltimore & Ohio Railroad. During the European War, J. J. Tatum was released to the Government for service by the Baltimore & Ohio Railroad and became General Supervisor of Car Repairs in the Division of Operation of the Railroad Administration. In this capacity he observed the unsystematized and haphazard manner in which the carriers throughout the United States were getting their repair work done, and came to the conclusion that in no sense were they keeping pace with the country's manufacturing establishments in the introduction of scientific methods of planning and routing their work, or in conserving their labor forces. In an effort to grapple with the situation, he began to evolve an industrial plan for maintenance of equipment operations, which later, upon his return to the Baltimore & Ohio Railroad, he completed, and put into effect for the first time at that carrier's Mount Clare shop in Baltimore during December, 1920. Satisfaction was expressed at the results attained at the Mount Clare shop after a period of trial, and the plan was finally extended to all feasible points on the Baltimore & Ohio Railroad on January 1, 1922. The popular title, spot system, was attached to the plan as it spread to other carriers.

It will be profitable to study the spot system first as it operates at a freight-car repair point, where for certain reasons it is least liable to the play of interfering factors.[2] Pursuant to the instructions given in the plan as originally outlined, it is necessary to organize from the labor force at any repair point one or more worker-units of corresponding size. A worker-unit, headed by a foreman and assistant foreman, is then subdivided into gangs, and the members of each gang allocated to a single spot where cars are taken for repairs. For instance, a freight-train car worker-

[2] See "The Spot System of Repairing Freight Cars," *Railway Mechanical Engineer*, July, 1928, pp. 396–399.

unit on the Baltimore & Ohio Railroad, except for refrigerator cars, now consists of 48 workmen or their equivalent, plus the two supervisors already mentioned. Six spots, arranged in alphabetical notation from A to F, are utilized, and therefore the 48 men, or their equivalent, are subdivided into 6 gangs, each with special work to perform at a designated spot. A worker-unit on the Baltimore & Ohio Railroad is made up of the following: 26 carmen; 13 carmen helpers; 5 carmen apprentices; 1 brake repairman; 1 shop laborer; and the half-time employment of 1 painter, 1 painter helper, 1 blacksmith, and 1 blacksmith helper. A car is repaired by stages, being stripped on spot A, and moved progressively through various operations until it is finished on spot F. A prearranged schedule of output must be drawn up, which will be dependent upon the facilities available at the repair point and the type of cars handled. If a worker-unit, employed at six spots, is expected to have an output of 15 cars a week, it will be essential that on an average $2\frac{1}{2}$ cars be moved from spot to spot each day.

The spot system, declare its advocates, is elastic enough to meet any contingency that may arise in connection with freight-train car maintenance. The time that a car is held on a spot may be lengthened or shortened to suit the type of repairs demanded, and the weekly output be regulated accordingly. Refrigerator cars, which require for their repair exceptional expenditures of labor, are allotted a worker-unit of 55 men on the Baltimore & Ohio Railroad, and normally only 6 of them are finished in a week. Should any gang in a worker-unit get behind in its schedule, the foreman can order another gang, less pressed for time, to render temporary assistance. A bulletin board may be affixed at the beginning of each spot upon which is inscribed a summary of the work processes to be accomplished on that spot, and no two boards are the same color. It occasionally happens also that the posts, scaffolding, and ladders of a spot will be painted green, red, orange, or some other shade, to indicate its location more precisely. Either shop or shop yard tracks serve the purposes of the spot system, unless inclement weather makes outside work impossible. It has often been found good economic policy to organize a worker-unit at a small repair point to which is committed the task of applying light-heavy repairs on the open track to certain models of gondola or box car. Where long, open-end tracks are available, spots may be nicely arranged in continuous sequences; but where short or stub-end tracks only are available, the spacing of spots will depend on switching facilities.

Passenger-train car equipment, as may be surmised, does not lend itself so readily to the application of the spot system. Although passenger-train cars are just as diversified in type as freight-train cars, their numbers altogether on the railroads stand in a ratio to the latter of only 1:42. Besides, portions of the repair work done to passenger-train cars must of their very nature be performed in segregated shops, especially fitted for the purpose. However, that a modified form of spot system may function successfully in connection with the maintenance of passenger-train cars is exemplified in the elaborate plan[3] which has been adopted by the Chicago & North Western Railway at its central shop in Chicago, Illinois. Although for purposes of repair, passenger coaches are only "pulled" between a few main spots in the Chicago shop, a strict estimate is made of the total number of man hours which have been expended in major and minor operations on them by workers in different sections of the plant. It has been found impossible to arrange worker-units on this railroad for passenger coach maintenance as has been done in the case of freight car repairs.

### The Spot System in Motive Power Repair Work.

MECHANICAL officers on the railroads are aware that, despite the practical worth of classification rules, it is expedient that they should regard each locomotive shopped for repairs as constituting a problem by itself. Seldom, if ever, do general repairs to

---

[3] For a detailed account of this plan read the article, "Passenger Shop Work Organized," *Railway Mechanical Engineer*, March, 1928, pp. 145–150.

the machinery or to the boilers of any two engines of like age and model involve an identical set of maintenance operations. This, and the relatively low volume of motive power output, has tended to retard or, at least, to complicate the introduction of the spot system at back or locomotive repair shops. Perhaps its use at the Baltimore & Ohio Railroad's locomotive repair shop in Cumberland, Maryland, is as good an example as might be offered of its possibilities in the motive power field. In an endeavor to cope with all eventualities, the Cumberland shop has completed an arrangement of twenty spots, three of which are located on outside tracks. Locomotives, having already been sandblasted before arrival, are washed and cleaned of sand on outside spot 1. Boiler, machinery, pipe, and miscellaneous stripping operations are performed inside the shop on spots 1A and 2, and locomotives unwheeled. From this point a routing plan is in effect which distributes engines to spots in accordance with the type of repairs needed or the class of power. Simple Mallet or other low pressure engines are sent to spots 7A and 9. Spots 10–12 inclusive are reserved for "fast" engines, so named because they can be repaired in from three to six days. All other power is moved for heavy repairs either to spots 3 and 4, which are devoted to frame, cylinder, and boiler work, or to spots 5–8 inclusive, reserved particularly for fire box operations. Eventually all locomotives congregate at a common wheeling spot, and thereafter travel the same course until at length they reach two outside spots where they are fired up, tested, and dispatched into service.

# Chapter IV

# Management and Men in the Mechanical Department

CONTROL of the affairs of a common carrier in the United States or Canada, as in the case of other business corporations, is conferred by the general body of its shareholders upon an elected board of directors. Then power to conduct and manage the enterprise is delegated by the board of directors, at least on all large railroads, to an executive group, consisting of a president, a number of vice-presidents, and other high-ranking officials. The subdivision of authority below this, which of necessity must be carried to the farthest limits of the carrier's property, becomes inevitably complex. The governance of a railroad calls for various grades of official dependence and interdependence, extending from its chief executive to the lowliest supervisor, and a drift to inefficiency will soon be marked, unless the regimen is strict.

## *Staff Officers of the Mechanical Department.*

THE vice-president in charge of operation on a carrier, by virtue of the wide range of jurisdiction belonging to his office, is generally thought of as occupying a position next in rank to its president. Appointment of an outsider to this office would be rated an absurdity, since only someone versed by experience in the essentials of train service, and fully acquainted with the equipment, roadbed, and structural needs of a railroad can assume its responsibilities. Under the vice-president in charge of operation a general manager may be appointed with authority over the entire system, or, should the carrier be split up on a regional basis, there may be a general manager for each region; occasionally the vice-president himself performs the duties of general manager. To the general manager is assigned complete control over train movements within the scope of his jurisdiction, so that all transportation officers are answerable to him. Sometimes staff officers of the mechanical and engineering departments report to him also, but on many roads these are directly responsible to the operating vice-president. This method is followed on all roads that have adopted union-management coöperation. The Baltimore & Ohio Railroad has a chief of motive power to whom is committed the task of fixing standards for the maintenance of old and the purchase of new equipment on its lines. This carrier has regional general managers, and its chief of motive power reports to the vice-president in charge of operation. The Canadian National Railway System, with a general manager for each of its three regions in Canada and the Grand Trunk Western Lines, and the Chicago, Milwaukee, St. Paul & Pacific Railroad, with two regional general managers, have staff officers of equal rank for motive power and train car equipment respectively, who again are both responsible to the operating executive. And, in spite of the fact that there is but one general manager with centralized authority on the Chicago & North Western Railway, its vice-president in charge of operation and maintenance has immediate jurisdiction over car and motive power officials in his department. As systematized methods of buying materials and equipment have become the practice on railroads, another staff officer, the purchasing agent, has appeared, who may be listed under the operating department or be given independent status. The purchasing agent has oversight of the storage facilities at central and local points on the carrier, and distributes supplies to its departments upon the receipt of properly signed requisitions; often subordinate to him is an officer known as the general storekeeper.

When labor issues of consequence arise on a railroad, such as proposals to alter wages or make important changes in working conditions, they are always given executive consideration. Minor questions, however, of daily recurrence affecting maintenance of way, shop craft, or train service employees, if not settled by local officials of the operating department, are ordinarily cleared through to the general manager having jurisdiction. The emergence of various plans on the carriers for the better ordering of industrial relations has frequently led to the appointment of special staff officers to whom the supervision of these plans has been intrusted. Union-management coöperation as it functions on the Baltimore & Ohio Railroad, including the apprenticeship system incidental to it, receives the undivided attention of an assistant supervisor of shops. The Canadian National Railway System refers all problems which relate to the functioning of its coöperative plan to a general supervisor and assistant general supervisor of shop methods. Some years ago, the Chicago & North Western Railway adopted the advanced policy of establishing a distinctive personnel department, with a vice-president in charge, to whom has been assigned the task of administering its form of systematized coöperation.

### *Line Officers.*

HEADING the roster of line officers in the mechanical department of carriers are general superintendents, or superintendents who furnish instructions to their subordinates respecting the actual work of maintaining equipment. These officers usually report to a general manager, but always have definite contacts with the motive power chief, or, if he exists, the car department chief. Some roads have a number of such officers, others have but one for each region, and still others but one for the whole system. The Baltimore & Ohio Railroad has two superintendents of motive power, appointed with jurisdiction respectively over its eastern and its western lines. The Canadian National Railway System has all told four general superintendents of motive power and car equipment, one for each of its three regions in Canada and a fourth for the Grand Trunk Western Lines. On the Chicago, Milwaukee, St. Paul & Pacific Railroad there is an assistant superintendent of motive power and an assistant superintendent of the car department in each of the two regions into which the system is divided. The Chicago & North Western Railway, in contradistinction, allows its staff officers of the mechanical department to exercise jurisdiction over the line.

Due to the expanse of territory that railroads in America cover, and the consequent need, in emergencies, for a measure of local control, it has been customary to block out systems from the operating standpoint into so many divisions. Departmental organization always tends to become somewhat blurred when the division is reached. A transportation line officer, the division superintendent, holds sway over a designated length of mileage, and all sections of the operating department within those limits are amenable to him in current transactions. Prompter action results from such an arrangement, which outweighs the disadvantage of occasional friction between the division superintendent and the departmental heads.

Preëminent among the subordinate maintenance of equipment officers of a division is the master mechanic, a typical product of railroading in America, around whom has often been thrown a certain romantic glamor. The master mechanic is in the difficult rôle of having to answer to the dictates of the line superintendent of the mechanical department on repair of equipment policies, and of having daily to collaborate with the division superintendent on matters pertaining to the availability of equipment for service. In some instances a master mechanic may exercise jurisdiction over every shop, car repair yard, and enginehouse in a division. There are two ways, however, in which his authority may be circumscribed. In the first place, an officer less well known to the public—the master car builder, appointed on a proportion of the carriers—may have exclusive control over train car maintenance. The master car builder is preferably chosen for a district, that is, he will have authority over two or more divisions, as is the case on the Chicago & North Western Railway. In the second place, it may be thought advisable to enhance the position of the superintendent in charge of a larger shop by letting him report directly to the system or regional officers. Always subordinate to either the master mechanic or the master car builder is the general foreman who may be in control at a lesser shop point, and invariably governs at an enginehouse or car repair yard. Between the general foremen and the well-defined forces of mechanical craftsmen stand a very important group, the supervisors.

## The Supervisory Class.

IMMEDIATE jurisdiction over the men who work with machine or hand tools in the mechanical department, and who make use of materials for repair purposes, rests with the supervisors, for the most part known as foremen. Difficulty is experienced in fixing the exact industrial status of supervisors who with very few exceptions have come up from the mechanical trades, and who, if demoted, simply resume their former occupations. The Interstate Commerce Commission in its record of wage statistics has included all supervisors as well as general foremen in the classification of employees. Yet supervisors in the mechanical department are given a measure of executive authority, are subject to a different discipline from craftsmen, and to a degree are the recipients of official confidences. For these and other reasons it is easy to regard them as forming a part of management in that department. Plainly the quality of leadership displayed by supervisors, whether in an economic or administrative sense, will be of marked significance to the carrier employing them. The peculiar circumstances under which they hold office in the mechanical department give them an excellent opportunity to interpret the managerial point of view to the workers and reciprocally to bring the needs of the workers to the attention of management.

The number of men allotted to a foreman in the mechanical department depends upon the character of the work to be done and the policies of the particular carrier. Oversupervision, it has been discovered, may breed indolence in the foreman, undersupervision leaves the way open for careless workmanship. An inefficient foreman may be one who moves about all day long, apparently working hard, but through his planlessness accomplishing relatively little. Such a type has been called "a material chaser, a blueprint checker, a shop clerk, and office boy, all combined." The capable foreman is more often the one who consults a work schedule before operations begin, and who throughout the day checks up regularly on his men and machines to keep work effort in proper sequence. He orders his supplies sufficiently ahead, and when any section of his force lags behind the schedule brings others to their rescue. The general foreman at an enginehouse or smaller car repair point rarely has more than a half dozen supervisors under him. Among those functioning in car maintenance operations may be: car unit, blacksmith shop, wood mill, coach yard, and track gang foremen; at enginehouses, the several metal trade shops may each have their representative supervisor, while a gang foreman will be in charge of shop labor. At larger car repair shops and back and locomotive repair shops supervision goes out to wider ramifications, and the foremen of main departments have assistants and acquire added importance. In all sections of the Chicago & North Western Railway's car repair shop at Chicago, the complement of foremen, according to figures published in 1928, was 17, and of assistant foremen, 24. Here a schedule foreman maps out the day's work for the whole shop with the aid of four assistant foremen.

### The Grouping of Worker Types.

TAKEN as a whole the railroads of the United States and Canada adhere quite closely to the same plan of differentiating between worker types in the mechanical department. No crumbling of trade boundaries worthy of mention, as might have been expected, has occurred in the department as a result of the shopmen's strike of 1922. Doubtless the worker-classification rules adopted for all Class I steam railroads in the United States by the Interstate Commerce Commission in 1915, and reissued to them in more extended form in 1921,[1] have been very effective in helping to establish and preserve this uniformity. It is now necessary that the commission's worker-classification shall be employed by the

[1] *Rules Governing the Classification of Steam Railway Employees, and Reports of Their Service and Compensation.* Interstate Commerce Commission, 1921.

carriers in making out both monthly and yearly reports for its Bureau of Statistics with reference to the compensation and hours of service of their employees. Data for the monthly report shall be furnished on what have been denominated Forms A and B, each of which has space for information concerning specified groupings of railroad employees. Maintenance of equipment and stores have been placed together as a separate reporting division under Form A where they have been allotted 29 subheadings for the tabulation of information, 21 of which are for workers and 8 for supervisors. The aim of the worker-classification of 1921, it has been stated, was not to formulate lines of jurisdiction for railroad employees, nor to standardize their occupational duties, but to make it possible for the carriers to have "the same general understanding" with reference to the types of occupation that they would include within a class. In no essential respect did the classification run counter to the apportionment of work set forth for the mechanical department by the national agreement of 1919 between the United States Railroad Administration and the federated shop crafts.[2] This apportionment of work is still the standard accepted by the shop crafts in negotiating their system agreements.

### The Carmen's Craft.

For the maintenance of train car equipment the mechanical department must chiefly rely upon the work of railroad carmen. This body of craftsmen, numerically the strongest among mechanical trades on the railroads, is quite unknown outside the field of transportation. According to the report of the Bureau of Statistics for the month of April, 1929, 99,203 journeymen carmen were then in the employ of Class I steam carriers in the United States. To find the aggregate number in the craft on these lines, many thousand carmen helpers, and regular and helper apprentices must be included in the total. Of peculiar interest is the varied character of the carman's range of activities. If he has re-

2 *Vide* chap. vi.

ceived a balanced training and has been judged competent, he is expected to perform all operations connected with the dismantling and reconditioning of train cars of any description. Under modern conditions this is placing a heavy burden upon one man's skill. The old-time carman, employed on cars of wooden construction, would pass muster if, added to his knowledge of wheels, brakes, and trucks, he was adept as a bench carpenter, could do duty in the wood mill, and was a bit of a painter and cabinet-maker. Now the introduction of the all-steel car and the composite car with steel frame or underframe, the inauguration of the unit system and other large-scale methods of repair, and the increasing use of heavier and more intricate tools and devices have nullified to an extent the carman's claim to many-sidedness. Although a measure of versatility will always be demanded of carmen doing running repairs in the train yards, it appears that those employed on the rip tracks and in the shops are faced with a permanently continuing specialization in their trade.

Plenty of illustrations might be given of the effect upon the carman's lot of newer developments in his trade. In dismantling a car, rivet heads were formerly struck off by main strength as sledge hammer fell on chisel; now a riveting gun, propelled by compressed air, and deftly handled at all angles by two journeymen and a helper, pierces each rivet in one or two blows and punches it from its hole. Bent or buckled parts of steel, such as end posts, plates, center and end sills, corner and side braces, are taken to the straightening table where they are heated with the blowtorch and shaped by hammer and air press; because of the differing form, thickness, and consistency of the metal, only experienced mechanics can properly perform these operations. When steel parts are ready for assembling, expert layer-outs indicate with mathematical precision where they are to be punched, sheared, drilled, or ground, and begin to fit them temporarily into position. Then come the riveters, usually working three together, who, having heated the rivets to the required temperature, set them in their intended receptacles and head their tips securely by the manipulation of an air hammer. Space will not permit of a description of the intricate work performed by carmen on air brakes and on different kinds of trucks, or of the specialized operations of veneering, lacquering, and upholstering done by them in the passenger coach department.[3]

Coach cleaners, who are largely women, though accorded a separate reporting division under Form A, may be regarded as an adjunct to the carmen's craft at passenger car repair points. These workers clean coaches on the outside with water, or water and acid, and spray their trucks with a distilled oil. They do light cleaning to the inside of cars while *en route*, blow out or vacuum clean and sweep, dust, and mop them while held at terminals, and at intervals renovate them more thoroughly. Among the scattered representation from other groups of craftsmen employed in the car department are sheet metal workers, and pipe fitters who repair the steam pipes and water coolers of passenger coaches and the ice boxes of refrigerator cars. Also in the department are electricians responsible for the installation and upkeep of lighting fixtures on passenger coach and other train cars; blacksmiths, machinists, and occasionally pattern makers who are retained for the performance of specific mechanical operations; stationary engineers and firemen who are engaged at power plants; and shop and common laborers.

## *Machinists Engaged in Motive Power Repairs.*

In describing worker types in the motive power section of the mechanical department reference may first be made to the functional activities of machinists because of their superiority in numbers. Class I steam railroads in the United States reported in April, 1929, the presence of 55,259 skilled machinists on their lines, apart from helpers and apprentices, the vast majority of whom are, of course, assigned to motive power repairs. Although the parts machined in a locomotive repair shop, back shop, or

[3] An outline of the status and duties of car inspectors has been furnished in chap. iii.

enginehouse are all distinctive of the railroad industry, only a portion of the machine or hand tools employed are adapted to special purposes. As a result the machining processes at a motive power repair point are largely identical with those found in manufacturing plants throughout the country. Several hundred machines, tools, besides other essential forms of equipment, may frequently be seen in machine shops at larger repair points, so that even to itemize these tools, let alone explain their uses, is beyond the scope of this volume.

Machine shop equipment is put to more variable uses at railroad repair points than in manufacturing establishments where standard goods are produced to stock. The foremen of railroad machine shops are therefore constantly confronted with the worrisome problem of relating the work effort of their journeymen and helpers in the most economic manner to the equipment at their command. Men must be kept busy though some machines stand idle. In most cases the policy of railroad management has been to demand continuous production from heavy-duty machine tools and to abandon those of lighter caliber to more intermittent use. This is one reason why machinists at railroad repair points are so often kept working at antiquated, light machines.

*Boiler Makers, Blacksmiths, and Other Motive Power Workers.*

ANOTHER body of craftsmen active in motive power repair work are the boiler makers. While figures for April, 1929, indicated that there were only 16,487 journeymen boiler makers on the Class I railroads of the United States, the services of this group of mechanics can scarcely be evaluated on the basis of numbers, since, together with their helpers and apprentices, they are mainly employed on what has been termed the "heart" of the locomotive. Boiler makers maintain in condition all sheets of the boiler and its fire box; blow out and test flues; remove and apply brick arches and arch tubes in the fire box, stay and crown bar bolts, and stay rods and braces. They are responsible, among other things, for the repair of water tanks and drums, steel cabs, running boards,

pilot steps, ash pans, and the netting and deflectors which arrest
sparks in the smoke box. They operate throat shears and punch
machines to cut metal, and roll machines to bend it as desired;
they develop projecting rims on metal for fitting purposes by
means of flange presses; they employ cutting off and cleaning
machines for flue work, and handle hydraulic power, yoke, and
other forms of riveting apparatus.

Hammersmithing and forging, and much of the welding work
necessary to motive power maintenance, is done by blacksmiths.
To their furnaces, closed or open, and fed by coke, coal, or other
fuel, are brought heavy slabs and billets of iron which, having
been subjected to intense heat, are then by the aid of steam or
power hammers or hydraulic presses shaped into replacement
parts for locomotives, such as driving wheel and engine truck
axles, frames, main and side rods, piston rods, pulling bars,
crank pins, and other large forgings. Preferably in special furnaces they attend to the case hardening, tempering, annealing,
and normalizing of metal. By means of welding apparatus they
repair guide yokes, put new ends on connecting rods, square
frames, and fill in frame sections. They perform more automatic
work with forging machines, Bradley hammers, bolt heading
machines, bulldozers, drill presses, and shears. Spring making
also belongs distinctively to the blacksmiths' trade. The development of autogenous welding has resulted in a considerable reduction in the number of blacksmiths employed on the railroads.
Whereas, at one time, five men in all, a hammersmith, a hammer
driver, a heater, and two blacksmith helpers, were needed to take
out and repair engine frames, two men now going to the engine
can recondition them with a welding device and cutting machine.

Sheet metal workers and pipe fitters instal and maintain parts
of locomotives and tenders that require the use of lesser gauges
of iron, and sheet copper, tin, and brass. They engage in brazing,
soldering, babbitting, and, to an extent, in welding operations, and
work with hand- or power-driven threading machines, vises, and
auxiliary hand tools. Electrical workers, besides attending to

engine headlights and the operation of overhead traveling cranes, have other duties to perform at motive power repair points in connection with electrical apparatus and fixtures. Where train control has been applied on carriers, as on sections of the Chicago & North Western Railway and Baltimore & Ohio Railroad, or where electric locomotives are used extensively, as on mountain divisions of the Milwaukee System, electricians are required in greater numbers and their work becomes much more diversified. Under these circumstances the inspection of electrical equipment is added to that of maintenance. At larger repair points a quota of molders may be retained in service to make castings of locomotive parts. Stationary engineers and firemen are regularly employed in the power plants at railroad shops and enginehouses. Also many workers are on the pay roll at motive power repair points whose activities are indicated in the names which they bear, such as water tenders, fire knockers and builders, coal passers, cinder pitmen, engine watchmen, sand house men, oil house men, turntable operators, coal chute men, shop chain gang men, material yard gang men, and common laborers.

# Chapter V

# Labor Organization in the Mechanical Department

LABOR organization, so far as it exists in the mechanical department of railroads in the United States and Canada, is almost entirely under international unions affiliated with the American Federation of Labor. In 1909, the American Federation of Labor, for the purpose of having an agency amenable to its jurisdiction, that might deal effectively and judiciously with craft problems arising on the railroads, authorized the creation of a Railway Employees' Department. All international organizations with an appreciable membership employed at motive power or train car repair work in the United States have been taken into this department with the exception of the molders' union and the pattern makers' league. Since 1924, the Railway Employees' Department, as will be explained further in chapter vii, has consistently sponsored the plan of union-management coöperation. Seven unions of mechanical craftsmen belonging to the department are at present subscribers to the plan: the Brotherhood Railway Carmen of America; the International Association of Machinists; the International Brotherhood of Boiler Makers, Iron Ship Builders and Helpers of America; the International Brotherhood of Blacksmiths, Drop Forgers and Helpers; the Sheet Metal Workers' International Association; the International Brotherhood of Electrical Workers; and the International Brotherhood of Firemen, Oilers, Helpers, Roundhouse and Railroad Shop Laborers. The first six unions, in the order mentioned, constitute the historic federated shop crafts whose representatives, together with the Director General of Railroads, were signatories to a national agreement, applicable to the mechanical department of all carriers in the United States, in 1919. The firemen and oilers' brotherhood, more recently admitted to the Railway Employees'

Department, though in no sense unfriendly to the federated shop crafts' program, has always negotiated its agreements independently.

### The Local Lodge and Its Members.

THE primary unit of organization among mechanical crafts on the railroads is the local or subordinate union or lodge. A specified number of qualified persons may apply for and obtain a charter from the international union of their craft to form a lodge with jurisdiction over a single repair point or over a wider territory. Journeymen and helpers are always eligible for membership in a lodge, but apprentices are only granted full membership rights after their term of service has been completed. Trade competency is accepted as the insignia of journeymanship by each of the crafts. Although apprentices are sought by each, of whom a four or five years' period of training is demanded, they will admit to their ranks as journeymen anyone who can earn the mechanic's wage and whose trade-worthiness is undeniable. However, this open-door policy of the unions in no wise explains why there are at present so many accredited journeymen in the mechanical department of organized carriers who have never been indentured as apprentices. It may be pointed out that in the days before the federal control of carriers in the United States, it was the custom of management on most roads to make full-fledged mechanics out of certain helpers who had shown a marked proficiency in one branch or in a single process of their trade. Railroads in the Dominion of Canada had followed the same practice. When William G. McAdoo was appointed to head the United States Railroad Administration in 1918 he decided, on account of the shortage of skilled labor, to systematize the plan of advancing helpers for the duration of the war. In February, he issued General Order No. 8 which provided that helpers who had had five or more years' experience in the work of maintaining equipment might be elevated to the rank of mechanics on the basis of a mutual understanding between union representatives and management. But in no case was the ratio of promoted helpers to journeymen already existing in a craft at any repair point to exceed 1:5.

Leaders of the mechanical crafts, though they did not openly quarrel with the terms of General Order No. 8, were convinced that an amalgam of the sort which it legalized between journeymen and helpers would result in a general debasement in skill. Therefore when opportunity offered after the war, they strove for and secured the insertion of clauses pleasing to them on this issue in the shop crafts' national agreement. According to these, helpers were emphatically barred from advancement to the status of journeymen except by way of a long apprenticeship. Any helper, two years active in his trade and desirous of moving up, might do so by enrolling as a helper apprentice and submitting to a three years' course of training. Two classes of apprentices, regular and helper, were thereby recognized in the mechanical department. Regular apprentices must be indentured between the ages of 16 to 21 years, but in the case of helper apprentices the maximum age at entrance was set at 25 years for electrical workers, 40 years for boiler makers, and 30 years for the other trades. Not more than 50 per cent of the apprentices at a local point might consist of aspiring helpers. The shop crafts now endeavor to adhere basically to these apprenticeship rules in drawing up system agreements with the carriers.

### Local Craft and Federated Shop Committees.

LODGES of the mechanical craft unions appoint from their membership a special committee which is empowered to deal with matters in dispute between them and the local management of the carrier. This is the craft "grievance" committee which may find it possible to settle a difficulty by merely conferring with a supervisor, or may decide that it must take its complaint to the office of the general foreman, master mechanic, or shop superintendent. In turn a supervisor or local officer may summon the committee into his presence whenever he has a charge to lay against one or more of the craftsmen whom it represents. As a rule the president or chairman of the local lodge heads the "grievance" committee of his craft and is its chief spokesman.

Under the machinery of government erected by the constitution of the Railway Employees' Department, lodges belonging to the international unions affiliated with it may unite to form local federations. These bodies hold meetings attended by delegates from the lodges, or, it may be, by workers *en masse* from all the lodges, for the discussion of problems of intercraft relationship and other propositions of mutual interest. For the settlement of questions of more vital importance, each lodge votes as a unit. Joint action, however, at local repair points is not solely for purposes of deliberation and the harmonizing of craft relations. A federated shop committee, consisting of the chairmen of the individual craft "grievance" committees at the point, treats with the local management on any issue of joint concern, whether petty or more entangling, that may arise under the working agreement between the crafts and the carrier. Whenever management and men are friendly to each other, fewer misunderstandings develop under the agreement, and the federated shop committee may relax its vigilance and mark time. But whenever one or both of the parties become distrustful, grow contentious, or refuse to deal fairly, or whenever the contagion of a deeper-seated trouble on the carrier spreads to local points, the sessions between committeemen and officials wax bitter and stormy.

### System Organization.

TRADE-UNIONS with a footing in the railroad industry have found it advisable to set up units of organization to correspond for the most part with the size of each carrier's property. Occasionally two or more small-type, contiguous railroad systems have been brought under one unit. In order to do business successfully with the carrier as a corporate entity, the unions have realized that they must have some body, representative of their lodges and familiar with the statistical and accounting records of the carrier, to carry on negotiations in their name. Hence the organized shop crafts with the exception of the firemen and oilers have inserted provisions in their constitutions rendering compulsory, or allowing for a grouping together, of their lodges on a system basis. The Brotherhood Railway Carmen of America, for instance, enjoins its subordinate lodges, after three or more have been created on a system to take steps toward the establishment of a joint protective board; should they defer action, intervention on the part of the general president of the brotherhood is in order. A carmen's joint protective board is made up of the chairmen of the local protective boards on the system, each of which has the right to cast one vote for every twenty members, or major fraction thereof, that it represents. On the other hand, the boiler makers' international union permits its local lodges to decide whether they are prepared to form a district lodge on a railroad system, and, if they are, allows them to arrange their own methods of representation.

The expenses of maintaining the system craft organization are defrayed from *per capita* assessments on the membership of the local lodges. Disputes, unsettled locally, go to the officers of the system organization, appointed at its regular sessions or conventions, who carry them for settlement to the management of the railroad, either alone and in person or accompanied by the chairman of the local lodge involved. Any matter that may affect the contractual relations existing between a particular craft and the railroad employing it may be threshed out in its system organization meeting. Responsibility for the declaration of a strike of its craft membership on a railroad rests with each system organization, but before the strike may be called it is constitutionally bound to await the receipt of a favorable referendum vote of the locals, and to obtain the consent of the international headquarters of the union.

Just as it has been indicated that lodges of the shop crafts may federate for local action under authority from the Railway Employees' Department, so too under the same auspices provision has been made for the formation of a parallel type of organization for the whole of a railroad system. This is the system federation, the "highest, tribunal" of craft unions belonging to the American Federation of Labor in the transportation industry. At the bidding of the Railway Employees' Department three or more of its affiliated crafts organizations that have gained an accredited standing on any carrier or associated group of carriers, must apply for a charter to establish a system federation. Latitude is given the crafts to develop a federation structure that will accord with the conditions on each system, but investigation will disclose that these bodies are governed much alike on the railroads of the United States and Canada. Legislative powers are exercised by the system federation's convention which generally is made up of delegates from each craft local, on the carrier. Occasionally, however, representation in the convention may consist of quotas of from 3 to 5 men from the executive boards of the several system craft organizations. The officers of a system federation are: a president, vice-president, and secretary-treasurer, appointed in convention; and an executive board, composed of the general chairmen of the respective craft organizations. Between conventions, administrative authority lies with the executive board, which as a conference committee represents the federation in all negotiations with the management of the carrier or carriers over which it has jurisdiction. This committee arranges a system agreement with management binding upon the crafts that adhere to the federation, and attempts to handle disputes under an existing agreement that may be referred to it for settlement. Strikes involving a system federation cannot be launched without the sanction of the Railway Employees' Department to which are sent the tabulated results of the strike poll taken by the individual craft organizations.

### The Consummation of Joint System Agreements.

No sooner had the Railway Employees' Department been formed in 1909 than a tendency toward united action became apparent among the shop crafts affiliated with it. In fact these crafts began early to advocate the conclusion of joint system agreements with the carriers, in preference to separate trade agreements, and already by 1913 had persuaded a number of the roads to their way of thinking. As a result the department, at its 1914 convention, placed the six organizations, described in the opening paragraph of this chapter as the federated shop crafts, in a special mechanical section, in order that they might act together and be possessed of a "clearly defined craft jurisdiction." Throughout its *régime*, the United States Railroad Administration looked upon the federated shop crafts as belonging in a distinct category, and as previously mentioned arranged a national agreement with them in 1919 having this in mind. Upon the return of the carriers to private hands and the abrogation of the terms of the administration's agreement with them, the shop crafts in the United States fell back upon their original plan of negotiating joint agreements through the medium of the system federation. In Canada, another method of parleying for terms between the shop crafts and carriers had been adopted during the war which has persisted in that country ever since.

Joint system agreements drawn up on railroad lines in the United States where union-management coöperation is practiced, exemplify in excellent fashion the alliance of the six mechanical crafts for the furtherance of their bargaining power. When the shop crafts' national agreement was about to terminate in 1921, conferences were held between executive officers of the Baltimore & Ohio Railroad, and Chicago & North Western Railway on the one side, and system federations No. 30 and No. 12 on the other, and agreements negotiated to take effect from the date of expiry, July 1. Similarly the Chicago, Milwaukee & St. Paul Railway concluded an agreement with its shop crafts on December 1, 1921, and the Grand Trunk Railway an agreement with the same crafts for the lines which it operated in the United States on January 1, 1922. All these documents were in abeyance during the summer of 1922, while the trades subscribing to them were embroiled in the

shopmen's strike, but, except on the Grand Trunk Railway, were
reaffirmed in the month of September when the workers were taken
back into service under the terms of the Baltimore Agreement.
For a time the Grand Trunk Railway experimented with a "company union," but, after a vote ordered by the Railroad Labor
Board had gone three to one for the shop crafts, decided to re-
new its 1922 agreement with them in February, 1923. Amended
to date, each of the agreements referred to incorporates clauses
on many subjects, such as: minimum rates of pay for the various
classes and grades of shopmen; wage differentials within classes;
hours of service and assignment to work shifts; overtime and
emergency employment; reduction in and restoration of forces;
classification of the work processes assigned to the crafts; apprenticeship rules and the status of helpers; seniority rights; and
machinery for the settlement of grievances.

For a period of years an ambitious attempt was made by the
Railway Employees' Department to institute machinery whereby
system federations located within certain wide geographical
areas, might bargain in common. Tangible effect was first given
to this policy in March, 1916, when, as the result of conferences
with a number of roads in southeastern United States, uniform
wage scales were set for some 35,000 to 40,000 shopmen. Thereupon it was announced that the country had been mapped out
into three divisions to systematize such negotiations, and subsequently another division, No. 4, was created for the Dominion
of Canada. A halt was put to sectional bargaining in the United
States by the shop crafts' national agreement. Then, upon the
lapse of that agreement, the situation soon became so inauspicious
for the shop crafts in this country that the three divisions, though
revived, were finally abandoned in 1926. Nevertheless, Division
No. 4, which, in 1919, had wrung terms from the Canadian Railway War Labor Board quite like those secured by shopmen in the
United States under their national agreement, lost neither its
identity nor its bargaining capacity. It is now party to a joint
agreement with the Railway Association of Canada which rep-

resents all the important carriers operating north of the international boundary. The Railway Association of Canada included
within its membership in 1929: the Canadian National Railway
Company, the Canadian Pacific Railway Company, and six
smaller railroads. The agreement between the association and
Division No. 4 resembles very closely the types of system agreement described above.

### Trade Jurisdiction.

WHILE the policy of federation has not eliminated the outbreak
of jurisdictional disputes among the shop crafts, it has at least
reduced their virulence. In 1918, at the request of these organizations the Hon. W. B. Wilson, Secretary of the United States Department of Labor, appointed a board of arbitration to formulate rules of demarcation for the classes of work which each of
the crafts might perform in maintenance of equipment operations. The board published its findings on July 18, only to rouse
the heated opposition of the blacksmiths' union which declared
that it could not understand the meaning of the board's decision
with respect to welding, and threatened a general strike of its
members. Reconvened in June, 1919, the board then issued an interpretation of its dicta on welding which caused the blacksmiths
somewhat reluctantly to accept the ruling. The findings of the
board were eventually incorporated into the national agreement
to which the shop crafts subscribed, and have continued to be a
standard of jurisdictional amity among them until the present
time. Whenever a demarcation controversy arises on any system,
it is a rule of the Railway Employees' Department that a committee composed of the general chairmen of the federated crafts
shall meet and render a majority verdict. The chief executives of
the crafts directly involved are then given an opportunity to state
whether they are satisfied with the verdict. Unsettled questions
may be referred to the president of the Railway Employees' Department for his decision, with the right of a final appeal to its
executive council.

The adjustment of jurisdictional difficulties in the mechanical department has been of singular defensive value to the Brotherhood Railway Carmen of America, since it has been fully guaranteed against the inroads of woodworking crafts from without, and firmly intrenched in the car repair section of the department, has found itself with little to fear from within. Against any claims that the metal trades might set up, it has established an almost exclusive jurisdiction over work on composite and all-steel train car equipment. According to a compromise reached between the carmen and sheet metal workers, the former repair all air-brake pipes on freight-train cars, and the latter all steam, air, and other pipes on passenger coaches. Friction of long standing between boiler makers and sheet metal workers was dispelled by the Wilson Arbitration Board when it confined the sheet metal workers to operations on sheet iron and steel of less than 16-gauge. However, the boiler makers were instructed that they must share a portion of the work in heavier metal with the machinists. Through a peculiar development in the railroad industry, jurisdiction over pipe work on locomotives in the United States, except the application of flues recognized as belonging to the boiler makers, has been accorded to members of the Sheet Metal Workers' International Association. Pipes on old-time locomotives, made of copper, were repaired by coppersmiths, whom the sheet metal workers' organization included when they entered the mechanical department. As the pipes on locomotives changed in their metallic content, this union asserted its jurisdiction over pipe fitters of whatever type. Meantime, the United Association of Plumbers and Steam Fitters of the United States and Canada, with a clear authority over pipe work in the building industry, made some headway in organizing railroad shopmen, and was soon in conflict with the sheet metal workers' international. As a result, the Railway Employees' Department, having decided in favor of the sheet metal workers' claims to jurisdiction, dropped the plumbers' union from its ranks in 1914, and has since repeatedly declined to readmit it to affiliation.

The Wilson Arbitration Board took the attitude that the exclusive use of oxyacetylene, electric, and other forms of welding or fusing apparatus should not be conceded to any one of the mechanical crafts. Rather the object sought by each craft in its proposed employment of these devices should furnish a basis for the determination of its jurisdiction. The board declared that true, autogenous welding only occurred where two separated pieces of metal were joined together to make a united whole. From the earliest days on the railroads blacksmiths had performed this operation by knitting the pieces together at their fires. Accordingly it was but right, the board stated, that despite the changes in processing that had taken place, blacksmiths should go to the engine and weld the parts together with the new tools at their command. But, where worn or hollowed parts were to be built up flush by using the oxyacetylene torch or electric outfit, which to the mind of the board was actually a fusing process, other mechanics than blacksmiths might be set to work. The principle to be followed was to allow each craft to perform tasks with the new devices that, before their introduction, it had accomplished by other means. In 1921, an agreement was reached between the Brotherhood of Maintenance of Way Employees, and the firemen and oilers' union, by which it was stipulated that in the mechanical department the latter should have jurisdiction over firemen and oilers in stationary plants, water tenders, fire knockers and builders, coal passers, cinder pitmen, and engine watchmen. This means that the Brotherhood of Maintenance of Way Employees may enrol not only common laborers in the department, but also various shop laborers such as material, yard, and chain gang men, sand and oil house men, coal chute men, and turntable operators.

### Seniority Rules and Furloughing.

THE organized shop crafts give unqualified approval to the principle of seniority and all that it connotes for their rank and file in the mechanical department. Seniority, as enforced under the terms of system agreements in the United States and Division No. 4's agreement in Canada, is applicable alone at local repair points, where lists of employees are retained according to grade or subdivisions of a grade for each craft. Distinct rosters are always kept for mechanics and helpers respectively. Four lists may be maintained for each grade of carmen according to their subdivision into painters, upholsterers, pattern makers, and other carmen, and in the electricians' trade a separate list in each grade may be employed for linemen, groundmen, and the operators of larger traveling cranes. The names of workers newly taken into the service, whether from outside or from among apprentices qualifying as journeymen, are placed at the bottom of a list and seniority begins at once. Workers who transfer to similar employment elsewhere forfeit their standing on a list and must start over again.

Reduction of forces in the mechanical department puts seniority to an important test. Whenever for financial or other reasons it has been decided at the executive headquarters of a carrier that employees in the mechanical department shall be furloughed, instructions are sent to the local officer in charge at the point or points concerned. These officers study the seniority lists, and then, commencing from the bottom upward, cut off men proportionately from each to meet the executive demands. Four or five days' notice must be given to men about to be furloughed, and the committee of their craft must be advised of the action taken. Conversely, restoration of forces is accomplished by starting with the last man checked from each list, so that workers are brought back in order of precedence until opportunities for employment at the time are exhausted, or all have returned to service. When the force at a local point has been reduced, the officer in charge may sorely need a mechanic or helper for some particular task. Seniority rules compel him to ask first the top lay-off man of the craft involved whether he will undertake the work in question. Should this man decline, he waives his seniority in writing, and the local officer goes down the list appropriate in the case, until the proper man is found. Such waivers to the advantage of junior men have only temporary effect upon those who grant them.

### Standard Wages and Wage Differentials.

THAT craftsmen in the mechanical department shall receive standard minimum hourly rates of pay is a feature of all agreements drawn up for that department by the railroads indorsing coöperation. Journeymen mechanics of the federated crafts, except freight-train car repairmen, car inspectors, and electricians who may be classified as of lower rank, are paid the same standard minimum rate. By wage awards made to their federated crafts by each of the roads committed to coöperation in 1929 the scale for journeymen mechanics in the United States, with the exceptions noted, was fixed at eighty cents an hour, for freight-train car repairmen and car inspectors at seventy-three cents an hour, and for helpers in all crafts at fifty-seven cents an hour. In Canada, where living on the average is cheaper, shopmen of all classes and grades on the Canadian National Railway System are paid one cent an hour less. Under the agreements in force, regular apprentices to the federated trades are paid a minimum hourly rate when indentured, which is increased at the expiration of each six months of their service, and helper apprentices start at the minimum helper's rate which in like manner is increased at corresponding intervals.

A certain percentage of workers in the mechanical department may earn more per hour than the prescribed minima. A differential amounting to an addition of five cents an hour is paid to all journeymen mechanics employed at fusing or welding operations. Other journeymen mechanics receiving a five cent differential are: flangers and layers-out in the boiler makers' craft; heavy-fire blacksmiths, and machinists and boiler makers who may be detailed to inspect engines to meet the government regulations. Also helpers on flange fires and helpers working with heavy-fire blacksmiths and hammersmiths are given five cents more than the regular helper's scale. The highest wages, however, paid in the department are to hammersmiths among journeymen and to those assigned to duty at heavy fires among helpers, known as heaters, each of whom receives a differential of ten cents an hour above the minimum for his class.

## Chapter VI

## Historical Background of Union-Management Coöperation

IT is patent to even a casual observer that human relations in industry have developed somewhat differently on the common carriers of America than in other forms of employment. This is a phenomenon which it would be unwise to overemphasize, lest it lead to false deductions, and yet which cannot be ignored in any quest for the origins of union-management coöperation on the railroads. The movement toward coöperation has without a doubt been aided by certain inherent characteristics of the railroad service. Once a person has entered that service he generally finds that he has chosen his life's work. Railroading has a peculiar magnetism which binds its personnel to itself. Its drifters are not those who wander in and out of the industry, but are rather those who are today on one carrier and tomorrow on another. Whether of high or low estate railroaders are inclined to recognize the responsibilities of kinship and to be industrially loyal. They are group conscious and occupationally reverent to a degree that one might expect would engender a will to coöperative effort for the common welfare. At all events it may be argued that preconceptions are such in the railroad industry that the initiation and carrying forward of a plan of coöperation should be materially assisted.

*Industrial Relations on the Carriers Prior to 1914.*

STILL, from the standpoint of human relations in industry, the history of railroading has had many dark pages which would seemingly render futile the hope that group consciousness or occupational respect and loyalty might ever result in coöperation. Before 1900, slight evidence is to be found of any occasions upon which management and men had united on the carriers for a coöperative objective. Delegation of authority from staff headquarters to line officers and thence to supervisors brought on too many railroads in earlier days a kind of semifeudalism, in which the worker was regarded as the undervassal. In his reminiscences of laboring conditions in the late eighties, Vice-President Peter J. Conlon, of the International Association of Machinists, has declared that master mechanics of that period were like czars in their domain, and that "the general foremen in 75 per cent of the shops were 'bullies'" who levied tribute from the men of the machinists' craft for their positions. Older workers often tell of the unhappy status of supervisors under this *régime* who were at one moment fawning upon their superiors and the next, in obedience to orders, spying upon or browbeating the men beneath them. Nor is the other side of the picture any more engaging. Though the average worker of the time was unquestionably dutiful and pliable, a strong element in all ranks was "hard boiled" and ready for almost anything from "pitch and toss to manslaughter." Cliques arose to rule and harass their fellow craftsmen, and possibly to sell them to the enemy. Many were work-shy and malingering was practiced with impunity. Vilification of those in authority was a common pastime.

During the ten or fifteen years immediately preceding the European War, industrial relations on the carriers of the United States and Canada improved perceptibly. More enlightened policies were adopted on various roads both by forces of labor and of management, resulting in an amicable intercourse unknown before. A few railroad executives might justifiably claim that by the beginning of the war, at least on a portion of their property, a naïve and informal sort of coöperation had come into existence. Nevertheless, the feudal spirit still reigned within the officialdom of many carriers in 1914, and had not been wholly extirpated even from the most forward-looking of them. The testimony of reliable workers would go to show that at this time mechanical officers in charge at local points, though suiting their mode of action to changing conditions, were often as arbitrary as ever. Supervisors, too, in the mechanical department, while generally speaking less abusive than they had been, might occasionally be expected to revert to their former type. Labor, for its part grown more confident through increase in bargaining power whenever it chanced to be "hard boiled," might at any moment prove refractory. A favored diversion among the crafts intrenched at local repair points was to "run out" officers or supervisors who did not please them. The annals of railroad companies are usually silent about the experiences of their representatives, who, vexed and badgered by continuous opposition, or possibly subjected to bodily injury, were forced to abandon their positions on the line.

### Organizational Advances in War Years.

EVENTS of far-reaching importance affecting the railroad industry occurred between 1914 and 1922. These in their interlacing sequence may be regarded as constituting a historic background for the emergence of union-management coöperation, and if the circumstances which gave rise to that form of coöperation are to be properly understood, they must be studied in some detail. At the beginning of the war, marked inequalities might be noted in the relative strength of railroad labor organizations. The train and engine service brotherhoods, heartened by the recent successful outcome of a "concerted movement" for wages in eastern traffic territory, had a high degree of organization on all Class I railroads. Unions in the mechanical trades, though lagging far behind the transportation brotherhoods' record, had, as pointed out in chapter v, been making steady progress, and were working under system agreements on a number of carriers. With the exception of the telegraphers and railroad clerks, most other crafts were organized in a desultory manner, and were weak in bargaining capacity. The first year and a half of war brought trade stagnation and dislocated markets in America, and consequent unemployment. The situation improved rapidly, however, in 1916, as orders for war goods began to pour in from abroad. High wages offered by special war industries drew workers away from the railroads, with the result that good shop mechanics were soon at a premium, and "handy men" had to be increasingly requisitioned for service. As conditions kept getting steadily better, the time seemed ripe for an organizational advance of all railroad labor bodies. In a few years, as will appear in the sequel, these bodies found themselves in difficulties that resulted in disasters and out of that union-management coöperation came into being.

The train and the engine service brotherhoods, first in motion, sought early in 1916 to secure the eight-hour day with time and half remuneration for overtime, and, having refused arbitration on the issue, prepared, if necessary, to call a widespread strike. Their demands were granted through the approval of the Adamson Act on September 3. Then after a lower court had declared this law unconstitutional, they threatened another strike to avert which President Wilson named a committee of four, of whom Daniel Willard, chief executive of the Baltimore & Ohio Railroad, was one member. Through the mediation of this committee the same terms as the law had bestowed were established. Meantime labor shortage was becoming more acute, and organization proceeding apace.

During the winter of 1916–17, by skilful bargaining, the shop crafts were able to draw up with thirty-one carriers in the southeast the so-called "southeastern agreement" which contained an elaborate set of rules very much to their liking. For more than eight months after the United States had entered the war, on April 6, 1917, the railroads were left in the hands of their private owners. But as congestion due to heavy freight traffic developing in the summer of 1917 became intensified by troop movements and the transportation of army supplies in the autumn, the President decided, by virtue of authority already given him by Congress, to take possession of all carriers in the name of the United States on December 31. It was during the twenty-six months of federal administration which ensued that the railroad labor organizations reached the zenith of their power.

### The Abandonment of Piecework.

MUCH has been written on the subject of the wage awards made to railroad employees during the era of government control, and this will be dealt with briefly. General Order No. 27, issued by the Director General of Railroads on May 25, 1918, started the up trend in wage scales paid to these workers, and recognized as well the principle of the basic eight-hour day in the railroad industry. Thereafter, supplements and addenda, etc., to General Order No. 27, which followed one another in succession until early in 1919, completed what the administration considered to be the legitimate "war cycle" of wage increases. Supplement No. 4, of July 25, 1918, was very gratifying to shopmen, as it increased the scales, both of mechanics and helpers, thirteen cents an hour, which brought the wages of all federated shop mechanics, except carmen, to the level of sixty-eight cents an hour, retroactive to January 1. A minute classification of shop workers was also made effective by this supplement, and overtime regulations introduced for them on all carriers, similar to those previously incorporated in the "southeastern agreement."

Less notice has been taken of the abolition of piecework and other forms of incentive wage payment in the mechanical department of railroads which occurred at this time and which the shop crafts regarded as highly significant. The piecework system of wage payment had been particularly favored on eastern carriers. Railroad managers who advocated it claimed that it stressed the native ability of the worker and stimulated effort, which meant greater productivity and decreasing labor troubles. The organized crafts in rebuttal pointed out: that repair work was so variegated at railroad points that the piecework system could not operate there efficiently; that the system had been found to be discriminatory in character; and worse still, that it encouraged a thieving connivance between foremen and such craftsmen as were prepared to be dishonest. Controversy over this issue came to a head in 1918, when representatives of the shop crafts began a vigorous organizing campaign on the Pennsylvania Railroad, whose great shop at Altoona, Pennsylvania, was a well-known center of piecework practice, which in the past had always successfully resisted organization of its mechanical forces, but which had now become vulnerable to attack through the attitude of the railroad administration and the war situation. Pieceworkers on the Pennsylvania Railroad were disgruntled because Supplement No. 4 had done no more than guarantee them that their wages would not go below sixty-eight cents an hour.

Midsummer of 1918 found the shopmen on the Pennsylvania Railroad clamoring for admission to the mechanical trade-unions, with the result that in one month the machinists' lodge alone at Altoona enrolled 3,700 new members. Gleefully, the crafts then took action to launch System Federation No. 90 on the Pennsylvania Railroad, and made arrangements to put a referendum to the membership on the question of whether they desired a discontinuance of piecework at the carriers' maintenance of equipment stations. Ninety eight per cent of the ballots cast were in the affirmative. This outcome on the Pennsylvania Railroad gave an impetus to a discussion of the problems of piecework and other incentive wage systems wherever they were in vogue, and the Railway Employees' Department importuned the Director General of Railroads for a finding on the question of their abolition. In December, the Director General accepted evidence in the matter, and rendered a decision by telegraphing instructions to his regional directors that, when the men on any road employing piecework and corresponding systems should by a substantial majority indicate their preference for an hourly basis of wage payment, these systems were to be discarded on that road and hourly rates established. Polls were then taken on all lines involved in January, 1919, which give overwhelming majorities for the hourly wages.

*The Shop Crafts' National Agreement.*

THE railroad administration was not long in office before it signified unmistakably that it would adopt and maintain a sympathetic attitude toward the aims of organized labor. In General Order No. 8, section 5, Director General McAdoo stipulated that no railroad worker should be discriminated against because of his membership in a trade-union. A Division of Labor was set up to harmonize relationships in the railroad industry with the president of the Brotherhood of Locomotive Firemen and Enginemen at its head, while three bipartisan adjustment boards were created to settle disputes which might arise under existing agreements, and to settle controversies occurring over wage determinations and the eight-hour day. Emboldened by these marks of recognition and by their rapidly mounting numbers, the shop craft organizations now began to urge upon the federal body the desirability of having a standardized form of contract in relation to their working conditions. They argued that a national agreement, drawn up between the administration and themselves and superseding the diversity of agreements already in force, would tend to lighten the administration's burdens by making for stability in their class of work and for uniform policies throughout the country.

Obstacles, however, stood in the way of an easy attainment by the shop crafts of such an agreement. Director General McAdoo at first scouted the idea, and apparently was only won over to it after much persuasion. On the eve of relinquishing his post as head of the administration to Walker Downer Hines, on January 1, 1919, he appointed a committee, equally representative of the federated crafts and the regional directors of the railroads, to frame an agreement, but after months of wrangling over details the committee could only reach a joint submission on about one-half the rules debated. Drafting of the agreement was left to a smaller committee composed of minor officials of the administration and certain labor representatives. Meanwhile leaders of the shop craft organizations were unable to keep their following in leash, and, early in August, unauthorized "rump" strikes broke loose on various carriers involving nearly 250,000 men, in protest against alleged tardiness in granting wage increases and in completing the national agreement. President Wilson in the emergency peremptorily bade the strikers return to their posts, or else, he asserted, all negotiations would remain at a standstill. Reluctantly, the shopmen drifted back to work in answer to this ultimatum, and on August 23 were given a flat advance of four cents an hour in pay, retroactive to May 1. The task of finishing the national agreement was expedited, so that it was approved by the contracting parties and ready for publication on September 20. Also, to satisfy demands that had arisen, four other agreements, national in scope, were signed by the administration between this date and February 1, 1920, with unions of the maintenance of way employees, stationary firemen and oilers, railway clerks, and signalmen.

The shop crafts, it would appear, had chosen the right time to gain their objective, yet, in their struggle for a national agreement, had minimized the dangers of the situation. The agreement as ratified had received the approval neither of the regional directors of the railroad administration nor of the federal managers in charge of railroad units. Delays had been costly, since already before the agreement had been completed, announcement had been made that the carriers would soon be restored to private ownership, with the result that it could be tested for but a short time before the railroad administration must go out of existence. Roads in the southeast and to an extent in the northwest and southwest, accustomed to collective bargaining of a more intensive sort, might not quibble over its terms. But there would be many carriers that would find obnoxious its rules on work apportionment, uniform wages, seniority, and overtime, and would seize the earliest opportunity to combat them. Moreover, the fact must be borne in mind that the national agreements signed by the administration covered the working conditions of only ten of the sixteen standard railroad unions. Nonparticipation especially of the train and engine service brotherhoods in the movement to establish national agreements, though attracting slight attention at the moment, was to be of grave consequence for the shop craft organizations within the next two years.

### Steps Leading toward Conflict.

LITTLE more than a summary can be given of the curiously interwoven, trouble-stirring incidents of 1920–21, which, it will be seen, were effectively to modify the shop crafts' position on the railroads. When federal control expired under the terms of the Transportation Act of February 28, 1920, a Railroad Labor Board was instituted to settle all controversies relating to wages, hours, and other conditions of employment, which after reasonable effort had not been adjusted between the operating companies and their employees. The Railroad Labor Board at once addressed itself to a consideration of long-pending wage issues, and ordered that while it was so engaged, working conditions should remain in *status quo*. This meant that the national agreements should continue in force until they could be investigated, and a decision reached as to their validity. On July 20, wages were brought to their highest peak in the history of the railroad industry, when increases amounting approximately to 22 per cent were granted by the board to all classes of employees. The rate for shop mechanics, except freight carmen, under this award was eighty-five cents an hour.

The latter part of 1920 marked a definite turning point in the fortunes of the shop craft organizations. A group of conservative railroad executives, irked by the presence of these bodies on the lines which they controlled, and industrially fettered, as they thought, by various restrictive obligations in the national agreement still in effect with the shop crafts, began at this time to launch counterattacks that eventually were to prove the undoing of the crafts. Through the medium of the Association of

Railway Executives, in which its members had great influence, the group inaugurated an aggressive campaign for the overthrow of all national agreements. In the case of the shop crafts' agreement, charges were made that it had standardized the wages of shop mechanics and their helpers throughout the country; that it had awarded them time and a half overtime for all work beyond eight hours and for work done on Sundays and holidays; and had classified them so minutely that several employees must often be assigned to duties formerly discharged by a single employee. It is interesting to note that these rules to which objection was taken had, except as they bore on wages, been substantially incorporated in the "southeastern agreement" of 1917, and been fully legalized by Supplement No. 4 to General Order No. 27.[1]

A strategic plan adopted by the hostile executives was to endeavor to drive an entering wedge between the shop craft organizations and the train and engine service brotherhoods. To hinder congestion, the Transportation Act had provided that intermediary boards of labor adjustment might be set up, according to any arrangement desired, to handle unsettled disputes on questions other than wages, that without these agencies would pass directly to the Railroad Labor Board. Conferences which took place between representatives of the carriers, and of the railroad unions looking toward the establishment of such boards became hopelessly deadlocked. The shop crafts, jealous of the integrity of their national agreement, advocated the formation of several boards on a labor group basis for the whole United States, akin to those that had functioned during the railroad administration. The opposing executives, striving for decentralization, recommended instead the location of a board on each railroad system. Though differences of opinion on the issue had existed in the Association of Railway Executives, decentralization policies, championed mainly by Col. W. W. Atterbury, then Vice-

---

[1] This point has been stressed by Walker Downer Hinés in his *War History of American Railroads,* printed for the Carnegie Endowment for International Peace, Division of Economics and History, pp. 175–179.

President of the Pennsylvania Railroad, had been carried in that body, when put to a vote, by 60 to 41. At the outset the train and engine service brotherhoods supported the shopmen's claims; but, as the conferences proved resultless, they grew diffident in the matter. At length, after the Railroad Labor Board had acknowledged that it had no jurisdiction to create boards, and the matter had reached an *impasse*, the Pennsylvania Railroad, alertly watchful for an advantage, summoned the officers of its train and engine service employees to a meeting at Philadelphia on December 21, 1920. At this the transportation men were told that they represented the "most responsible" class of railroad workers, and were won to the acceptance of a system adjustment board on the Pennsylvania Lines. The intimate relations that had persisted for some years among standard railroad organizations now showed signs of weakening and in January, 1921, were strained when the four transportation brotherhoods came out officially for regional, in preference to national, boards of adjustment. With misgivings, the shop crafts spoke of a "break in the chain."

Hearings with respect to the national agreements were under way before the Railroad Labor Board early in 1921. Each side came well prepared with memoranda on the subject, so that a battle royal followed. In essence the employees' representatives contended that the rules in the agreements were reasonable, and that there was good evidence that they had been instrumental in creating more uniform and satisfactory working conditions. The railroad executives in answer claimed that various rules had unjustly penalized their companies, and that agreements which took into account the local situation on the individual carriers would work out to greater advantage. On April 14, the board handed down Decision No. 119 in which it ordered the abrogation of the national agreements on July 1, 1921, but remanded to the carriers and to their employees the duty of seeking in the interval to negotiate new and substitute agreements in conformity with sixteen basic principles which were attached to the decision as an exhibit; the settlement of disputed points was to lie with the Railroad Labor Board. In the ensuing negotiations the parties clashed with varying degrees of intensity, as the workers clung to rules which they cherished and the executives sought to eliminate those deemed peculiarly burdensome to the companies. The board, as a result, was submerged with controversies, and in the process of winnowing the wheat from the chaff amended, by Decision No. 222 and addenda thereto, seven rules in the shop crafts' national agreement that the mechanical trades regarded as distinctly "favorable." Of these seven rules, as amended, five were concerned with the annulment of overtime payments for work done on Sundays and holidays, and of payments for time spent in waiting and traveling by men assigned to special services; a sixth arranged for the physical examination of applicants for employment in the mechanical department; and a seventh allowed helpers and apprentices to be promoted to do carmen's work, when the latter were not available, without any stipulation as to the length of time they had been in the trade. If the carriers were willing, they might adopt all rules as they stood in the shop crafts' national agreement; otherwise, the amendments of the Railroad Labor Board became effective.

The fifteenth principle of those attached to Decision No. 119 stated that the majority of any craft on a railroad should have the right to determine the organization that would represent its membership in drafting agreements. Strife developed on the Pennsylvania Railroad when, in compliance with this principle, System Federation No. 90, declaring that it represented 75 per cent of the shopmen on that carrier, indicated its desire to negotiate an agreement. Officials of the road complained that they had no adequate proof that the system federation represented a majority of their shop workers, and after balloting had been proposed on the question, disagreed with the federation on the method of taking a vote. Each party tried its own way of balloting before the dispute was finally referred to the Railroad Labor Board where took place a keen struggle between the board and carrier. Representatives of the carrier, when summoned, refused to attend a meeting of the board in September, 1921, asserting that it was without prerogative to "invade the domain of management." The quarrel was at length taken to the courts, and after one reversal of judgment, reached the Supreme Court of the United States where a decision favorable to the board was rendered in February, 1923.[2] System Federation No. 90 soon became a shadow, as the Pennsylvania Railroad set itself firmly against dealing with any labor officials not in its own employ, and began to lay the foundations of the first of a throng of "company unions" that were soon to emerge on the railroads.

There was a great deal of unemployment among the mechanical trades in 1920 and 1921, occasioned in large measure, said their leaders, by the policies of the railroads in contracting out their maintenance work and even sometimes their repair facilities. Upon the abandonment of federal control, guaranty of income for a period of six months was granted to the carriers accepting the government's terms, by which they were assured of operating revenues equal in amount to what had been paid them in rentals under the railroad administration. A number of carriers at this time sent out much of their equipment repair work to "contract" shops, pleading that economy resulted through having it done where wages were lower, and where they avoided the objectional rules of the shop crafts' national agreement. Later, certain of the railroads leased one or more of their repair shops to dummy, auxiliary corporations, which simply rehired the old working force or took on new men at suitable rates of pay. The shop craft organizations claimed that the institution of these practices was intended as a blow to their membership who were either driven from employment or removed from the protection of the Railroad

2 See *Pennsylvania Railroad Company* v. *United States Railroad Labor Board et al.,* United States Reports, CCLXI, 72–86. In that it found that the board might not be enjoined for publishing violations of its decisions, the Supreme Court in this case may be considered to have upheld the board in principle. However, the court recognized that since the board had not been created as a tribunal to determine legal rights and obligations, its decisions had no other sanction than that of public opinion.

Labor Board; that repair costs had been increased thereby rather than lessened; and that through financial collusion between the carriers and outside concerns during the guaranty period the Government had been robbed of many million dollars. Spokesmen for the carriers pointed to the limited scope of these transactions, adding that the roads involved in them had acted on their own initiative in good faith, after having been advised that their methods were legal. Prior to the shopmen's strike in the summer of 1922, the Railroad Labor Board had handled but one case on this issue involving a small railroad which it decided was guilty of improper conduct in contracting out certain car repair work. The Interstate Commerce Commission, on the other hand, had in 1921 begun a series of investigations into specific cases of contracting out on larger roads, and in March, 1922, had ruled that the costs incurred by these practices had in some instances been grossly wasteful and in others excessive. The commission had expressed no opinion with respect to the motives dictating the carriers' policies.

### The Shopmen's Strike of 1922.

By Decision No. 147 and its addenda, effective on July 1, 1921, the Railroad Labor Board lowered the wage rate of all workers on the railroads approximately 12 per cent. The scales paid to shop mechanics and their helpers as a consequence suffered a flat decline of eight cents an hour. After the fashion of other railroad employees, the shopmen protested this reduction, and listed it among the grievances that had been adding fuel to their discontent. Still firm in their advocacy of national adjustment boards and a national agreement, the shop crafts were now feeling the impact of the attack being centered on them by the group railroad executives opposed to their views. Early in 1922, a further wage reduction was proposed, and the situation grew worse. It became evident that should a strike of the federated crafts be precipitated, it would likely be of general application, and even those roads which had no desire for a break with their shop workers would be drawn into one. The sixth convention of the Railway Employees' Department met in Chicago, Illinois, on April 10 with the mechanical trades in a belligerent mood. Overshadowing everything else was the necessity of taking action to redress injustices under which they believed that they were suffering. Though a few daring spirits suggested that in the event of a decision to strike, withdrawal from work should only occur on those roads that had given the greatest offense, the view of a majority of shop craft delegates favored action extending to all carriers. According to instructions given in convention, the executive council of the department then issued two strike ballots to the shop crafts on June 8, one of which covered the question of the seven amended rules, and the other, questions of contracting out and piecework. A third ballot was prepared by the council on its own initiative dealing with Decision No. 1036 of the Railroad Labor Board, of June 5, which had cut the wages of shopmen by amounts ranging from five to nine cents an hour. Tabulation of the votes cast on these ballots indicated that 95 per cent of the trades voting were ready to cease work. The executive council, therefore, authorized a countrywide strike of the shop crafts to begin on July 1.

In the neighborhood of 400,000 workers belonging to the six federated shop crafts answered the strike call, and were officially joined by the organized firemen and oilers on July 10. The Railroad Labor Board, on July 3, adopted by resolution the extraordinary and incongruous stand (in the face of eighty years of legal striking in the United States) that the shop crafts by their stopping work had definitely severed their connection from the carriers that had employed them. While strike leaders may have loosely stated that they were leaving the carriers' employ, this constituted neither excuse nor justification for the ill-advised decision of the board. The resolution also made public the fact that in the future the board would be ready to deal with craft groups on the railroads composed of those who had remained at work or of others newly enlisted for service. The carriers secured workers by establishing employment agencies, picking up drifters, and attracting mechanics and helpers from industries where they were less favorably situated. By superlative effort they kept their terminals operative, though few of them could maintain their equipment in safe condition.

As the strike gained momentum the carriers applied for, and were granted, injunctions by federal and other courts which were served both on local and higher officials of the craft unions. Altogether some seven hundred to eight hundred injunctions were issued against executive officers of the Brotherhood Railway Carmen of America. On July 11, President Warren G. Harding opened conferences lasting for several weeks with the parties involved in an endeavor to halt the strike. The shop craft organizations agreed on August 2 to accept terms of settlement proposed by the President which called for their return to work with seniority rights unimpaired. The railroad executives, however, objected to this settlement on the ground that they had taken thousands of men into service to whom they had promised seniority from the date of their admission. President Harding finally advised that the strikers go back to work, leaving the tangled question of seniority to the decision of the Railroad Labor Board. This in turn was inacceptable to the unions. Thereafter the handling of the issue from the standpoint of the administration, passed to Attorney General Daugherty who, on September 1, obtained a sweeping temporary injunction against the striking organizations from a federal district court in northern Illinois, which was continued after the presentation of voluminous evidence. Demoralization now set in among the strikers, pinched financially and overborne by legal action, so that they began to break ranks and cross to such carriers as might be willing to employ them.

Meanwhile the transportation brotherhoods had been parleying with the Association of Railway Executives in the hope that they might win honorable terms of settlement for their fellow unionists. Though their efforts had proved unavailing, it seemed that a portion of the executives were in a frame of mind to negotiate. Bent on creating a diversion of advantage to the shopmen's cause, the Railway Employees' Department entered into conversations with this group dominated in the main by the presidents of the Seaboard Air Line, Baltimore & Ohio Railroad, and New York Central Lines. The result was the drafting and signing in conference of the Baltimore Agreement, or as it has been sometimes called, the "Willard-Jewell Treaty" which became effective on eleven railroads and their subsidiaries on September 14. Other carriers later adopted a similar basis of settlement, but the number was disappointingly small. The gist of the Baltimore Agreement was that as many men as possible, not proven guilty of acts of violence, should be returned to their former positions at the wage rates established on June 5 by the Railroad Labor Board. Disputes as to seniority were to be referred to a commission of twelve, equally representative of the carriers and shopmen. The mechanical trades had emerged battered and spent from the struggle, and their organized strength on a majority of railroads in the United States was gone. Under the Railroad Labor Board's decision of July 3, many carriers, having successfully filled the places of men on strike, had begun to set up "company unions" on their properties, disclaiming any further relationship with the international craft organizations.

## Chapter VII

## Origin and Development of the Coöperative Plan on the Railroads

WHILE union-management coöperation first actually appeared on an eastern carrier early in 1923, it will be necessary, for a thorough understanding of it, to narrate events that began four years or more before the shopmen's strike. The stimuli that made possible the coöperative movement were supplied in the days of the government control of railroads. When William G. McAdoo became Director General of Railroads on January 1, 1918, he assumed the responsibility of endeavoring to secure coördinated action from all carriers in the United States in the face of an unprecedented traffic congestion which had developed in 1917, and the impairment of workers' morale that undoubtedly had taken place since the country had entered the war. That he was alarmed when he viewed the situation was obvious from the tone of letters which he immediately sent out to the executives of several railroads whose lines were in a strategic position, demanding that they introduce more effective transportation policies. Daniel Willard, president of the Baltimore & Ohio Railroad, who received one of these letters, in a reply dated January 21, candidly admitted that his forces had grown quite discouraged, a circumstance which, he affirmed, was "reflected in a certain let-down of effort." The director general, as a remedial measure, had already on January 18 appointed a Railroad Wage Commission with the assurance that wage rates would be raised, retroactive to the beginning of government control, and that employment conditions would be improved. Additional reasons have been given in the preceding chapter why railroad workers in general should look upon the government administration of transportation services with distinct favor, and should be ready to leave the adjustment

of their industrial difficulties in its hands. Director General Mc-
Adoo has stated that he and his assistants in office observed a
steady up trend in workers' morale throughout 1918, and Walker
D. Hines, his successor, has testified similarly for 1919. It was
during this time that proposals were originally made that management and men in the mechanical department of the railroads
should coöperate in some formal way for their individual and
common welfare.

*The Railroad Administration Indorses a Coöperative Program.*

THE nurturing ground of the coöperative movement on the railroads was provided by the International Association of Machinists. In an important sense this resulted from the fact that
the chief executive officer of that organization at the time was
William Hugh Johnston. Though rarely thought of as neglecting
practical considerations during his term of office as president of
the machinists' association from 1912 to 1926, Johnston was perhaps most widely known, both within and without the ranks of
trade-unionists, for his speculations on the industrial order. He
was a lay preacher *par excellence* of what he considered were the
ideals and high purposes of organized labor. As the war drew to
a close, and for several years after it had ended, the air was filled
with appeals for new and recreative forms of industrial democracy which should be introduced in the place of outworn systems
of economic policy. President Johnston joined in these appeals,
and was earnestly desirous of allying the machinists' organization with any movement that would assist in making industrial
democracy a reality. Shortly after the armistice had been signed
in November, 1918, he met at Washington, D. C., a man who was
to play a very significant rôle in connection with the evolution
and spread of union-management coöperation on the railroads;
he was Capt. Otto Sternoff Beyer, Jr., then in the service of
the ordnance department of the United States Army. President
Johnston was greatly delighted with their interchange of views

on industrial issues. "A most interesting and illuminating conference followed," he has stated, "which revealed a remarkable coincidence of thoughts, theory and experience on the part of Captain Beyer and myself with respect to the development of democracy in the government of industry."[1] Soon these two men were to be closely associated in fathering a scheme of industrial relations on the railroads which was to call for joint action on a coöperative basis between management and craft workers in the mechanical department.

Both by education and years of practical training Captain Beyer was excellently equipped to deal with the problem of bettering industrial relations on the railroads. He had been graduated as a mechanical engineer from the Stevens Institute of Technology in 1907. Then, after a period of service with an iron and steel company, he had become in 1911 technical assistant to the mechanical superintendent of the Erie Railroad. The following year, he had accepted a position as special motive power engineer on the Chicago, Rock Island & Pacific Railway, which he had held until 1913. Next, in order to acquire administrative experience, he had gone for a time to the Horton, Kansas, shop of the Rock Island System as general foreman in charge of medium-heavy and heavy repairs to locomotives. In 1916, he had left railroading to assume control of the locomotive testing laboratory, and to do experimental work in engineering, at the University of Illinois. Upon the outbreak of war he had entered military service, and had soon been assigned to the ordnance department, where commissioned captain in January, 1918, he had been given oversight of the technical training of all ranks. While the war was in progress, he had been one of those directly interested in fostering a spirit of coöperation between official supervisors and organized workers in the government's arsenals, notably in the largest of these at Rock Island, Illinois. An arrangement was effected with the arsenal workers whereby they were allowed to submit recom-

[1] Report of International President William H. Johnston, *Machinists' Monthly Journal,* September, 1924, p. 467.

mendations through their committees for improvements in working conditions and methods of production, and which required
that they be fully consulted whenever it was proposed to make
changes in their piecework scales.[2]

The United States War Department began in the winter of
1918–19 to reduce the personnel of its ordnance department
which led to the discharge of large numbers of mechanical and
other craftsmen from the arsenals. With a view to increasing
their work opportunities, the crafts concerned sent forward a request to army headquarters that an arsenal orders branch be
established within the ordnance department. The Secretary of
War approved of the formation of this branch which was set up
in May, 1919, with Captain Beyer in charge. The idea was that
the arsenals, as manufacturing units of the ordnance department,
might be used to produce goods economically for the War, Post
Office, and other government departments, after orders had been
solicited by the newly created branch. Two representatives, appointed by the crafts employed at the arsenals, remained continuously at the office of the orders branch in Washington, D. C.,
and were given a voice in determining its policies.[3] Workers were
also placed on local, joint advisory committees to deal with problems of manufacturing at five of the arsenals. During a little over
a year the branch obtained about three million dollars' worth of
additional business for the arsenals, and supplied employment to
many craftsmen, including some 2,000 machinists, who otherwise
would probably have been discharged. However, the War Department was still bent on retrenchment, and in the autumn of
1920 decided to confine the manufacturing activities of its ordnance department within narrower limits. In his administration of

[2] Cf. Vigilans, "Industrial Democracy at Rock Island," *The Nation,* September 13, 1919, pp. 366–367; William L. Chenery, "Arsenal Employes' Organization," *Survey,* May 8, 1920, pp. 205–207.

[3] Cf. John A. Fitch, "Manufacturing for Their Government," *Survey,* September 13, 1919, pp. 846–847; "Industrial Education in the Arsenals," *The
Dial,* September 20, 1919; Newton D. Baker, "Employees Advisory Plan of
the Arsenals," *Industrial Management,* November, 1919, pp. 400–402.

the orders branch, Captain Beyer had unquestionably had an opportunity to test out the value of joint action between management and workers in the conduct of industrial affairs, and besides had caught a vision of what might be done to stabilize employment in other fields of endeavor.

While acting as supervisor of technical education in the ordnance department Captain Beyer had already begun to evolve a coöperative program which he thought might be applied with advantage more or less generally among organized industries. In March, 1919, he had submitted an immature draft of this for critical comment to Arthur O. Wharton, who the year before had left the presidency of the Railway Employees' Department of the American Federation of Labor to become a member of the Board of Railroad Wages and Working Conditions. Then, as he had rounded his program into more coherent and satisfactory form, he had determined, in part because of his railroading experiences and in part because of assurances of support which he had received from the machinists' union, to seek its introduction on the government-controlled carriers of the country. With this in mind, he had laid it before the chief executive officers of the standard railroad labor organizations, each of whom had approved of it in principle. At about the same time he had entered into conversations with Walker D. Hines, Director General of Railroads, and certain of his assistants, in which he had urged its adoption, as far as might be considered feasible, on the lines under their jurisdiction.

The railroad administration thought well of Captain Beyer's program, and agreed to recommend its application at once in the mechanical department of the carriers. In a letter of November 10, 1919, to the regional directors of railroads,[4] Director General Hines requested that they should bring the program to the attention of the federal managers in their respective terri-

[4] For this letter and comments thereon see *Official Proceedings,* Fifth Biennial Convention, Railway Employees' Department, American Federation of Labor, Kansas City, Missouri, April, 1920, pp. 132–134.

tories who might see the wisdom of introducing it in the mechanical department of the lines under their immediate control, in
which department, he believed, there was "less of a spirit of cordial understanding" between management and men than anywhere else on the railroads. It is significant to note that the form
of coöperative procedure by joint, local committees advocated
in this letter corresponded very closely to that adopted several
years later on a carrier restored to private control. Aware that
the railroad administration would soon go out of existence, the
federal managers appear to have done little to give effect to the
Director General's suggestions, although he has declared that a
number of them were decidedly interested in the program. Officials of the shop crafts have reported that according to the information which reached them the letter obtained slender response. On three or four railroads only were their committeemen
summoned into conference by management, prior to the termination of government control, with a view to discussing the possibility of a coöperative arrangement.

### Where among Private Enterprises Would Coöperation Be First Adopted?

THE measure of support lent to Captain Beyer's coöperative program by the standard railroad labor organizations had largely,
no doubt, been motivated by their attitude of friendliness to the
railroad administration, whose success in directing the transportation services of the country on a basis of economy they
would gladly have facilitated by any means in their power. From
1920 to 1922, when upon the lapse of government control the
fortunes of the railroad labor organizations were waning, responsibility for furthering the coöperative program was almost
entirely assumed by the International Association of Machinists.
The account given in chapter vi of the events that occurred in
these years adversely affecting the status of the shop crafts
would show them being gradually thrown more and more on the

defensive. Their national agreement had been assailed as hindering production, and seven of its rules expunged as nonessential to the negotiation of system agreements. The national adjustment boards which they esteemed so highly had been dissolved for good. Work had been taken from them by the contracting out of motive power and train car repairs. An important group of railroad executives had developed a growing antagonism to the trade-union method of organization, an unhappy augury for the shop crafts on their lines. To the machinists' union these evidences of opposition to the shop crafts were due to a misapprehension of their purposes. Advocacy of a program of coöperation, it was thought, would create a different impression of the shop workers' aims; at least it would allow them to disprove the claim that they were uninterested in production.

The idealism which had flourished so remarkably before and after the armistice declined during the years 1920–22. Postwar deflation became acute in the autumn of 1920, and, as the value of trade fell off, wage-cutting was soon being practiced. Railroad management, busy at first in 1920 with the adjustments made necessary by the retransfer of the carriers into private hands, was then faced by one of the severest traffic slumps in the history of American transportation. Railroad workers, on the other hand, had grown more or less disillusioned as they had observed their lofty aspirations of the war period come to naught. While combating proposed reductions in the wages of members of the machinists' association, President William H. Johnston took occasion to advise a number of manufacturers, among whom was a well-known maker of printing presses, to introduce a scheme of coöperation in their plants as a means of harmonizing industrial relations and of cheapening, and bettering the quality of, production. None, however, of the manufacturers saw enough merit in the suggestion to adopt it.

At length in the spring of 1922 President Johnston and Captain Beyer turned to the railroads in the expectation that certain of them under private operation might be won to the acceptance of a coöperative program similar to that which Director General Hines had transmitted to the regional directors in 1919. They had decided to select first for approach only carriers whose management, judged by their past record, should be inclined to look with favor on the program, and whose shop workers, it was hoped, would raise but minor objections to its introduction. They made their initial appeal to the New York Central Railroad Company, with the president of which, the late Alfred H. Smith, William H. Johnston had for some time had very cordial relations. President Smith, it has been stated, was in sympathy with the program, but a conference held with operating officials of the carrier respecting its adoption for the mechanical department proved abortive. Next, President Johnston and Captain Beyer sought out Daniel Willard, chief executive officer of the Baltimore & Ohio Railroad, who already had established a reputation for broadmindedness on labor issues, and for the scrupulous care with which he had endeavored to adhere to the letter of trade agreements. They conferred with President Willard at his office in Baltimore and found him quite willing to hear their proposals. At the outset he was a trifle dubious of the program, which, coming in the manner that it had from the workers, he regarded as distinctly unusual. But, when he had asked several searching questions about it, and had discovered that its main purpose was to allow the workers along with management to express their opinions on matters relating to the more efficient conduct of industry, he said that he was ready to advise that it be given a trial on the Baltimore & Ohio Railroad.

These conversations with reference to the acceptance of coöperation held on the eve of the shopmen's strike doubtless assisted in paving the way for the Baltimore Agreement which rescued the crafts from a worse fate than they otherwise might have suffered as a result of that conflict. Maintenance operations had been thrown into a state of disorder during the strike at nearly all railroad shops in the country, and it was partly in gratitude to the Baltimore & Ohio Railroad for the rôle that it had played in making possible this agreement, that the machinists' organization again appealed to it in the autumn of 1922 to adopt the coöperative program as an aid to restoring efficiency in its mechanical department. President Willard who had given considerable thought to the matter of coöperation while the strike was in progress, expressed himself as prepared to resume negotiations with the crafts where they had been left off. In discussing the program with him Captain Beyer pointed out that it might be best to launch it at a shop where conditions seemed auspicious. President Willard half jokingly replied that the most unpromising maintenance of equipment station on the Baltimore & Ohio Railroad was its Glenwood shop at Pittsburgh, Pennsylvania.[5] If coöperation could succeed there, he said, it would succeed any place. Oddly it was then resolved, without material protest from labor, that coöperation should be first tried out at the Glenwood shop. System Federation No. 30, representing the shop crafts on the Baltimore & Ohio Railroad, pledged its support to the movement and joined with the International Association of Machinists in completing arrangements with the management of the carrier for the introduction of the program. Captain Beyer was retained by the machinists' organization to guide the development of the movement at Glenwood and in general to act in the capacity of a mediator between officers of the company and the crafts.

### Testing the Coöperative Program on the Baltimore & Ohio Railroad.

WHEN, several months later, Captain Beyer arrived at the Glenwood shop, he quickly learned for himself that it had earned the disrepute into which it had fallen. Due to a variety of retarding influences productiveness at the station had declined to about two-thirds of what its plant facilities would have warranted. Racial and religious differences had each had their share in bring-

[5] Refer to address of Daniel Willard before the National Civic Federation, reported in *Industrial Management*, May, 1927, p. 261.

ing this result, but perhaps the most deleterious effect upon output had been exercised by local politics. The Glenwood shop is located in Pittsburgh's second ward, noted in the history of the municipality for its boss rule. The ward politician had intrusted the carrying out of his policies in the shop to henchmen who might be either workers, or supervisors or men higher up, and anyone who showed too independent a spirit would generally find that his working conditions became very disagreeable or so intolerable that he was driven from employment. Gangs were arrayed against each other in the shop, and roistering and breaches of discipline were common. If, for example, the lie had been passed between groups of workers at the lunch hour, missiles might fly across the shop in the afternoon. Under these circumstances trade-union organization, in spite of the fact that it was firmly intrenched at the station, had been mainly held to the task of trying to settle disputes and grievances, and morale had sunk to a low level.

Before the strike, although the Glenwood shop was fully equipped to perform heavy maintenance operations both on train cars and locomotives, the company had at intervals, in order to save money, contracted out much of the work that it might be expected to do, thereby creating an irregular state of employment among its workers. Some 800 men were put to work after the strike and retained in service until the latter part of November, when suddenly all were furloughed. Then, as senior men were taken back by stages, by the New Year a force of 100 to 125 men were being steadily employed. Had it not been for the amount of capital invested in the shop the company would have been disposed to shut it down altogether. If the men at the station, whether at work or on furlough, were to be in a mood to support the coöperative program, it appeared essential that a binding guarantee should be offered them with respect to employment. At a conference held in Baltimore on February 9 executive officers of the carrier sanctioned the announcement of a definite policy on the question of employment, provided the men at Glenwood would agree to the program. Three days later a mass meeting of the crafts was assembled in Harmony Hall, Glenwood, near the shop, at which the company's proposals were put squarely before the men by their local officers and higher official representatives of the machinists' organization. While they were instructed in the ideals of coöperation, they were also given to understand that, if they were prepared in good faith to accept the movement, 300 furloughed men would be restored to service when the whistle blew the following morning. Other quotas were to be called back in order of seniority as coöperation became effective. By a standing vote the men pledged their assent, and the coöperative movement was under way.

Captain Beyer went to the Glenwood shop to supervise the introduction of the program toward the end of February, where he was assigned a desk and given what clerical help he deemed necessary. Shortly afterward, a preliminary get-together meeting of management and men was held in the master mechanic's office. At this were present four of the company's mechanical officers at the station, the local chairmen of the seven shop crafts, the secretary of local shop craft federation No. 10, and Captain Beyer. In the course of the proceedings Captain Beyer delivered an address explaining the aims of the coöperative movement; the basis upon which it was hoped that a joint committee representative of management and men would function at Glenwood; and the manner in which it was intended that suggestions should be received from both parties relative to operations of the shop and other questions of mutual concern.

It was one thing, however, as Captain Beyer discovered, to expound coöperative principles to the workers at the Glenwood shop, and quite another to get them into a properly receptive attitude. Contentiousness had prevailed so long at the shop that its speedy elimination could not be expected. Captain Beyer has referred to the many petty disputes and misunderstandings between management and employees which he was obliged to straighten out before coöperation had a chance to thrive. To handle the type of men who had been a source of trouble under the old *régime* was an outstanding difficulty. Committeemen of their craft, held responsible for such men, would alternately chide them and entreat them to do better, when they failed to coöperate, and finally, if they remained headstrong, ask for their removal to a less desirable location in the shop. Transferred workers, it has been said, would generally after a time come penitently asking for a return to their former positions. Discharge or permanent demotion of "troublemakers" was, so far as possible, skilfully avoided, with the result, as Captain Beyer has expressed it, that they "were saved for their shop and railroad, and perhaps for themselves and their families."[6] By degrees a routine method of procedure was worked out for joint, coöperative meetings, so that when Captain Beyer left the Glenwood shop after almost a year, union-management coöperation on the railroads was no longer merely a program but might be more properly spoken of as a plan. Through his training and experience as an engineer, Captain Beyer had been able to instruct the local committee in the classes of suggestions that would most likely lead to improved workmanship and increased production.

A year's trial of coöperation had served to place output and morale alike on an entirely different plane at the Glenwood shop. Furthermore, the Baltimore & Ohio Railroad had given a large complement of workers regular employment at the station in fulfilment of its promise. In February, 1924, section 2 of the executive council of the Railway Employees' Department, representing exclusively the mechanical trades, met and adopted union-management coöperation in the form in which it had been evolved at the Glenwood shop as its official plan of industrial relations. Captain Beyer was taken into the employ of the department to act in its behalf as a technical adviser to railroads when introducing or extending the plan. By this time systems of employee representa-

6 Address by Captain Otto S. Beyer, Jr., reported in the printed proceedings of the Fifth Convention, Division No. 4, Railway Employees' Department, Montreal, Quebec, March, 1924, p. 29.

tion, of varying significance, were being developed as a feature of the "company unions" that had been set up on carriers where the shop crafts had been worsted in the strike of 1922. Although the Railway Employees' Department made no specific mention of systems of employee representation on the railroads when indorsing the Glenwood plan, it may be assumed that the action which it took was largely intended as a countermove to these.

On February 24, 1924, a memorandum of understanding was reached between the management of the Baltimore & Ohio Railroad and the officers of System Federation No. 30, wherein were embodied in detail the rules according to which joint local committees and also a system committee should be established and function on the carrier. The institution all told of forty-five local committees was authorized for stations under the jurisdiction of its maintenance of equipment department. Moreover, an arrangement was consummated by the railroad about the same time with other crafts on its lines, as will be further explained in chapter xix, by which committees might be set up for each of its divisions that would be unitedly representative of the transportation department and the department of maintenance of way and structures.

In July, 1924, an agreement was drawn up between officers of System Federation No. 41 on the Chesapeake & Ohio Railway, and its chief mechanical officer, for the inauguration of a plan of coöperation in its maintenance of equipment department. A beginning was made by forming a committee in the motive power department of the 17th Street shop at Richmond, Virginia, the personnel of which was later widened to include representation from the car department at the same point. However, the carrier's management, though not disavowing the plan, has been unwilling to extend it to other maintenance of equipment stations. Meetings are still held at the 17th Street shop, but suggestions are rarely presented by those who attend, and coöperative procedure on the Chesapeake & Ohio Railway may, therefore, be regarded as dormant.

*Establishment on the Canadian National Railway System.*

DURING the years 1918–22 four distinct transportation groups
were coördinated to form the Canadian National Railway Company. First, a unified management was set up in 1918 for the
Canadian Government Railways and the Canadian Northern
Railway Company, and then to these were added the Grand
Trunk Pacific Railway Company in October, 1920, and the
Grand Trunk Railway Company in January, 1923. The Canadian mileage of the last-named carrier and its mileage in the
New England states were made a part of the central region of
the Canadian National Railway System. Its mileage in the states
of Michigan, Indiana, and Illinois was erected into a separate
region, which in 1929 acquired single, corporate existence as the
Grand Trunk Western Railroad Company. Instituted during a
period of war-time and post-war stringency, the Canadian National Railway Company was struggling along with a very
meager operating revenue and a huge deficit shown annually in
its income account when Sir Henry Worth Thornton consented
to assume office as its president in October, 1922.

Henry W. Thornton had begun his railroad career as a
draftsman in the department of maintenance of way and structures of the Pennsylvania Railroad, on which carrier he had risen
to the rank of division superintendent and eventually in 1911 had
been made general superintendent of its subsidiary, the Long
Island Railroad. When the European War began, he had been
called to Great Britain to become general manager of the Great
Eastern Railway, a run-down carrier which for years had been
the butt of music hall ribaldry. While in Great Britain he had
succeeded in rejuvenating the Great Eastern Railway, had been
commissioned with important tasks by the British Government,
and knighted for his various services. The invitation which he had
received to take control of the Canadian National Railway Company had been issued in the belief that he was the man most likely
to be able to put that public enterprise on an economically sound
and progressive basis.

When the Grand Trunk Railway Company had been included as part of the Canadian National Railway System, it was employing a bonus plan of remunerating its shop workers at all its major repair points both in Canada and the United States. Opinion developed on the Canadian National Railway System, especially among officials, in favor of inaugurating the bonus method of payment on other sections of the company's lines, a proposal which at once gave rise to vigorous controversy. Though many formerly in the employ of the Grand Trunk Railway Company were satisfied with the operation of the bonus plan, it soon became evident to officers of the shop craft organizations that hostility would be shown to its wider extension by a large proportion of workers on the system as a whole. In view of this fact, J. A. McClelland, a vice-president in Canada of the International Association of Machinists, considered a move to establish some form of coöperation between management and men on the Canadian National Railway System which might stop, or at least discourage, the spread of the bonus method of payment. He communicated with William H. Johnston, seeking to learn more of the objectives of coöperation as it was being advocated by himself and Captain Beyer, and took occasion to sketch for Sir Henry W. Thornton what he thought it might mean if applied in the mechanical department of the Canadian National Railway Company. Sir Henry W. Thornton, immediately receptive to the idealistic tenets of coöperation, foresaw the advantages which its introduction might have in establishing improved industrial relations on the great carrier that had recently come under his supervision. Early in the summer of 1923 he wrote to President Johnston stating that he would be glad to discuss the coöperative movement with him if he would make a trip to Montreal. President Johnston could not go at the time, and for six months the matter was in abeyance. In December J. A. McClelland again talked with Sir Henry W. Thornton about coöperation and received his assurance that he was willing to give it a trial on the lines of the Canadian National Railway Company. Moreover Sir

Henry went with J. A. McClelland to the office of S. J. Hunger-
ford, vice-president in charge of operation and construction on
the carrier, where he expressed the desire that there should be no
further extension in the mechanical department of the bonus
plan.

On January 11, 1924, a meeting of general managers, mechanical superintendents, and other officers of the Canadian National Railway System was held in Montreal, Quebec, at which
William H. Johnston and Captain Beyer were present. By an
informal method of question and answer the officers were acquainted by the two visitors with the leading aims and administrative features of the coöperative movement. The meeting was inclined toward an acceptance of a plan of coöperation, but before
its conclusion agreed that no steps could be taken to introduce it
on the carrier until the approval of each of the shop crafts involved had been secured. With this in mind the Railway Employees' Department of the American Federation of Labor arranged to have the claims of coöperation presented before the
fifth annual convention of Division No. 4 when it assembled at
Montreal on March 24. B. M. Jewell, president of the department,
William H. Johnston, and Captain Beyer, attended the convention and early in its proceedings delivered addresses dealing with
the coöperative movement from almost every angle. A special
committee of fifteen members was then appointed to study the
issues which the adoption of a plan of coöperation would present
to the shop crafts in Canada. In a report, submitted on March
28, this committee advised that Division No. 4 go on record as
indorsing the principle of coöperation, but that each system federation adhering to it should decide, from the standpoint of labor,
whether it was ready to have a plan put into effect on the lines
under its jurisdiction. The policy might be advisedly followed, of
first agreeing with management upon one particular shop where
the plan would be given a fair test. No action, however, should
be taken before the membership at that point had signified its
approval. Though the report elicited a barrage of inquiries and

criticisms it was finally adopted on a roll call ballot of the convention by 85 votes to 29.

Indorsement of coöperation by Division No. 4 had cleared the way for its acceptance, so far as labor was concerned, on any Canadian carrier, but only on the Canadian National Railway System was management willing to go along with the movement. *Pourparlers* between officers of the Canadian National Railway Company and its System Federation No. 11 continued throughout the remainder of the year. In the interval Captain Beyer made a personal survey of the leading repair points on the system in Canada and prepared a report covering his itinerary which he submitted to the company for consideration on August 23. Finally the shop at Moncton, New Brunswick, a point on the former Canadian Government Railways, was selected as an appropriate spot to launch the movement. In contrast to what has been described as the situation at the Glenwood shop of the Baltimore & Ohio Railroad, industrial relations had always been harmonious at Moncton, but nevertheless production was at a relatively low ebb. Political influences had impaired efficiency on the Canadian Government Railways, and Moncton was a station where under the old *régime* patronage had left baneful traces. After a sanctioning vote of the local crafts had been taken, the first joint cooperative meeting on the Canadian National Railway System was held at Moncton in January, 1925. The plan was next extended to the carrier's locomotive repair shop at Stratford, Ontario, and thereafter by degrees to other of its major shops in Canada. The sentiment of the men at the different points was generally discovered through what to railroaders is known as "caboose talk," the tenor of which would indicate when a favorable vote might be secured and the plan successfully inaugurated.

As early as August, 1925, the coöperative movement was carried to the western region of the Canadian National Railway System, but only at first to its Fort Rouge and Transcona shops at or near Winnipeg, Manitoba. In consequence of the spread of One Big Union doctrines in western Canada after the war, leading to the famous general strike at Winnipeg in 1919, the shop crafts affiliated with the American Federation of Labor in that area had been reduced to skeleton proportions. One Big Union advocates showed their dislike for coöperation, when its introduction was discussed, by calling it "the Canadian National slave pact." However, as the management of the railroad entered into coöperative relations only with representatives of the international craft unions, and as it adopted a policy of slowly weeding out more troublesome persons from employment, a change was gradually effected in the labor situation at its Winnipeg shops. All the craft unions began to experience a marked accession of strength after the inception of coöperation. In January, 1927, management and men agreed upon a constitution for the joint coöperative plan, which according to orders issued in April of the same year was to be extended, if locally acceptable, to all enginehouses and smaller car repair points in eastern Canada where approximately fifty or more men were employed. Following a visit paid by Captain Beyer to Battle Creek, Michigan, in 1926, the plan was introduced at that station and then transmitted by stages to other points on the Grand Trunk Western Lines and to the strip of mileage belonging to the Canadian National Railway Company in New England. In 1926 and 1927 provision was made for the selection of a regional committee in each of the carrier's three regions located mainly in Canada, and for the formation of a joint system committee, the composition and powers of which will be described in chapter viii. Further expansion of coöperation on the western region was begun in the summer of 1928, with the result that by the autumn of 1929 the plan was functioning at fourteen points outside the Winnipeg area.

The unqualified support given to the coöperative movement on the Canadian National Railway System by Sir Henry W. Thornton has without question contributed immeasurably to the firm hold that it has secured on the carrier's economic life. Sir Henry's zeal for the creation of more harmonious relations between management and men on the lines under his supervision would seem to be due in part to his native traits of character, and in part to the variability of his railroading career. During an interview which he granted the writer at Montreal, Quebec, in November, 1928, he acknowledged that as an official in the service of the Pennsylvania Railroad Company before the war he had never been exactly satisfied with its labor policies. His duty, he said, to the railroad had carried him in one direction, while his heart was bearing him in another. In discussing his experiences as a railroad executive abroad, he paid a high tribute to the industrial compatibility of the British railroad workers. Their intelligent willingness to unite with him for a common end, he believed, had helped to crystallize ideas already in his mind of the proper relations that should subsist between management and men on the railroads. Concerning the attitude which he as the chief executive officer of a great railroad system might be expected to hold toward organized labor he spoke succinctly and without hesitation. Trade-unions, he asserted, were in industry to stay, and for him to combat them would be like rowing a boat against the stream. His policy, therefore, was to pull with them.

### The Chicago & North Western Railway Adopts Systematized Coöperation.

ALTHOUGH the plan of coöperation formulated for the mechanical department of the Chicago & North Western Railway is in no essential respect dissimilar to those in effect on other carriers its evolution has been to an extent separate. The question of establishing a formal type of coöperation on the Chicago & North Western Railway was first broached shortly after the termination of the shopmen's strike. It happened that when one day in the autumn of 1922 B. M. Jewell, president of the Railway Employees' Department of the American Federation of Labor, was in conference on various matters with William Walliser, vice-president in charge of personnel on the railroad, he commented upon the very friendly relations that, in spite of the strike, appeared to prevail between its management and shop workers. Upon the basis of this chance expression of opinion the two men began to debate the possibilities of organizing a system of joint machinery for the road whereby more tangible results might be secured from the coöperative spirit already in existence. William Walliser had quite original ideas to offer on the subject, and may be considered the main author of the coöperative plan eventually accepted on the carrier. Inasmuch as Jewell and Walliser had an understanding with respect to the introduction of a coöperative program on the Chicago & North Western Railway previous to the erection of the committee at the Baltimore & Ohio Railroad's Glenwood shop in February, 1923, it may fairly be claimed that from a historical standpoint the movement on the former road had an independent beginning.

Certain hindering factors intervened, however, to prevent action being taken to set up a form of union-management coöperation on the Chicago & North Western Railway during the balance of 1922 and throughout 1923. But the question was given an important place in the agenda for discussion when William Walliser met system officers of the shop crafts in conference in the early part of 1924. The pros and cons of the movement were then debated in lodges of the federated crafts, letters on the subject were interchanged between them, and further parleys in relation to the elaboration of a plan of coöperation for the carrier held with management. Early in 1925, Captain Beyer went to Chicago to assist in forwarding the movement on the carrier although by this time the plan being drawn up was in its final stages of completion.

On March 6, 1925, a mass meeting of the federated shop crafts was held in Wicker Park Hall, Chicago, at which the details of the proposed plan of coöperation for the railroad was subjected to a lengthy consideration. Some opposition to it was voiced by one or two crafts, but on the specific question as to whether it should be adopted or not the meeting took an affirmative stand. A program of systematized coöperation, maintenance of equipment departments, was then signed by William Walliser, representing the company, and by the general chairmen of each of the federated crafts, and copies prepared for distribution to local repair points. In this were set forth the aims of the movement, the composition of the local and central coöperative committees to be formed on the carrier, the subjects that might be beneficially dealt with in coöperative meetings, the necessity of keeping a record of all proceedings under the plan, and the company's policy with respect to the stabilization of employment. The first local coöperative meeting on the Chicago & North Western Railway was convened at Clinton, Iowa, in the month of April. Fred. W. Sargent, president of the carrier, spoke favorably of the movement; William Walliser and craft officials traveled from point to point to explain its objectives; and by 1926 it had been extended to all repair stations on the company's lines. Coöperative committees now function at some thirty shops, enginehouses, and car yards on the railroad.

### The Deer Lodge Experiment and Acceptance by the Milwaukee System.

To trace the origin of the coöperative movement on the Chicago, Milwaukee, St. Paul & Pacific Railroad, it will be necessary at the outset to direct attention to its Deer Lodge, Montana, shop, situated at the western end of its Rocky Mountain Division. In 1923, E. Sears, master mechanic of the Rocky Mountain Division, while on a trip to Missouri, had an opportunity to investigate the activities of a joint welfare committee made up of representatives of management and employees, which had been established at the plant of the Commonwealth Steel Works near St. Louis. Upon his return to Deer Lodge, he told Eric Peterson, a district delegate of the machinists' organization on the carrier, of his observations, whereupon the latter furnished him with a brief account of the results, which according to his information had already been obtained through coöperation at the Glenwood shop of the Baltimore & Ohio Railroad. Master mechanic and district delegate found themselves equally desirous that some form of organization should be adopted at Deer Lodge by means of which administrators and workers might act in unison to increase efficiency, enforce shop regulations, and improve working conditions. With a view to achieving this, a meeting attended by representatives of the crafts was held in the master mechanic's office in December, 1923, at which preliminary steps were taken toward the institution of a satisfactory joint plan. At length on February 18, 1924, was created the mutual welfare bureau, or committee as it was subsequently termed, of the Deer Lodge shop, which continued to meet once a month for almost three years with marked success until superseded by the official acceptance of union-management on the carrier in 1927. The mutual welfare committee functioned in almost the same manner as a local coöperative unit. Unlike a coöperative committee, however, it had very explicit rules for the maintenance of shop discipline, and had a worker as its chairman in alternate months. It is interesting to note that during its lifetime this committee made a conscientious attempt to estimate, in so far as possible, the gains accruing from its recorded suggestions.

Although it would be an error to state that the existing coöperative movement on the Chicago, Milwaukee, St. Paul & Pacific Railroad grew out of the venture at Deer Lodge, a certain relationship between the two must be distinguished. When in 1925 the Milwaukee System, due to circumstances that will be outlined in chapter xvi, went into the hands of receivers, its management was ready to entertain any idea that might lead to the betterment of its financial position. A proposal, therefore, advanced by the shop crafts that the introduction of a plan of coöperation in its mechanical department might increase production was regarded by management as one means toward the goal of economy. While little rancor had been left on the Milwaukee System as an aftermath of the shopmen's strike, it was nevertheless known that a combination of laxity and friction among its personnel at various repair points was impeding output. The mutual welfare committee at Deer Lodge had afforded a prototype of what might be accomplished by joint endeavor on the railroad, and it would for this reason seem unnecessary to put coöperation to a further test at any particular shop. Action looking to a more general acceptance of coöperation on the carrier was first taken on August 2, 1926, when the vice-president in charge of operation and other staff officers went into conference on the matter with the system chairmen of the federated shop crafts. The history and experiences of the committee at Deer Lodge were among the subjects discussed at this meeting. The general chairmen, believing that they voiced the attitude of the shopmen on the company's lines, agreed to assume the responsibility of indorsing coöperation without the necessity of a referendum vote. The initial meeting under the plan was held at the carrier's Milwaukee, Wisconsin, shop in September. Then on November 29, a formal memorandum of principles, embodying rules of procedure for the plan and a statement of its main objectives, was signed by staff officers of the carrier and the craft chairmen. No central coöperative committee has as yet been created on the Milwaukee System.

# Chapter VIII

## The Technique of Coöperation

THERE is no sound argument against informal or unsystematized types of coöperation on a railroad or in any other business enterprise. The function of coöperation, as the word is used in this study, is to harmonize in a progressive manner the relationships existing between management and men as human factors in industry, with the end in view that both may be benefited socially and economically and the industry itself be advanced in the process. Results of such a character have been attained, and, doubtless, still will be attained without the employment of any functional machinery through which coöperation may work. For some years, as both parties will testify, a splendid spirit of coöperation has prevailed between management and organized workers on the Southern Railway System which, in spite of the fact that no joint meetings are held, has redounded to the distinct advantage of the company and its personnel. A somewhat corresponding state of affairs may be found on several other carriers. Proponents of union-management coöperation have not been in the habit of belittling these illustrations, but rather have commended them, claiming that they are merely indicative of the richer and fuller measure of benefits that may be secured through the adoption of their plan. A most attractive feature of union-management coöperation, they assert, is the simplicity of its functional machinery, which renders them confident that its spirit will never be lost in the form. Whether their assurance on this point is justified, can only be decided after the rules of procedure governing union-management coöperation on different railroad systems have been surveyed in detail.

### Participation of Organized Labor.

THE principles of union-management coöperation involve the

"full and cordial recognition" by a carrier's management of any
or all of the craft organizations on its lines, as one party committed together with itself as the other party, to action under cooperative rules of procedure.[1] The Railway Employees' Department of the American Federation of Labor, whose affiliated
unions, as related, have been so instrumental in fostering the
plan, has not minced words in defining what is meant by recognition. Henceforward, it has affirmed, those organizations that
participate in coöperation shall not be regarded by the carriers
as a sort of "necessary evil" with whom they must bargain concerning wages and working conditions, but as a helpful and constructive force, intent on bettering railroad performance. Old
ideas must be surrendered, and the unions accepted as assets instead of as liabilities in the daily operation of the railroads.

Carriers, it may be assumed, will be disinclined to enter into a
coöperative arrangement with any craft or federation of crafts
that does not embrace within its membership a substantial majority of employees on their lines. Yet, for one reason or another,
it may sometimes happen that at a given repair point a craft or
local federation participating in coöperation commands a bare
majority, or even represents a minority of the workers. Where
"home guards" are in evidence at smaller points, and workers
less migratory, the degree of organization is likely to be relatively high. At central shops, especially if located near a large
city, owing it may be to a greater labor turnover, radical movements, due dodging, personal antagonisms, or a combination of
a number of things, organization will often be at a lower ebb. The
federated crafts, for example, have a membership in the extensive Mount Clare shop of the Baltimore & Ohio Railroad within
the environs of the city of Baltimore, Maryland, estimated at
only 50 to 60 per cent of the total working force. Several crafts

[1] See American Federation of Labor's pamphlet, *The Coöperative Policy of
the Railway Employees' Department,* 1926, pp. 7–8; and *Official Proceedings,*
seventh convention, Railway Employees' Department, Chicago, Illinois, 1926,
pp. 69–74.

in the Fort Rouge and Transcona shops of the Canadian National Railway System at or near Winnipeg, Manitoba, were notoriously weak for a length of time after the introduction of the coöperative plan, mainly on account of the influence of radical thought. Coöperation would be ineffectual under these circumstances, unless feebleness of organization at certain points were offset by healthy union growth at others.

Procedure under union-management coöperation in the mechanical department of railroads in the United States includes in all instances the six federated shop crafts, according to their allocation for service at maintenance of equipment points. The basis upon which one of the federated crafts has been taken into the plan varies in the Dominion of Canada, as will be noted. To date, the Chicago & North Western Railway, and the Chicago, Milwaukee, St. Paul & Pacific Railroad have admitted only the six trades to participation in their coöperative arrangement. The Baltimore & Ohio Railroad, on the other hand, has allowed representation on local coöperative committees to the International Brotherhood of Firemen, Oilers, Helpers, Roundhouse and Railroad Shop Laborers, wherever that organization has become established on its lines. Also, the firemen and oilers' brotherhood has a representative on the committee of the Grand Trunk Western Railroad Company's central shop at Battle Creek, Michigan. The widest form of participation in coöperation by shop workers, however, occurs on the lines of the Canadian National Railway Company operated within Canada. When, after 1922, the three divisions subordinated to the Railway Employees' Department in the United States began to lose their importance, Division No. 4, created for Canada, drifted to a semi-independent position, and formulated by-laws in its conventions expressly to suit the needs of shopmen in its territory. The constitution of the Railway Employees' Department as revised in 1926, it may be pointed out, took no cognizance of the existence of Division No. 4, so that it has become in effect a national institution for Canada, though always careful to maintain friendly relations with the parent body in the United States. Because of a peculiar jurisdictional situation in Canada arising from distinctions drawn between pipe work and sheet metal work, which allows control over the former to the United Association of Plumbers and Steam Fitters of the United States and Canada, and over the latter to the Sheet Metal Workers' International Association, Division No. 4 has granted affiliation to both of these unions. Furthermore, to the extent that they have become organized on the railroads of Canada, it has taken in lodges of the International Molders' Union of North America, the Pattern Makers' League of North America, and the firemen and oilers' brotherhood. The Canadian National Railway Company in developing its coöperative plan within the boundaries of Canada has followed almost identically the policies of Division No. 4. It admits to its coöperative meetings not only representatives from the six shop crafts, but also pipe fitters who belong to the plumbers' association, and members of the pattern makers' and molders' internationals. Owing to the circumstance, however, that the firemen and oilers' organization has had to face competition from an aggressive national union in enrolling shopmen of its craft in Canada, its inclusion under coöperation is held in abeyance.

### Basis of Representation.

In its application to the mechanical department, union-management coöperation's chief sphere of action is the local joint committee. As the aim of the plan is to bring management and men together for the discussion of problems of mutual concern, meetings are held periodically at maintenance of equipment points to which are summoned, so far as is possible, an equal and balanced representation from each. Authority is vested in the ranking officer at a repair point, or of the district in which a repair point is situated, whether he be shop superintendent, master mechanic, master car builder, or general foreman, to see that the plan functions according to agreement, to preside, either in person or by deputy, at all meetings, and to keep a chronological record of the accomplishments of local coöperative effort. On all railroads committed to coöperation a group is chosen from the supervisory staff at a local point, by the mechanical officer in charge, to speak for management. In practice, at small stations he names all his staff, but is forced to pick a certain number from among them at larger shop points. In the latter case, when a supervisor has served on the joint committee for some time, he is generally dropped from it and another supervisor appointed in his stead. Except on the Chicago & North Western Railway, it is compulsory that a representative of the stores department shall be placed on the committee.

On the Baltimore & Ohio Railroad and Grand Trunk Western Railroad it is stipulated that the workers' group attending joint coöperative meetings shall be made up of the local federated shop committee. Under the plan of systematized coöperation effective on the Chicago & North Western Railway it is essential that this group be selected from that committee. In other words, the principle has been accepted by each of these carriers that the men who represent the crafts at local points in connection with the working agreement between them and the company shall also act in their behalf at coöperative meetings. On the two first-mentioned roads, of course, a representative of the firemen and oilers' brotherhood may also be invited to attend. Both the Canadian National Railway Company in regulations covering its lines in Canada, and the Chicago, Milwaukee, St. Paul & Pacific Railroad, have adhered to the policy of letting each craft body appoint its own representative or representatives, without question as to membership in the federated shop committee. The former directs that the workers' group on coöperative committees in Canada shall consist of: one representative from each craft at major shops; three representatives of the employees at larger enginehouses and car repair points; and two representatives of the employees at smaller stations. Local officers on the Milwaukee System in forming coöperative committees have merely to enforce the rule that the workers shall choose "one representative for each craft or subdivision thereof." Canadian shopmen apparently prefer that the men chosen for "grievance" work and their coöperative committeemen shall for the most part constitute two distinct groups. In July, 1928, for example, among Ontario shops on that carrier, only two out of six coöperative representatives at London, three out of seven at Stratford, and two out of nine at Leaside near Toronto, were also on the local shop committee. Experiences with respect to this issue have been more variable on the Milwaukee System. At its western terminal shop in Tacoma, Washington, the workers have been scrupulous in sending their shop committee as a body to represent them on matters of coöperation, and at its central locomotive repair shop in Milwaukee, Wisconsin, a majority of the coöperative committeemen have always been "grievers." But at Minneapolis, Minnesota, shopmen on the Milwaukee System have made it a rule to name an entirely different slate to meet the management in a coöperative way from that which comprises the shop committee.

Examination of methods of representation will indicate that joint coöperative committees are regularly limited to less than twenty members, except at one station on the Milwaukee System. At its passenger coach shop in Milwaukee, Wisconsin, by reason of a liberal inclusion of supervisors, and an extensive subdividing of crafts, the committee has reached a total of about thirty persons. Making use of his discretionary powers, the master mechanic at the Miles City, Montana, shop of the same carrier has provided room for an apprentice on the local committee. He also invites additional craftsmen to each meeting as guests, in the belief that this will stimulate their interest in coöperation, and prepare them to serve as committeemen at a later date. Craftsmen guests are allowed a voice in the proceedings but do not vote.

The Baltimore & Ohio Railroad, when it inaugurated its coöperative arrangement, decided that it would be advisable to hold local committee meetings twice a month. Other roads, when they indorsed coöperation, followed similar policies with the exception of the Chicago & North Western Railway, which from the beginning authorized its meetings to be convened monthly. In August, 1928, under pressure of low earnings the Baltimore & Ohio Railroad was forced to economize in every direction and for that reason took occasion to put its meetings in the mechanical department on a once-a-month basis. The carrier was persuaded that nothing deleterious to the movement would result from the change. Wherever locomotives and train cars are maintained in close proximity to each other on its lines, the Baltimore & Ohio Railroad has established one committee to cover both phases of the work. This has been the procedure on other carriers with respect to maintenance points of lesser or intermediate importance, but at their major shops they have generally recognized separate departmental interests. Independent committees for motive power and car departments have been set up at each of the large shops of the Canadian National Railway System at or near Winnipeg, Manitoba. In like fashion two committees have been established both at the Chicago, Illinois, shop of the Chicago & North Western Railroad, and at the Milwaukee, Wisconsin, shop of the Chicago, Milwaukee, St. Paul & Pacific Railroad.

### Local Committees at Work.

THOUGH always assembled when workers are held for day duty, local joint coöperative committees meet oftenest just before or after the lunch hour. The work of committees is done on "company time," and in no sense affects the compensation of employee members. The Baltimore & Ohio Railroad has signified a desire that committeemen from the crafts shall indulge in a "wash up" before appearing at meetings. Shopmen on the carriers committed to coöperation are inclined to hold differing views as to the necessity for a "wash up." A proportion of them think that because they do not leave the company's property to attend meetings, and because considerable effort must be spent in removing the traces of grease, dust, and fumes, incidental to their employment, that a "wash up" should be unessential. The feeling, moreover, is abroad that the management, if really bent on coöperation, should meet the workers in the condition that they come from toil. Opposed is the argument that committeemen for the crafts enter a coöperative meeting intrusted with an important undertaking by their fellow workers, and that they will be on a better footing to discharge their task if they first wash themselves and, figuratively speaking, leave the shop behind. This action, too, it is said, is advisable in order that papers passed about among committeemen shall not be soiled or smudged by dirty hands. The sessions of coöperative meetings generally consume from one to, at the most, three hours. Nicely appointed quarters may be especially provided for the committee, but more commonly it assembles in the head office at the station, or in the men's lunch or recreation room.

As soon as one joint committee meeting has been adjourned at a local point, under union-management coöperation, preparations should be under way for the next. It is expected that the interim between meetings will be fruitful of ideas relating to the betterment of the industry which will be presented for discussion at the next session. Craft committeemen are intended to be representatives in the true sense of the word. They are to give heed to every idea coming from journeymen, helpers, and apprentices of their trade and they must bring them, together with their own ideas, to the attention of the joint committee. In so doing, they should be careful to receive and submit the views of men who do not belong to their organization, but who may have evinced an interest in the coöperative plan. In their early advocacy of coöperation from labor's point of view, Captain Beyer and other craft leaders emphasized the value of having matters that might logically come before the joint committees debated in local lodge meetings. This has become the practice at various points, but by no means to the extent that was anticipated.

Proceedings in local joint coöperative meetings are usually

direct and undelayed. Communications, if any, are read, and then the chairman turns to a consideration of all items of business that have been settled in one way or another since the last meeting or are still pending. It is a cardinal principle of union-management coöperation that, whenever a proposition has been inserted in a local committee's minutes, it shall be carried forward from meeting to meeting until finally disposed of with the full knowledge of the membership. The chairman, therefore, must keep track of each item and be in a position to advise the committee concerning it at any time. Should it have been dealt with conclusively between meetings, or action on it have been found impossible, the committee must be so informed, and it is dropped forthwith from the minutes. A typewritten or mimeographed copy of the minutes of the preceding meeting is placed in the hands of committeemen before they assemble, so that they may follow the comments of the chairman, and ask questions when anything is obscure.

Next, the chairman addresses himself to each representative in turn, asking him if he has any new suggestions to offer. Here it is that coöperation finds expression in an effective and tangible manner. Ideas that have originated either with management or men are now presented to the committee in the form of suggestions. The aim is to secure as plentiful a supply of good suggestions as the circumstances prevailing at any maintenance of equipment point will allow. In other words, emphasis is laid upon the quantity of suggestions, as the more there are, the wider the distribution of coöperative effort, and upon their quality, as this reveals the alertness and application of mind of the coöperators. The capabilities of the chairman are put to a test in drawing out suggestions and guiding discussion. Representatives of the management offer as a rule less than a third, sometimes, in fact very few of the suggestions, but their participation in discussion and their counsel and advice in shaping decisions can be of great value. Debates, though, are generally let run their course, unless they become too acrimonious. Without exception, the introduc-

tion of questions pertaining to the federated craft or other working agreements between the railroads and their employees is
strictly barred from all coöperative meetings. So too, owing to
the fact that Safety First meetings are held at local repair
points, an attempt is made to keep safety items out of the cooperative committee's minutes. This is difficult, as many items
seem to occupy a sort of borderland between coöperation and
safety. Investigations are frequently necessary to determine the
merit of certain suggestions for the conduct of which a subcommittee may be appointed by the chairman. Subjects of a more
general character relating to the welfare of the industry may be
taken up toward the close of a meeting, provided that this does
not interfere with the regular order of business. Itinerant officials
of the railroad often drop in at the sessions of a coöperative committee, while the attendance of a limited number of credentialed
outsiders is permitted. Short speeches from visitors are solicited
as a stimulus to coöperative endeavor.

### The Maintenance of Local Records.

EACH railroad system indorsing union-management coöperation
has its own method of registering the various suggestions offered
at local repair points on its lines. Since, as has been pointed out,
unsettled items must be retained on the local minutes until closed,
the problem with the carriers has been to adopt some expedient
that will allow for continuity of record and at the same time facilitate reference. On the Milwaukee System the individual committees have simply numbered the suggestions presented in consecutive order from the date of their initial meetings. In every
instance the name of the person responsible for a suggestion is
given in the minutes. A similar plan of numbering is used on the
Chicago & North Western Railway, but always with a notation
of the exact date upon which the suggestion was registered.
Where car and motive power departments have one meeting on
this carrier, the suggestions originating from each department

are enumerated separately. Coöperative minutes on the Chicago
& North Western Railway do not mention those who make suggestions by name, but merely state that they were offered by, for
example, "the chairman of the electrical workers," or "the tinner
foreman." Local committees on the Baltimore & Ohio Railroad
itemize suggestions by the month, always chronicling the names
of those who have submitted them. Item number, 6-19-28, in the
minutes kept at Ivorydale, Ohio, would refer to the nineteenth
suggestion made in the sixth month of 1928 at that point. Numbering of suggestions on the Canadian National Railway System
is done on a yearly basis, although the month when they are introduced is also specified. By a system of alphabetical notation
it is designated whether a representative of the management or
of the employees brought in the suggestion, but the actual maker
of it remains anonymous. 7-E-31 set opposite a suggestion presented at the Port Huron, Michigan, car shop of the Grand
Trunk Western Lines would show that it was the thirty-first of
the year at that point and that it had been introduced in the seventh month by an employee; whereas, use of the letter M, instead
of an E, would have indicated that the suggestion had come from
a representative of the management.

Examination of the records of coöperation discloses the fact
that the normal ratio of suggestions found unacceptable is quite
low. A few of those that are disapproved reach a higher committee before being finally dropped, but for the most part elimination is accomplished locally. In a period of over four years, from
March 5, 1924, to June 20, 1928, the Baltimore & Ohio Railroad
received at all its repair points a grand total of 21,582 suggestions; of these, 18,237, or 85 per cent, were classified as having
been adopted. Statistics kept by the car department of the Chicago & North Western Railway for the first six months of 1928
show the approval of 2,270 items out of 2,431 disposed of at
local car repair points, or approximately 93 per cent. Rather
noticeable fluctuations occur from point to point on all railroads

with respect to the proportion of suggestions dropped, which may be accounted for in large measure by the influence of local policies.

Three leading reasons may be cited why some coöperative suggestions fail of approval. Many ideas, expressed before committees, are of course mown down under discussion, and never appear upon the minutes. Others, which are recorded as suggestions, having come to the attention of officials, are subjected to investigation, or given a preliminary trial, and then declared to be impracticable. Accordingly they are reported in the minutes as having been dropped. Again, the financial outlay required to put a suggestion into effect may block its acceptance. Coöperative propositions whose aggregate cost is less than $100–$150 may possibly be sanctioned by local officers, but, whenever a larger sum is involved, a special "authority for expenditure" must be sent to company headquarters. The higher railroad officials have a well-reputed and hard-headed aversion to paying out money under an A.F.E., as it is commonly styled, unless substantial returns are anticipated. Even though they relax this attitude somewhat, particularly when traffic conditions are good, as the price of coöperation, they will hardly agree to expensive suggestions if their economic worth is at all in question. In the third place, there are certain types of suggestions which are outclassed because they are said to be in conflict with the general policies of the carrier, or because they introduce what is considered to be an unwise modification of the equipment standards in force on its lines.

## Joint Regional and System Committees.

PARLIAMENTARY relations are lacking between local coöperative committees on the one hand, and the joint regional and system committees formed under the plan of union-management coöperation on the other. The joint system committees, for example, which function on the Baltimore & Ohio Railroad, the Chicago & North Western Railway, and the Canadian National Railway

System, are in no wise delegate bodies but are made up of staff officers representing the management and leading shop craft officials representing the men. On the Baltimore & Ohio Railroad, the committee consists of the staff of the Chief of Motive Power and Equipment and the executive board of System Federation No. 30. On the Chicago & North Western Railway, it includes "designated railway officers" and the general committee of System Federation No. 12. Selection of a list of officers to serve on the system committee authorized by the Canadian National Railway Company is made by the vice-president in charge of operation and construction, while the workers' group comprises the chairman of Division No. 4, the general officers of System Federation No. 11, and several other selected federation representatives. The three regional committees on the Canadian National Railway System include officers chosen by the general managers of the carrier, and executive officers (mainly belonging to the region) of the shop crafts.

Always on the agenda of regional joint committees on the Canadian National Railway System are included items that have been carried on minutes of local committees, and have been thought worthy of submission to a central conference for discussion and possible settlement. The regional committee is essentially a coöperative board of reference rather than in any sense an appeal tribunal from local points. Certain questions, it is believed, will receive an ampler and more authoritative consideration when they reach the higher committee. On the Canadian carrier, matters may be taken from the regional committee for further treatment before the system coöperative meeting, although this is done only to a limited extent. In practice, by far the greater number of items transferred from the local committees is finally disposed of by the joint regional committee.

Since the Baltimore & Ohio Railroad and the Chicago & North Western Railway do not have regional committees, their central committees in each case act as a board of reference to which unsettled items are brought from local stations. A spirit of local self-sufficiency is manifest on the Chicago & North Western Railway, and in consequence very few items are taken to its central committee. Uniformly an opportunity is afforded by system cooperative meetings for staff officers of the carrier to confer with the shop crafts' system officials on all the broader questions of policy affecting coöperation. Stabilization of employment has until the present been the chief topic for debate at central meetings. Closely associated with this have been the issues of building new or converting old equipment in the company's shops, and utilizing its plant or foundry facilities to manufacture additional equipment parts. Other matters that have commanded attention are apprentice education, faults in the administration of the technique of coöperation, and a method of estimating coöperative gains. Regional committees on the Canadian National Railway System are convened once in six months, and the joint system committee once a year. On the Baltimore & Ohio Railroad and Chicago & North Western Railway the central committees are scheduled to meet every three months.

## Chapter IX

## Attitudes of Management and Men toward the Plan

THE circumstance, that under the technique of coöperation no binding tie exists between local committees and regional and central committees, seems at first glance to be a violation of democratic principles, but on a moment's thought the reason for this will become clear. The management of a railroad constitutes a sort of hierarchy in which the power to settle matters of general policy is lodged with officials of executive rank. Although a system of representation might be visualized in which line officers and supervisors would go as delegates from a local to a higher committee, the difficulty would be that, once there, they would be wanting in authority to transact the more important items of business. The shop crafts, for their part, appear convinced that local labor opinion will almost invariably reach a higher committee as a result of the elective methods prevailing within their system federations. It may be urged that neither this nor any other structural weaknesses possessed by the technique of coöperation should be enough of themselves to prevent its successful outworking. Human factors, it may be contended, should always have a greater rôle to play in determining the fate of union-management coöperation on the railroads than should the vehicle of government devised for it. Assuming this to be so, it will be advisable to examine more closely the attitudes of mind which have been displayed by management and men in embracing and furthering the plan. Furthermore, to complete the survey, it will be essential to indicate some of the causes why obstructions were offered to coöperative arrangements at their introduction, and have occasionally since been imposed to retard their progress.

### Attitudes of Management.

BASICALLY, the avowed purposes of railroad executives in sanctioning the inauguration of union-management coöperation on the lines under their jurisdiction have been similar to those of other executives in the transportation or manufacturing industries who have supported forms of employee representation. Whether the group favoring coöperation has been more sincere than the group favoring employee representation is in the realm of controversy. Many leaders of organized labor have held steadily to the opinion that advocates of employee representation have been introducing, with a remarkable degree of finesse, one type of artifice or another merely to pacify the workers in their employ and at the same time to stultify the aims of craft unionism. Wiser spirits among them have been less condemnatory in their judgment. The fact remains that the primary objectives of the new *régime* planned for industrial workers, organized by trade, are much like those which, through the instrumentality of employee representation, have been planned for workers, organized by company. The relative extent to which these objectives have in each case been gained is another matter.

Both of the new managerial groups have painted an ideal picture for the workers. A place in industry is to be given them, it is said, which they have never occupied before. The old attitude of dominance is to be relinquished by management, and a quite different status conferred upon the hitherto subservient workers.[1] This, according to Henry S. Dennison, a prominent member of the group espousing employee representation, is "the management of men on a non-autocratic basis." Just as citizenship in the state, with all its accompanying privileges, lends dignity to its possessors, so, it is claimed, a citizenship is being erected in industry which brings to the workers a new conception of the meaning of their tasks and changes their vocational demeanor. Speaking of the coöperative movement on the carrier over which

[1] For a discussion of the newer attitudes of management in industry read: William M. Leiserson, "Employee Representation—A Warning to Both Employers and Unions," in the *Proceedings* of the Academy of Political Science, June, 1928, pp. 96–109.

he presides, Daniel Willard has said: "It gives to every employee an enlightened and enlarged view of his own worth and importance as a part of the great organization known as the Baltimore & Ohio Railroad."

Then as a corollary to lifting the workers' status, management assures them of increasing opportunities for self-expression, a voice, in fact, in the conduct of industry. Divergent points of view have been taken by exponents of employee representation on this issue. Some have made liberal overtures to their employees with the end in view that they should become articulate in industrial matters, while others have moved cautiously, evidently fearing the impingement of working class power upon the field of management. The area within which the carriers receive the intellectual contributions of their shopmen under union-management coöperation has been marked out in the preceding chapter. A passage in the Baltimore & Ohio Railroad's coöperative program of 1924, which was followed almost word for word by the Milwaukee System in its memorandum of principles of 1926, is typical of management's attitude on this subject. It briefly guarantees to the craftsmen that in the course of a "frank discussion of questions relating to the planning and carrying on of work" the ideas that they advance "will be given the fullest consideration." The manner in which representatives of the organized shopmen have trenched upon the domains of management in the treatment of problems such as the stabilizing of employment, the extension of manufacturing in the company's shops and foundries, and the financial distribution of coöperative gains, will be detailed later on.

Again the doctrine of fellowship in industry has become a credo with a portion of business executives. Here personal attributes tend to thrust themselves into the foreground, and the way is less certain for the majority. Autocratic methods may be abandoned in an enterprise and the workers given more influence in shaping industrial policies, but fellowship, though earnestly desired, is generally harder to make effective. Where large scale businesses are administered, not all executives have the ability to establish close contacts with their men, and at the same time maintain the necessary discipline. Sir Henry W. Thornton has consistently taught fellowship on the Canadian National Railway System, but he is an exceptional figure in the transportation world. "We are all employees—you, I, and everyone else," he exclaimed to a system coöperative meeting on the carrier at Montreal, Quebec, in January, 1928. Happily Sir Henry can express his natural urge to fellowship, and in so doing not lose one whit of authority. Similar tenets appeal to J. T. Gillick, vice-president of the operating department of the Chicago, Milwaukee, St. Paul & Pacific Railroad, who is regarded as a counselor and friend by all that carrier's maintenance of way, shop, and transportation men, hundreds of whom he knows by name. Nor in this connection should John Howe, superintendent of the Baltimore & Ohio Railroad's locomotive repair shop at Cumberland, Maryland, be forgotten. Careless of the comfort of office chairs, "Jack" Howe spends the most of every day on the shop floor with his men who carry their difficulties to him in person. Once a month he gives them a straight-from-the-shoulder talk, standing on the flat area of a large machine, when he tells them exactly what he thinks about anything and anybody in the shop. The Cumberland plant is a model of efficiency and discipline. Though fellowship in industry is a splendid ideal for progressive management, experience has shown that it is but relatively attainable.

In return for what it concedes, management expects from the forces of labor a clearer apprehension of their responsibilities to industry. This, prescribed to a greater or lesser extent under schemes of employee representation, has become a definite rule under the plan of union-management coöperation. The management of the Chicago & North Western Railway in its systematized coöperative program of 1925 is "interested in the constant and efficient use of its shop facilities" and for the achievement of these aims is dependent upon the freely given help of its shop workers. Sir Henry W. Thornton has affirmed that the Canadian National Railway Company's purpose to secure "a maximum of efficiency" in all its services would only be obtainable through a combined effort on the part of management and men. Daniel Willard, president of the Baltimore & Ohio Railroad, believes that the widened vision and feeling of responsibility which employees should acquire under coöperation ought surely to inspire them "personally to do good work, to do honest and dependable work."[2] The genuineness of management's loftier proposals for labor are naturally called into question by this descent to a realistic attitude. The inference is readily drawn that management when entering into "uplift" covenants with the workers is merely disguising its foremost purpose which is economic gain. In answer, management can do no more than admit its desire to secure industrial efficiency and resultant economic gain, but at the same time assert its sincerity in giving to labor a new status and new aspirations.

The two managerial groups, however, as has been said, stand rigidly apart on the question of the character of the labor organization upon which they are willing to confer the benefits of their humanizing policies. The railroad companies indorsing union-management coöperation have formally and unequivocally acknowledged certain organizations built on craft lines as the sole agencies with which they will make an arrangement looking toward mutual helpfulness and understanding. Each road has with these bodies a simple coöperative agreement which, in a sense, is ancillary to the main working contract or contracts they have signed with them, but is just as binding. Evidences, indeed, are not far to seek that the interpretation placed upon working contracts both by the railroad companies and their employees has been visibly modified by coöperative practice. According to

2 Golden jubilee of the city of Garrett, Indiana. Address by Daniel Willard, October 30, 1924, p. 7.

Daniel Willard business corporations are either antagonistic to trade-unions, tolerate them, or take steps to coöperate with them.[3] He has candidly confessed that, during his earlier years as chief executive officer of the Baltimore & Ohio Railroad, toleration of unions, in so far as they were organized on its property, was the rule. Whenever representatives of the craft unions came to see him on any business, he held friendly parley with them, but, in his own words, was anxious "to have it over with," and, as they filed out, hoped "that it would be a long time before they came again." Nevertheless, he had become dissatisfied with merely tolerating the unions some time before he had decided that it would be wiser to embark upon a coöperative venture with them. Under coöperation, he has stated, working contracts and the tasks to be performed on the railroad have remained fundamentally the same, but "a different state of mind" has been observable since its introduction, both among management and men.

### Attitudes of Labor.

THE workers who have committed themselves to the adoption of union-management coöperation have brought to it their own particular philosophy of organization. They emphasize the fact that they enter into the plan as members of free and voluntary associations of labor. These associations, they assert, are voluntary, because men of certain craft qualifications, who have exercised their powers of willing and choosing, have come together spontaneously for their formation. Though fraternal and economic impulses may have been, in some measure, responsible for the will to associate, the act of association itself is uncompelled. The characteristic of freedom which they claim as inhering in their organizations may be separated into two phases. In the first place, their unions belong to the category of associations that

[3] From the report of a speech delivered by Daniel Willard on February 17, 1927, before the National Civic Federation, published in *Industrial Management,* May, 1927, p. 262.

have received positive legal recognition, and, therefore, while constrained by the law, have specific rights of action under it. However, it is to an economic rather than to a legal sort of freedom that they mainly refer in discussing their admission to coöperation. Established on a craft basis, each of their organizations, they point out, has contractual relations with a number of business corporations, not with any single corporation. Each association accordingly has a reality of existence quite independent of the industries in which its membership is employed. All its contracts might be annulled, and yet its essential integrity be still preserved. No economic dictation, it is contended, can force it to take a course that it does not care to take. Great store is set by trade-unionists in this capacity for self-direction which they believe to be a fixed and inalienable possession of their associations.

Zeal for their philosophy of organization has ordinarily led craft unionists, including those who adhere to the plan of coöperation, to utter upbraidings against unions of the "company" type. Their free and voluntary associations, they declare, differ from the "company union" which is formed at the instigation of the employing corporation, and remains largely amenable to its direction. The very term, "company union," itself is intended by many to convey the impression that freedom of action is hampered by corporation control. It is true that the establishment of only a few "company unions" has been solicited by the workers, and that the great majority of them have been proposed by the employing concerns, or in some instances even forced upon the workers. But the question of their freedom of action in contrast to the question of spontaneous origin is of profounder significance, and cannot be lightly dismissed with generalizations. No judgment would be fair in the matter unless a study were made of the exact situation of each "company union" on the railroads or elsewhere, and a decision reached by contrasting many individual cases. Evidences are accumulating that "company unions" are oftentimes much more self-reliant than craft unionists imagine.

The railroad craft organizations, in agreeing to participate in union-management coöperation, have retained intact all their rights of collective bargaining, and, officially at least, have not relinquished any of their militant methods. They nevertheless engage, as has been already related, to abstain from bringing before coöperative meetings any matter which might affect the schedule of rules governing their wages and working conditions. Concerted withdrawal from work, that is, the strike, which the craft unions consider a legitimate expression of their freedom of action, may take place as heretofore, but the hope is entertained that the possible grounds for action of this sort may be confined to much narrower limits. In other words, it is expected that where coöperation flourishes, the strike will become, more than it ever has been, a reserve weapon. Inasmuch as unions in the railroad industry have not tried to enforce the union, or closed, shop, this issue has been in no way related to the introduction of coöperation. The shop crafts have been quick to realize, however, that as they occupy a preferred position in the eyes of management under the coöperative plan, their organizational difficulties should be lessened. It would seem that an advanced condition of unionization is likely to result from coöperation, although technically the non-union, or open shop, will prevail. Most "company unions," it may be mentioned, have also been formed on an open shop basis. Strikes have been called of late by some "company unions" in spite of the forecast of advocates of employee representation that such occurrences were highly improbable.

The craft unions subscribing to union-management coöperation believe themselves competent, then, to send representatives to meet with management for purposes of mutual helpfulness, above all else because of the free and voluntary character of their associations. To their way of thinking the ideals of management can best work out to advantage where a quality of self-dependence is thoroughly inbred in the men who meet with management on common ground. By virtue of the assent which they have given to the coöperative plan, it is incumbent upon their membership to take a definite interest in all matters of which they have an immediate knowledge in the railroad industry. Through the channel afforded by the technique of coöperation, the shop crafts endeavor to obligate their members to bring forward recommendations for the purchase and grouping of hand and machine tool equipment; the methodizing of repairs and scheduling of work through shops; the introduction of devices to hasten and cheapen production; the distribution and economic use of new material; the reclamation of scrap; the outfitting of shops for comfort and sanitation; and the condition of shop grounds. Other railroad unions joining in coöperation assume responsibilities characteristic of their sections of the industry. All trades consider that they owe it to the railroad which employs their membership to help it improve service to the public, and, when possible, to attract new business to its lines, thereby augmenting its total operating revenues. Reciprocal advantages for this diversified outgo of effort are expected from the companies. Besides the unsubstantial gratifications which will ensue as the result of coöperation, the workers await a more tangible recompense in the form of "a fair sharing of the gains of coöperation" between the companies and themselves. Especially shall this recompense include more wholesome and less laborious working conditions, the regularization of employment, and additions to income, so far as they may be judged appropriable.

## Opposing Views of Management.

Has union-management coöperation, it may be asked, developed in consonance with the official attitudes and avowed objectives of the parties who have gone into it? Management, while proffering its ideals to the workers, has firmly insisted on contributions in return that will enhance efficiency. Labor, though agreeing to further intelligently the practical aims of management, has clung fast to its trade-union policies, exalted its philosophy of autonomous organization, and stipulated that it must share equitably in all the gains of coöperation. Here is an admixture of philosophy and ideals with materialistic considerations which may, it is true, have the capacity to work well, but seemingly is bound to meet with difficulties. The motives which commonly actuate one party to coöperation are called into question in the ranks of the other, whereupon influences inimical to the movement have a chance to thrive. If coöperation is to succeed, it is plain that its foundations must be deeply bedded in mutual confidence. Only when the parties agreeing to it have a firm faith in each other's sincerity of purpose, and at the same time are fully persuaded that it offers a sound method of bettering industrial relations, is the outcome likely to be favorable. Distrust and disbelief have proved themselves to be twin foes of the coöperative plan.

From the standpoint of management on each railroad, as will have been noted, just a few executive or other staff officers were actually concerned with the promotion of union-management coöperation in its inceptive stages. Fortunately for the plan, the carrier's chief executive officer was among those fostering it in every instance, except, of course, on the Milwaukee System which was in receivers' hands. Various staff officers who had little or nothing to do with the introduction of coöperation looked upon it as a sort of routine innovation, developing strong opinions neither for nor against it. But others were quick to array themselves in opposition to it so that a certain amount of dissension among high officials was experienced on all roads when coöperation was adopted. These manifestations of hostility often sorely tried the patience of advocates of the movement. Perhaps the most difficult situation encountered and straightened out was on the Canadian National Railway System, where, because of its composite formation, a disposition toward self-autonomy has lingered in administrative circles. To secure compliance with its coöperative agreement, first as it was applied regionally in Canada, and then as extended to the Grand Trunk Western Lines, was a task of no mean proportions. One officer in particular was quite obdurate in his hostility, gained a considerable following, and was only brought to book through executive pressure. Sir Henry W. Thornton has been disinclined to deal severely with any of his staff who cannot see eye to eye with him on this question. Daniel Willard has spoken of the reluctant support received from certain officers during the early period of coöperation on the Baltimore & Ohio Railroad, though adding that the ill will shown was not as keen as had been anticipated. A number of the original adversaries of the plan, it may be pointed out, have since come to acknowledge its merits, after it has been given, what they consider to be, a fair trial. Not a few of them, however, though outwardly conforming, still sit sullen in their tents, and apparently would be glad if they could renounce the whole movement. Continuing antagonisms have retarded the progress of systematized coöperation on the Chicago & North Western Railway.

In part the unwillingness of staff officers to accept the plan of coöperation has been due to the persistence of feudalistic principles in the railroad industry. The dyed-in-the-wool autocrat in high office on the railroads has been loath to entertain recommendations even from his subordinates on the line, let alone, to receive workers' ideas. While none of the roads indorsing coöperation has, within recent years at least, belonged to the more conservative group of carriers, traces of dictatorial methods of rule have not been lacking among their staff officers. Of greater significance is the opposition engendered by dissatisfaction with the visionary nature of the coöperative plan. Officers who for the most part are ready to treat the working force justly have nevertheless held that the railroad industry is better served where management and men are kept functionally apart. To them the formulae of union-management coöperation are too fine spun for the purposes it has in view. Like any novelty, the plan, they say, may work out for a time, but will succumb, whenever the responsibilities attached to it grow monotonous, and its illusory character becomes evident.

Line officers and supervisors have also shown enmity to coöperation, because it often has meant the surrender of what has remained of the old-time, arbitrary methods of rule, in which they have been schooled, and to which they may have clung at local points. So, too, they have been prejudiced against it because of its content of idealism, or, because it appears to be another "efficiency fad" transmitted from headquarters, the details of which they must administer. Moreover, they have found personal grounds for complaint against coöperation which have led them to manifest ill will toward it. Local executive officers are responsible for the effective use of all facilities at a repair point; supervisors, in turn, are responsible for the performance of a department or subdepartment, or for special work processes assigned to their control. Each of these in his everyday activities is brought into close touch with the workers from whom ideas are sought under the coöperative plan. Meetings are held at which suggestions from the men are recorded that presumably will lead to changes and resulting economies in plant operation. May not the inference be drawn that officers or supervisors should already have made these changes, and that, therefore, they may possibly have been lax in the discharge of their duties? The fact that shortcomings may be imputed to them, of which they may or may not be guilty, has unquestionably caused a goodly number of administrators at local points to combat coöperation. Yet by tactfully acknowledging the help that they have received from their men through coöperation, most local officers and supervisors have met this situation, and avoided any serious reflections being cast upon their own work. Indeed, at places where coöperation is most effective, a spirit of give and take seems to emerge, and fault-finding from either side to be reduced to a minimum.

*Workers' Opposition.*

ASSURED of a more estimable place in industry as a result of co-operation, and awaiting their share of its accruing gains, shop workers might be expected to have accepted its introduction with greater alacrity and uniformity than has management. But this, at least in the earlier stages of development, has not been the case. Though, generally speaking, craft union leaders have been favorable to the plan from the outset, no sooner has its adoption been discussed than various objections have always been raised to it, by lesser craft officials and by the rank and file. A great deal of education has invariably been needed before labor has gotten into the swing of the coöperative movement on any railroad. Most of the objections, when analyzed, are found to go back to suspicions of one kind or another. Chief among these is the suspicion which workers so often have of the motives impelling management to sign the coöperative agreement. Bargaining episodes out of the past flock into the workers' minds, and in view of real or fancied wrongs inflicted upon them, they ask why the railroads have suddenly become so magnanimous. Even after suspicions have been lulled and coöperation has been proceeding smoothly for a time, there is always danger of something happening either locally, or on the system as a whole, to rearouse distrust.

Workers' suspicions with respect to the motives of the railroad company tend to focus on its desire for efficiency. Trade-unionists in America have no liking for the word, efficiency, but will put up with it if, from their angle, it does not imply a vitiation of craftsmanship. The continuous introduction of power machinery, they regretfully admit, is limiting the boundaries of trade competence, and tending to reduce the workers' position. When as an accompaniment to this, business corporations cold-bloodedly speed up production, thereby making men subservient to the machine, they have only intensified, they believe, the craftsman's predicament. Fear has been expressed among railroad workers that coöperation, with its emphasis upon efficiency, may ultimately demote them to the same abject condition. They distinguish between the railroad company and its management, indicating their belief that, while the latter may of itself be high-minded, it is answerable to the former which has been established essentially as a profit-making venture. To the credit of management it may be stated that it has accepted labor's disquietude on this subject as, under the circumstances, a normal manifestation, and has carefully and soberly tried to instil the idea that no lowering of the standards of craftsmanship is contemplated by the employing company. The interest shown by the Baltimore & Ohio Railroad in the question of apprenticeship training under coöperative auspices has given assurances of a brighter future for craftsmanship on that carrier, and has done much to temper distrust. Suspicions, nevertheless, slumber on all roads practicing coöperation, as is sometimes revealed in conversations with shopmen at local points when quite ingenuously they may declare that their company will still bear watching.

Again, a dread has often been expressed by craftsmen that the union organizations to which they belong will be put in jeopardy through being robbed under coöperation of their old-time aggressiveness. Coöperation, they assert, demands a lamblike attitude of the unions that tends to make them forget their basic aims. Craft leaders, replying to these objections, have referred to the increased importance which they believe will be attached to the unions through their participation in coöperation, and have given pledges that their bargaining strength shall not be impaired. Lastly, a hesitancy to accept the tenets of union-management coöperation has been shown by some who cannot disabuse their minds of the opinion that it must have an adverse effect upon employment conditions. Since many coöperative suggestions are of a labor-saving type it is plain that, unless their influence is somehow counterbalanced, they will result in a lessened need for man power in the railroad industry. By the methods which they have adopted to stabilize employment, as will be disclosed in chapter xvi, the carriers have been steadily endeavoring to grapple with this situation.

Occasionally the view has been expressed that workers' opposition to the coöperative plan is more manifest at stations where men of alien races are employed in relatively large numbers. This, except in instances where the foreign element is imbued with radical thought, is discovered upon investigation to be scarcely true. Coöperative principles, for example, are well understood, and lively coöperative meetings held, at the Galewood car repair shop of the Milwaukee System, Chicago, Illinois, in spite of the fact that many nationalities, especially those from eastern and southern Europe, are represented among the workers. Similarly at the Baltimore & Ohio Terminal Railroad Company's shop in Chicago, where many languages are spoken, harmonious and effective coöperative relations prevail. Contrary evidences may be adduced to indicate that workers who favor the doctrines of the One Big Union or kindred organizations of syndicalistic leanings, and all communists, will have nothing to do with coöperation. Modern industrial slavery, they believe, can never be permanently ameliorated by damaging compromises with the ruling, economic classes. Unsuccessful attempts, it may be pointed out, have constantly been made to disrupt coöperation at the Chicago, Illinois, shop of the Chicago & North Western Railway by an ultraradical faction, largely of foreign extraction. The difficulties faced by the Canadian National Railway Company in extending coöperation throughout its western region, because of the presence of very advanced ideas among its shopmen, were briefly alluded to in chapter viii. Perhaps the toughest problem met and overcome by the carrier in that region was in taking the plan into its shop at Edmonton, Alberta, where one man of extreme views, but withal an excellent mechanic, who held a large section of the workers in the hollow of his hand, was accustomed to speak of it with withering scorn. Socialists, on the other hand, have regarded union-

management coöperation on the railroads as a progressive movement, and have generally accorded it their whole-hearted support.
Though the Chicago, Milwaukee, St. Paul & Pacific Railroad had
some trouble with Pacific Coast syndicalism in instituting co-
operation at its Tacoma, Washington, shop, at Milwaukee, Wisconsin, a city where socialism is rampant, it found its shop
workers eager for the plan.

### *Opportunities for Success.*

ENOUGH has been written to indicate the hazards which beset
union-management coöperation through the interplay of human
factors. Clearly, from labor's point of view, the future of the
plan on each carrier rests with the membership of the craft unions
who may give it their continuing approval, or, at any time, if
hostility should be sufficiently aroused, may order its discontinuance through their organization channels. It may be expected, however, that the influence of craft union leaders will always be great in shaping the policies that the membership will
follow. As experience has been gained under the plan, the suspicions of labor appear to have measurably abated, although symp-
toms of discontent sometimes flare up quickly when the carrier is
thought lax in fulfilling its obligations. From the point of view of
management, the higher staff officers representing each railroad
corporation may be regarded as mainly controlling the future of
its coöperative plan. If their favor for it should cease, the movement on the carrier, irrespective of the desires of labor, must at
once topple. Still it may be remembered that these officers are
bound to be swayed in their opinions regarding the merits or
demerits of coöperation by information which they receive from
their associates at headquarters or from subordinates on the line.

The assertion is often heard at maintenance of equipment stations that coöperation, in order to be effective, must be a "fifty-
fifty" proposition. In other words, when confidence is mutual
between the parties engaging in coöperation, when an even balance

of interest in the plan is maintained between them, and when, in taking action under it, each endeavors to bear a fair share of the responsibilities, the likelihood of its bringing uniformly successful results is greatest. But in visiting repair points the observer is soon led to the conclusion that such an equation is rarely attained in actual practice. More frequently he discovers that the movement at local points is being hampered to some extent by the fact that the coöperative effort and understanding of one party is weaker than that of the other. The contributions of the committees at such stations are generally found to be less valuable than they would have been had a more equable balance existed. Executive officers of a carrier, keeping the coöperative movement in mind, should sometimes be able to strengthen a local committee, when they transfer an administrator from one point to another within the mechanical department. The right officer or supervisor shifted to a certain station may provide the very influence needed to give balance to coöperative action. Shop workers, however, are held so closely to the same repair point that transfers of them seldom occur except when the railroad may carry out centralizing policies. The only adequate way to stimulate their zeal for the movement, therefore, would seem to be by instruction as to its advantages, although upon examination it may occasionally be revealed that their lack of coöperation has been largely due to lack of judgment displayed in choosing the men for the local joint committee.

# Chapter X

# Suggestions Dealing with Repair Point Equipment

THE ideas presented to local joint committee meetings in the mechanical department of carriers, in the hope that they may be registered as suggestions, have been very heterogeneous in character. As yet only one carrier, the Canadian National Railway Company, has authorized a definite plan of classifying coöperative suggestions, although now and again other roads have grouped them roughly under certain headings as an aid to interpretation. Statistics of the plan of classification adopted by the Canadian National Railway Company were issued for the first time as a supplement to the minutes of its system coöperative committee's meeting of February, 1929. By an analysis of existing records it has been found possible to tabulate under twenty-five subject headings all suggestions advanced on the carrier since it entered the coöperative movement. Any official classification of suggestions must of necessity be more or less arbitrary. Some suggestions, because they have a single or leading purpose which is unmistakable, may be referred to their class with ease, whereas others, having composite aims, must be listed at the discretion of the cataloguer. A proposal effecting a change in shop methods, for example, may also lead to a saving in materials, or one occasioning a structural repair may shorten the time of transfer and thereby economize in labor. Because of such hindrances to accuracy in classification the description of suggestions to be offered in this volume will be on a topical rather than on a strictly analytical basis. To begin with, an account will be given of the various types of suggestions that have been recorded with respect to machine and hand tools, and other forms of work equipment used at repair points. This will include a treatment of proposals relating to the purchase of new tools and other equipment; the transference of equipment between departments and between repair stations; the reconditioning of worn equipment; the grouping of equipment about the plant; and the storage and issue of cutting, measuring, and auxiliary tools.

### Purchase of New Tools and Equipment.

MISCONCEPTIONS have been rather common in connection with the procedure followed by railroads in buying tools and other equipment for the mechanical department. It has generally been thought that the purchasing department has more important functions assigned than actually belong to it. Early in 1928 the *Railway Mechanical Engineer* published in its columns the results of an investigation made by certain of its editors into the manner in which new equipment is selected by the carriers.[1] Though the investigation took no account of the policies of roads indorsing coöperation, it brought to light considerable data in relation to equipment buying that should be illuminating for this study. It disclosed the fact that almost always it is the foremen over departments or, in some cases, the general foremen at repair points who originate requests for new equipment. These men are expected to have an intimate acquaintance with problems affecting the divisions of maintenance work over which they hold jurisdiction, and, therefore, should know what kind of equipment is needed. With each request which they present for new equipment supporting information must go forward, explaining clearly why it is desired, its approximate cost, the percentage of savings it will probably effect, and the disposal that will be made of the equipment replaced. Occasionally the request will be canvassed by a so-called tool committee, or an officer designated to inquire into shop equipment needs, before it goes for ratification or rejection to the chief mechanical officer of the railroad. The latter depends upon his subordinates to furnish him with reliable advice in each

---

[1] "How Railroads Purchase Shop Equipment," *Railway Mechanical Engineer*, June, 1928, pp. 305–306.

case, but to satisfy his mind may often give it his personal attention.

Railroads enter the supply market to purchase shop equipment for the mechanical department with their own particular customer's point of view. They must buy, as has been explained in chapter iv, many machine tools of the same standard models as those employed in manufacturing establishments. Again, they must spend money for other tools that are specially adapted to machining the parts of locomotives and train cars. In general their tools and other forms of equipment are used more intermittently than in continuous process factories, and they, therefore, must approach the market with the idea that for the most part they are buying production goods that should provide facilities over a lengthy period. It has been computed that well-designed machine tools, if kept in proper repair, should last on the average in railroad shops about twenty years. Selection of the right kind of tools to do the class of work for which they are fitted during this extended period is a matter requiring a great deal of forethought and careful study. Some lighter machine tools and the majority of hand tools are subject to more frequent renewal. Special shop equipment in the way of overhead or portable cranes, blacksmith forges, and annealing furnaces should be reasonably durable. Tractors on the other hand, which jolt in and around shops, should wear out sooner.

Local supervisors, and to an extent general foremen, the investigation has pointed out, do not only originate most requests for tools and other equipment but also exercise considerable influence upon their selection. As soon as the chief mechanical officer has sanctioned a request, the purchasing department is notified, and it immediately sets to work to get bids from manufacturers. The purchasing department scrutinizes the bids received, and sends the more suitable of them on to the mechanical department. Consultation of the opinion of the local supervisor or general foreman who may have originated the request is customary before one bid is finally accepted. Then a formal requisition is made out in accordance with the terms of the bid which receives the approval of the chief mechanical officer. When in the market for more durable equipment, the railroads are inclined to accept those bids which more nearly meet the standards they have set, regarding cost as of secondary importance. Manifestly supervisors or general foremen have significant functions to perform on the majority of carriers in helping to fill by proper methods of selection the equipment needs of the mechanical department. It is accordingly necessary that they should be constantly watchful of the state of all tools and other equipment coming under their jurisdiction, that they should keep themselves well informed in relation to all developments in the supply market for such equipment, and that they should be able to substantiate their claims for new equipment with logical arguments and carefully prepared data.

### Relations of Coöperation to the Buying of Equipment.

Advocates of union-management coöperation have not proposed any radical alteration of the equipment-purchasing methods usually employed in the mechanical department. They take the position, however, that the methods in use are incomplete, and that they can best be rounded out through the introduction of the coöperative plan. Requests for new tools and other equipment should not necessarily have to originate in the ranks of supervisors or general foremen, but oftentimes might begin quite advantageously one step lower, that is, with the workers. The men, they say, who work directly with machine tools or engage in day by day operations with hand tools should know a great deal about their mechanical condition, their capacity for output, and their need for renewal. They should be familiar with the state of usefulness of other shop equipment with which they have a constant working experience. It is true that supervisors and general foremen often leave themselves open to approach by shop mechanics who have views concerning new equipment, or may consult with one or more of them before sending in a request, but such procedure is casual and unauthoritative. Union-management coöperation, it is claimed, provides a formula which will allow for a much more comprehensive appeal to labor opinion on the subject of new equipment, and give to that appeal the stamp of official indorsement.

The pith of the argument, then, is that the views of shop workers regarding the purchase of new equipment are likely to be worth while, and that coöperative meetings, if successfully conducted, should afford a splendid opportunity for their discovery. Here the officer who presides, and the other representatives of management who attend, may at short, consecutive intervals receive an unsolicited statement of what the workers are thinking on the subject of new equipment. Problems bearing on this issue may be threshed out in meeting, or a committee formed to give closer study to a particular situation. Various smaller purchases, agreed upon as necessary and not involving authority for expenditure, may be effected by reference to the official in charge at the local point. Otherwise, when larger appropriations are required to buy equipment, the voice of labor along with that of management will be heard upon the question.

Technically these prescriptions of coöperation are not intended to veto the initiating rights of supervisors and general foremen with respect to the purchase of new equipment, but, nevertheless, have served to vitiate the exercise of such rights. Suggestions relating to the advisability of buying equipment originate in coöperative meetings and go forward in substantially the same manner as do the requests of supervisors and general foremen. Consequently supervisors and general foremen, as participants in coöperation, have felt constrained to make their equipment wants known through the means afforded by its technique, and have been letting their individual powers fall into disuse. This, no doubt, is in accordance with the desires of the carriers. In the program for coöperation issued by the Baltimore & Ohio Railroad in 1924, "tool equipment" was specifically mentioned as a topic that might be profitably discussed at local coöperative meetings. A coöperative bulletin, released at a western region shop of the Canadian National Railway System in 1927, pointed out that more harmonious relations would be maintained between management and men if all important changes in machine and other tool equipment were fully treated by coöperative committees before being put into effect.

Up until now shop workers on none of the carriers committed to coöperation appear to have fully utilized their capacity for influencing the purchases of more costly types of equipment. For one thing, they have evidently been a bit timid at the novelty of expressing their views at a time when thousands of dollars must be spent for equipment purposes. Failure to grasp the responsibilities which they are expected to assume in the matter has doubtless also retarded action. Besides, the crafts have hardly yet accustomed themselves to the severely calculating attitude generally adopted by railroad headquarters when expenditures of such a character are under advisement. Smaller points, as will be seen, are restricted in this sort of discussion by the fact that they secure much of their equipment secondhand from other points. However, the combined list of recommendations presented by management and men at various stations on the subject of buying more expensive articles of equipment has already been significant. And even when the workers have refrained from advancing ideas, it may be contended that they have derived some benefit from taking part in the discussion.

An exceptionally good illustration of a full-fledged use of the technique of coöperation in connection with equipment buying is afforded by the records of the passenger coach department of the Milwaukee, Wisconsin, shop of the Chicago, Milwaukee, St. Paul & Pacific Railroad. During a period of thirty-two months from April 19, 1926, to December 26, 1928, about ninety articles of equipment, large and small, were purchased for this department on the advice of the coöperative committee. No form of shop equipment, indeed, according to the testimony of the superintendent in charge of the department, is now secured except with coöperative approval. Questioned as to whether many ideas on this subject are presented by the men or whether they mainly come from the management, the superintendent answered: "Both originate ideas for both are vitally concerned." The men, he stated, were definitely interested because they were desirous of obtaining equipment that "would not only make work easier and safer for them but permit them to turn out a better grade of work at a lesser cost." Besides, in competition with contract shops the department had bid for, and been awarded, the privilege of building ten new all-steel baggage cars, and for this reason the men had been especially anxious to have good tools in order to perform a high quality of workmanship. Whenever a doubt has existed as to the need for a machine or the results that it would effect, an investigatory subcommittee has been appointed, since, as the superintendent said, "It is necessary to give the management facts." With coöperative assistance a survey was made of requirements of the cabinet shop when it was known that eighteen old-style sleeping cars were to be converted during 1928 into modern, steel-sheathed suburban coaches. As a result a glue spreader was manufactured in the shop, and five new machine tools were bought: a hydraulic press; a hand-stroke belt sander; a tapping machine; a jointer; and a drum sander. The total outlay for these tools was $7,504. In the operations which they performed in making and forming headlining, ply-wood paneling, and in sash work during five and a half months until the eighteen cars were completed in November, 1928, it is estimated that $7,456 was saved, or almost the entire cost of the tools. During this period the tools were also employed for other purposes.

On the Canadian lines of the Canadian National Railway System, as has been explained in chapter viii, suggestions relative to the purchase of more costly articles of equipment are likely to be taken to a regional joint committee for final settlement. For example, one suggestion submitted by the employees that a new dry kiln for lumber be erected, and another by management that two portable rivet heaters be bought for use in repairing freight-train cars, were carried on the minutes of the car department's committee at the Fort Rouge shop, Winnipeg, Manitoba, for many months without result. Eventually both propositions, involving in each case an estimated expenditure of about $3,000, were referred to the joint coöperative committee of the western region in December, 1926, where assurances were given that they would be taken care of in the appropriations for 1927. In like manner the locomotive repair department of the Transcona shop, near Winnipeg, obtained a crane for its foundry, and a machine for facing horn jaws, after suggestions advanced by employees' representatives had been considered by the regional committee. Again, authority was granted to the Point St. Charles shop at Montreal, Quebec, to secure an electric vacuum apparatus especially designed for cleaning coaches at the joint coöperative committee meeting of the central region in July, 1928.

The range which discussion may take in local coöperative meetings on types of equipment of intermediate importance is exemplified where the following have been granted: an electric driven emery wheel at Belle Plaine, Iowa, and fifty feet of gas line for the boiler shop at Clinton, Iowa, points on the Chicago & North Western Railway; an electric crane for machine shop No. 1 at Mount Clare, Baltimore, Maryland, and a pipe stock for the pipe shop at Chillicothe, Ohio, on the Baltimore & Ohio Railroad; and on the Milwaukee System, a power hack saw at Dubuque, Iowa, and two one-ton chain hoists at the Galewood shop, Chicago, Illinois. Many recommendations leading to the acquisition of lighter machine tools, cutting and measuring tools or of other odds and ends of equipment are mere matters of shop routine. The need for these kinds of equipment is generally apparent, and the coöperative meeting becomes a clearing house to bring it to the attention of the administrative officials. The equipment required, it is argued, is often secured more expeditiously and the workers are better pleased if they help conduct the business. Should an emergency arise between meetings, making it necessary that some article be obtained at once, both parties can be informed of the situation, and the purchase recorded at the next meeting. To illustrate the manner in which proposals may accumulate on the coöperative minutes with respect to lighter machine tools, cutting and measuring tools, etc., there is the following citation from the records of the Ivorydale, Ohio, shop of the Baltimore & Ohio Railroad. In the coöperative minutes at that point of July 5, 1928, suggestions had either been granted or were pending for four flute drills, four buffer wheels, and twelve thread taps for grease cups on rods, each of stated dimensions; blades for the power hack saw; diaphragms and gauges for the regulators; mill files, Toledo ratchet dies, drills and castle nuts, each of specified sizes; parts for the Ohio injector and force feed lubricators; a saw for cutting twelve- and fourteen-inch timbers; a saw for the carpenter shop; a double-faced Ashcroft steam gauge; new pipe racks, and a ladder rack. It is customary on the railroads to charge out small auxiliary and other hand tools to work done, which means that their purchase price is included along with labor costs. Quite often a shortage of hand tools in general, or in a particular department, or of a certain kind, is reported to a coöperative meeting for correction.

## Transfers of Used Equipment.

QUITE a traffic in productive equipment is carried on between the repair plant units of American railroads. This may simply involve the transposition of movable tools or other equipment from points where for some reason they have become superfluous, to other points where there is an undersupply, by which means an effectual counterbalancing of equipment between stations is obtained. Or, more important, it may involve the stepping down of equipment from larger to smaller points, or it may be from points more favored to such as have been stinted in the appropriations. It is a policy of wisdom for the mechanical department of a carrier to keep all its equipment active until each article has performed its last use. When a new machine is ordered for a certain shop, the machine it displaces may still do sturdy service at some other point on the company's lines. Hence in keeping their accounts the carriers always deduct the estimated value of the old machine from the price of the new one installed in order to discover the actual or net outlay. Transfers of standard types of equipment between departments at a repair point is also common practice. Most specialized equipment, however, cannot be shifted between departments and when displaced must be sent elsewhere.

Mechanical officers have long been aware of the economic advantages of equipment transfers, although they sometimes can be accused of dilatoriness in effecting them. In times when a carrier's gross income has fallen, and its operating ratio tends to rise, it is noticed that in order to curtail expenses, mechanical officers become expert in moving equipment from point to point. Union-management coöperation has no doctrine to add on this subject. Its exponents, nevertheless, may aver with some justice that through the plan, transfers become less fitful and more systematized. The needs of individual repair points are set forth in the minutes of regularly occurring coöperative meetings, and a stimulus given by this method of publicity to the circulation of part-worn equipment. A staff or line officer of the carrier, reading these minutes, may quickly mark an outlet for an idle machine or other bit of unused equipment. Craft-union officials are able through the channels of the system organization to disseminate information concerning equipment that is available. Moreover, at local points, representatives of both management and men become alert in detecting opportune ways in which equipment may be traded from department to department.

Searches afield for secondhand equipment to satisfy coöperative proposals have been often requited. Records of the Dubuque, Iowa, car shop on the Milwaukee System provide a simple case in point. This station had only one electric skill saw which was much in demand, so that time was lost in transporting it about the shop. A requisition was submitted for an additional saw but was turned down at headquarters. The matter was pressed coöperatively, and as a result an officer of the mechanical department made inquiries at different points on the system to locate, if possible, an electric skill saw for Dubuque. Finally, an idle saw was found at Sioux City, Iowa, and shipped to Dubuque, which closed the item on its coöperative minutes. A drill press was suggested as urgently needed in the blacksmith shop at Cone, East St. Louis, Illinois, on the Baltimore & Ohio Railroad. One was available at the larger shop in Washington, Indiana, and having been reconditioned was forwarded to Cone. Less fortunate was the coöperative proposal at the Mount Clare shop of the same carrier in Baltimore, Maryland, that a lathe be secured for its No. 2 machine shop. Inquiries elicited the information that no lathe could be spared anywhere on the company's lines. Likewise, when an employee's suggestion at the London, Ontario, car shop, of the Canadian National Railway System, specified that a heavy sewing machine was needed to sew carpets and repair diaphragms for coaches, and that a used machine would answer the purpose, advices were received that a part-worn machine of this type was unprocurable on the road, but that the price of a new one would be included in next year's budget. However, a demand from the machine shop at Point St. Charles, Montreal, Quebec, on the Canadian National Railway System for an electric center grinder was quickly met when information came through from the machinists' local at Ottawa, Ontario, that a serviceable grinder lay unemployed at that station and was ready for transfer. Hoisting appliances seem to figure most prominently among recommendations for the transfer of equipment at repair points, with lighter, standard machine tools ranking next in order. An interesting suggestion originating with management at the Fort Rouge shop of the Canadian National Railway System, Winnipeg, Manitoba, designated a use that might be made of a surplus incinerator. It was set up at one end of the rip tracks, and all the accumulated rubbish of the freight car shop consumed in it daily. The labor of two men, it is estimated, was thereby saved, as rubbish had formerly to be loaded on cars and taken to the dumping ground.

## The Reconditioning of Equipment.

A CONSIDERABLE percentage of suggestions inscribed on the minutes of local coöperative committees refer to the question of repairs to shop equipment. As line officers and supervisors are responsible for the upkeep of equipment within the scope of their jurisdictions, they rely for their knowledge of its condition, where union-management coöperation does not appertain, upon their own observations or upon what the workers tell them. It is axiomatic that too frequent maintenance tends to be uneconomical. On the other hand, if an article of equipment gets into too great disrepair before receiving attention, its productivity will have invariably diminished in the meantime and its restoration to form have become cumulatively more expensive. Shop workers who have little thought for the well-being of the company employing them have often been known, in spite of the alertness of official superintendence, to let equipment suffer through undermaintenance. Coöperation, it is argued, should forestall this danger in that it changes the workers' attitude toward the company that they serve. As a matter of fact it may sometimes operate in the direction of having equipment overmaintained. If no other ideas occur to the workers prior to a coöperative meeting, it is generally easy for them to discover some article of equipment that might stand reconditioning, and an untimely suggestion may result.

A few suggestions, gathered at haphazard, may be regarded as typical of those presented to coöperative committees on the subject of repairs to shop equipment. At points on the Baltimore & Ohio Railroad in 1928 repairs such as the following were sought: general overhauling of the steam hammer in the blacksmith shop at Benwood, West Virginia; relining of the rivet heating forge for use in boiler makers' work at Willard, Ohio; restoration of the ground connections of the electric welder, at Cone, Illinois; and reconditioning of the Bradley hammer at the Mount Clare shop, Baltimore, Maryland. Again, on the Chicago & North Western Railway, the boiler makers' representative on the coöperative committee at Boone, Iowa, reported that repairs were necessary to three Ingersoll-Rand motors used for tapping out stay bolt holes; the machinists' representative at Missouri Valley, Iowa, asked for an overhauling of the cylinder boring bar; while at Fremont, Nebraska, the carman on the coöperative committee urged that the hand pump be fixed upon which the car department depended for its supply of drinking water.

*The Question of Equipment Grouping.*

So interconnected are the work processes requisite to the maintenance of train cars and locomotives, that the grouping of tools and other equipment at a repair point is always a matter of vital concern. This question, as it bears on shop methods, will be treated from another angle in chapter xi. Honest differences of opinion have customarily prevailed among line officers on the subject of equipment grouping, with the result that when a new administrator has taken charge at a local point, one of the first things he often has done has been to make a general reallocation of equipment. Supervisors, too, have usually been inclined to have their own favorite system of arranging equipment in the department under their control. Mechanical craftsmen, for their part, once they have become habituated to working with a machine tool or other article of equipment at a certain spot, have usually been averse to any change in its location. Hence when coöperative procedure has been related to the problem of equipment grouping, it has not only taxed to a degree the forbearance of management, but has demanded a more progressive viewpoint from the men. As a sequel, management has been rather slow to surrender its prerogatives in this regard, and the workers somewhat frugal in their presentation of ideas.

Suggestions on the grouping of equipment have, perhaps, been registered most plentifully with respect to the juxtaposition of lifting devices, such as jib cranes, air hoists, etc., and the larger-sized machine tools. Among proposals of this type accepted at local points have been the following: that a special crane be installed at the Liberty planer to avoid dependence on the facilities provided by the overhead crane, submitted by an employee at Battle Creek, Michigan, on the Grand Trunk Western Lines; that a fast-moving air hoist be applied to the post near the bulldozer machine in the blacksmith shop, an employee's suggestion at the Fort Rouge locomotive repair shop, Winnipeg, Manitoba, on the Canadian National Railway System; and that a crane be brought to the spot where the gear cases were handled in the boiler shop, presented at Deer Lodge, Montana, on the Milwaukee System. In order to insure maximum tool capacity and to economize in the use of acetylene gas, a suggestion has been made by the boiler makers' representative at the Clinton, Iowa, shop of the Chicago & North Western Railway, that the angle shears be set up next to the drill press, and that the bevel shears be then moved to the spot formerly occupied by the angle shears. At the same station as the result of a foreman's proposal, all the welding operations performed by the mechanical crafts have been localized at one central spot. For the purpose of eliminating transfers of material, a suggestion of management has been adopted at Port Huron, Michigan, on the Grand Trunk Western Lines, that the bolt threading machines be taken from the machine shop and erected close to the bolt heading machines in the blacksmith shop.

## The Storage and Issue of Shop Tools.

BASICALLY, repair points on the railroads have the same problems to face with respect to the storage and issue of shop tools, as have manufacturing establishments. Cutting and measuring tools, various portable devices, and auxiliary hand tools, if they are to be properly cared for, must be systematically brought in, reconditioned, and put for safe-keeping in a place where they will be readily accessible, when not in use. Major railroad shops, as a rule, have a well-appointed tool room, or crib, with an attendant in charge for each important department. Lesser repair points, however, are not always so favored. Productivity is hampered if tools cannot be found when wanted or if they are out of condition. Scientific storage facilities include racks, shelves, drawers, and bins where the teeth and edges of tools are retained undented and they are otherwise protected. Tool room attendants must grade and classify their equipment, pack it away as conveniently as possible, and keep a close record of all articles handed out or delivered for use.

Through coöperative agency numerous improvements have been effected in the methods of tool storage and issue employed at shop points. Under the plan the car department of the Chicago & North Western Railway's shop at Missouri Valley, Iowa, has been provided with adequate tool room facilities, and a checking and reconditioning system for tools has been put into operation. Formerly hand tools and other appliances were left scattered about promiscuously at Missouri Valley, and could be traced only with difficulty. From both shops of the Canadian National Railway System at or near Winnipeg, Manitoba, have come reports of the introduction of better-defined policies of tool storage and issue since the beginning of coöperation. At the Cumberland, Maryland, enginehouse of the Baltimore & Ohio Railroad as the result of a boiler maker's suggestion, revolving tool holders on roller-bearing axles have been constructed to take the place of the long tool racks formerly in use, a device which has spread to other points on the line. Again, at the Cumberland, Maryland, bolt and forge shop of the same carrier the coöperative committee has enjoined its craft representatives to urge upon the men the necessity of returning all tools promptly to storage, and at its Ivorydale, Ohio, shop in answer to a coöperative suggestion an inclosed wagon has been built to convey electricians' tools and appliances to the neighborhood of locomotives undergoing repairs. Proposals advanced by management at the Glenwood shop, Pittsburgh, Pennsylvania, of the Baltimore & Ohio Railroad have also led to wagons being designed and constructed, auxiliary to the stores, which are supplied with portable equipment especially needed by the engine stripping and frame gangs.

## Chapter XI

## Suggestions with Reference to New Construction, Shop Methods, and Appliances

ALL structural work performed for the mechanical department of any railroad in the United States or Canada comes under the jurisdiction of the department of maintenance of way and structures. Most suggestions, therefore, recorded in local joint coöperative meetings that are of structural import are first carried for action to the ranking line officer of the latter department, the division engineer. If, however, the proposals involve but a few hours of labor and are otherwise inexpensive, they may be taken for quick handling to a supervisor of that department. As a consequence, bridge and building, track and roadway, electrical transmission, and other crews of the department of maintenance of way and structures help to put into effect many coöperative suggestions. An idea of the extent of suggestions of this sort may be gathered from the illustrations which follow.

### *Structural Proposals.*

LOCAL coöperative committees have as yet been rather modest in sending forward requests for new construction that must entail larger financial outlay. Oftenest under this heading they have asked for buildings of limited size or for additions to or the remodeling of older buildings, in order to provide locker, lunch, or toilet facilities, or to improve the ventilating system, etc., in submitting demands for which, as will be outlined in chapter xii, they have been reasonably successful. But only in minor ways as a rule has structural work been undertaken at their solicitation which has been intended to furnish increased opportunities for production at maintenance of equipment points. Through coöperative agency authority for expenditure was obtained by the passenger coach department of the Milwaukee, Wisconsin, shop of the Milwaukee System to allow for the erection of an inclosure in the upholstery shop where material might be blown, and to build a special canopy at the west end of the truck shop. At the London, Ontario, car shop of the Canadian National Railway System, it had been found that the cabinet shop was too cold and damp, at certain seasons of the year, properly to complete veneering operations. After investigation, upon the basis of a coöperative suggestion, it was decided to partition off a section of the cabinet shop, thereby constructing a "glue room," in which the air could be kept dry and a warm even temperature maintained.

Among other structural suggestions of more or less routine character have been those relating to the building of new or the restoration of old platforms, floors, racks, doors, and windows; the installation or mending of air lines, steam pipes, electrical fixtures, and telephone apparatus; attention to improper drainage and roof leaks; and the painting of buildings or shop equipment. Representative proposals taken up in coöperative meetings at points on the Baltimore & Ohio Railroad have asked for: repair of various spots in the enginehouse floor, a new steam coil pipe for the drop pit, and mending of roof leaks in the pipe, machine, and blacksmith shops and in the enginehouse at the Cleveland, Ohio, terminal; repairs to the engine-washing platform, the drainage system in the train car yard, and the water line behind the enginehouse stalls at Benwood, West Virginia; the installation of electric lighting in the lumber shed at the New Castle, Pa., shop; mending of leaks in the air lines on the repair tracks and in the enginehouse blow back system at Storrs, Cincinnati, Ohio; and painting of the water-treating plant and air tank of the company's property at Dayton, Ohio. Samples of structural proposals from the minutes of points on the Chicago & North Western Railway, have been those requesting new window space in the carpenter shop at Belle Plaine, Iowa; repairs to doors in the machine shop at Boone, Iowa; and the installation of a company telephone in the storeroom at Council Bluffs, Iowa. Again, on the Grank Trunk Western Lines, through coöperative action the telephone system has been overhauled at Port Huron, Michigan, and approximately five thousand square feet of new flooring laid at the shop in Battle Creek, Michigan.

Further types of structural suggestions which have dealt with the building or maintenance of standard gauge and service tracks, turntables, transfer tables, walks, driveways, crossings, elevators, and subways have often borne also upon the problems of shop methods and later in this chapter will be treated from that point of view. A few such recorded at the stations specified have sought action as follows: at Miles City, Montana, on the Milwaukee System, that five pits in the enginehouse be lengthened to take care more efficiently of larger power, and that steps be taken to straighten the track south of the machine shop; at Port Huron, Michigan, on the Grand Trunk Western Lines, that a spur service track for lorries be run to the shears in the blacksmith shop to prevent congestion; and at Benwood, West Virginia, on the Baltimore & Ohio Railroad, that a new walk be constructed leading from the slag pipe to the second story of the river pump house, that the crossing behind stall No. 20 in the enginehouse be repaired, and that necessary repairs be made to the turntable, giving special attention to the condition of the idlers.

### Plant Layout, Facilitation of Transfer, and Work Scheduling.

THE recital of differing classes of suggestions has included, first those recorded with respect to machine tools and other forms of equipment, and, second, those submitted with respect to buildings and their appurtenances. Next in order it would seem fitting that a study be made of the relationship of coöperative suggestions to the methods by which work processes are performed. Back of all the diverse problems that arise in any shop on the broad question of work methods stands the issue, constantly increasing in importance, of production control. Most industrial managers, and a growing percentage of industrial workers, have come to realize that the older, rule-of-thumb methods of "getting the work done" in shops must be discarded. Words like planning, routing, and scheduling as applied to work performance, though a trifle hackneyed, have evidently gained a permanent place in the language of industry. No matter what modern scheme of production control is adopted, a well-arranged plant layout will be incidental to its success. Whenever a plant, in order to achieve its industrial aims, is dependent upon the processing effectiveness of two or more departments, it is essential that these departments be so located in reference to each other that a proper flow and interchange of work may occur between them. Machines and other equipment, too, should be grouped in departments in such a fashion that wasted time and effort will be reduced to a minimum. Equipment is so multiform, and production so diversified at railroad repair points, especially in the motive power section, that to group or align equipment most economically to meet the needs of production is a matter of grave concern.

Those who designed many of the plants still in use for maintenance of equipment purposes on American railroads had little conception of the meaning of production control. Hence the structural layout, from the present point of view, is incongruous, and the completion of necessary departmental readjustments is often very difficult. Yet, if room is available, it should always be possible to arrange equipment in appropriate production units. While it cannot be said that the accomplishments of coöperative committees have been pretentious in regard to plant layout, they at least have manifested a laudable interest in the subject. No sooner had the coöperative plan been launched at the Milwaukee, Wisconsin, shop of the Milwaukee System in 1926 than this problem arose for discussion. The ninth suggestion, in fact, registered in the motive power department, submitted by a machinist's representative, alluded to the antiquated and uneconomical layout of the plant and asked for remedial action which was shortly afterward taken. The coöperation committee in the passenger coach department at Milwaukee has secured the removal of the pattern shop from the upper floor of the wood mill because of cramped conditions, and the transfer of the silver plating department from one building to another. As several examples of proposals with respect to the grouping of equipment have been furnished in chapter x, only one need be added under this heading. At the Mount Clare shop of the Baltimore & Ohio Railroad in Baltimore, Maryland, it was pointed out in coöperative meeting that the drill press located in the combined paint, hardware, and pipe shop was too large for the work operations performed in that shop, and therefore should be moved to the passenger coach erecting shop where it would be much more serviceable. This suggestion was accepted, and a lighter capacity drill press supplied to the paint, hardware, and pipe shop.

Routing, which as an element in production control seeks to discover the shortest and most economical way from raw materials to finished product, has in its fuller aspects received scant attention from coöperative meetings. Nevertheless, they have entertained many proposals having as their object the facilitation of transfer about the plant, always a necessary adjunct to a routing program. In the passenger coach department of the Chicago, Illinois, shop of the Chicago & North Western Railway, as the result of a suggestion offered by an assistant foreman, additional tracks and hoisting machinery have been provided in the truck shop which greatly assists the handling of trucks that were formerly pushed to position by manual labor. At Council Bluffs, Iowa, on the same carrier a new crossing has been installed over two repair tracks, in order that rivet heater forges and acetylene wagons may be moved to a work location more easily; hitherto the nearest crossing had been at a distance of six car lengths. Again, obstructions have been removed through coöperative agency. When larger power came into use on the Baltimore & Ohio Railroad, extensions were built to a number of stalls in the enginehouse at Washington, Indiana. This left a square corner where the new wall on one side met the unextended portion of the building, around which portable cranes could not travel unless a locomotive was shifted. A machinist helper's suggestion that the corner be eliminated by the erection of a slantwise wall, allowing for additional space, has been accepted and has resulted in a considerable saving in time and labor. Because wheels stood too close to engines undergoing repairs and interfered with work in the boiler shop, a proposal has been adopted at Miles City, Montana, on the Milwaukee System whereby a double track has been put in outside the "dead" track in the machine shop to provide room for the wheels in another location.

Coöperative committees have dealt more understandingly with problems of work scheduling than they have with routing. Undoubtedly their experience with the spot system of repairs has contributed toward this end. To illustrate, it may be mentioned that operations on engine cabs are performed at the Cumberland, Maryland, locomotive repair shop of the Baltimore & Ohio Railroad in an old roundhouse still utilized as a part of the plant. Carpenters and boiler makers employed on the cabs found their work overlapping so that one craft interfered with the activities of the other. In answer to a carpenter's suggestion a schedule has been arranged giving the craft to which he belongs four hours' clear time on a cab before the boiler makers may begin operations. At Chillicothe, Ohio, on the Baltimore & Ohio Railroad, the committee complained that cars were not being spaced on the stripping track in conformity with spot system regulations, and as this hindered progress under the schedule, they requested corrective action by the yard forces. The schedule drawn up for the car department of the Dubuque, Iowa, shop of the Milwaukee System in 1928 called for the repair of one caboose a day. A carman's suggestion alluded to the difficulty of maintaining this schedule unless more cabooses were brought in and held on the tracks in a preparatory stage of repairs. The committee at Dubuque has also discussed the economy of keeping cars of the same class together for maintenance purposes, and the delays which their schedule had suffered through sending blacksmith work to be done in the motive power department.

## Localized Shop Economies.

THE focal point of union-management coöperation on the railroads is the individual craftsman, supervisor or local officer who, from personal observations at his particular place in the industry, should be able to impart ideas for the better performance of work and the improvement of working conditions. There have resulted a multiplicity of suggestions of a localized character, some types of which have already been studied. Among the most worth while of these suggestions have been those aiming at the more economic performance of a single industrial process, or of a brief series of processes. To assign suggestions of this kind to appropriate subgroups is a difficult matter. They may be illustrated, however, by first treating of the class which emphasizes the method to be followed, but which has little or no regard for the question of the equipment employed. Next, consideration may be given to the types which have sought by the introduction of newly invented, or other shop-made contrivances, to hasten and cheapen production or to improve the quality of workmanship.

On the Milwaukee System, due to a machinist's suggestion at its shop at Deer Lodge, Montana, the rails in the enginehouse pits have been raised in order to facilitate the removal of shoes, wedges, and binders from locomotives undergoing repairs. Also at Deer Lodge, a helper apprentice's suggestion has been approved to the effect that electric locomotives should always be brought into the shop with No. 1 end ahead, to lighten work for the electricians and air brake men and to economize on time. When shipped in from outside points to the car department of the Chicago & North Western Railway's shop at Chicago, Illinois, two kinds of truck bolsters used to be indiscriminately mixed

together. The blacksmiths' committeeman stated that from four
to six helpers, called from the fires, generally spent a whole day
sorting out from the shipment the class of bolster intended for
the blacksmith shop. His proposal that the bolsters be billed to
Chicago in separate consignments was accepted. At Fremont,
Nebraska, on the Chicago & North Western Railway, to save
equipment the machinist representative on the coöperative committee suggested that the hose on portable acetylene outfits
should be reversed, as the trailing end tended to wear rapidly
through contact with abrasive objects.

How meaningful an apparently trivial matter of shop practice
may turn out to be, has been exemplified at Battle Creek, Michigan, on the Grand Trunk Western Lines. A sweeper in the Battle
Creek shop asked for and received permission through the coöperative committee to test out the relative merits of two different
makes of broom, each costing the same price. He discovered that
with one he could work over approximately a third more floor
space in a given length of time. As his occupation called for
rough sweeping, eight hours a day, a purchase of the more effective make of broom was clearly advisable. Certain changes in
shop methods that have been introduced on the Baltimore & Ohio
Railroad through coöperation appear in the following examples.
At Washington, Indiana, on that carrier, a pitman was constantly at work shoveling ashes into a gondola car for removal.
A system has been devised at a small cost, as the result of a
supervisor's suggestion, whereby the ashes are now blown from
the pits up into each car through its hopper. Sheet metal workers
at the Ivorydale, Ohio, shop found that the stand to which a vise
was fastened for the bending of pipe lacked firmness. Their representative brought this matter to the attention of the coöperative committee and succeeded in getting the base of the stand imbedded in concrete. An electrician at Dayton, Ohio, referred in
committee to the thriftlessness of fueling a stationary engine to
keep two boilers in operation at the coal hoisting dock. Near by,

he pointed out, was the water-treating plant to which was transmitted electric current. If motors were installed to run the coal hoisting machinery, power costs would be materially reduced. The initial outlay necessary when this suggestion was put into effect was soon balanced by the savings. A proposal submitted at the Locust Point, Maryland, car shop has led to an air line being rigged up on the wood boring machine with which the operator may scatter the shavings as he works, allowing him to discern with precision his markings on the wood. The carman on the coöperative committee at the Glenwood shop, Pittsburgh, Pennsylvania, questioned why so much time should be lost on outside repair work due to stormy weather, when space for cars might be available in an old enginehouse belonging to the plant, which was standing idle. The general foreman has acted on this suggestion and secured the use of the enginehouse for stormy days. At the Tenth Street repair yards, Pittsburgh, Pennsylvania, complaint was made in meeting that cars billed for reconditioning were not delivered promptly enough by the transportation crews, and that the men loitered about in the morning waiting for work. This matter was corrected by interdepartmental arrangement, so that the cars are switched to the repair tracks overnight.

### The Invention of Mechanical Devices.

BOTH supervisors and craftsmen in the mechanical department of railroads have long had a reputation for ingenuity in bringing into existence new appliances as aids to production. Their efforts in this regard have not always been encouraged, nor have their accomplishments been given merited recognition. Here union-management coöperation, declare its proponents, has a splendid opportunity to display its effectiveness. It offers a challenge, they assert, to the inventiveness of management and men alike, stimulating their creative faculties, and causing them to originate forms of shop equipment that will redound to the advantage of the industry and make work easier. All manner of contrivances will be instituted that will provide short cuts in processing, and bring a saving in man hours and often in material. For the performance of definite operations, for instance, new fixtures will be developed to locate and hold work in position, movable jigs will be put together to mark out work specifically and speed the action of cutting tools, and dogs will be made as grips or clamps on lathes and planers.

A fragmentary picture only can be given of the numerous equipment devices that have been proposed and put into use through coöperative agency. The jolting of a box car over the rails is very hard on the carline castings in its roof structure, which oftentimes break. At East Clinton, Illinois, on the Chicago & North Western Railway, it ordinarily took from 32 to 36 man hours to drill and reinforce these broken castings with the assistance of an air motor. A millwright in the shop planned a cylinder to feed the air motor which relieved the strain of holding and keeping it in play at required angles. It has been estimated that now only eight man hours are consumed in repairing the castings, while the shop-made cylinder was paid for in three days' operation. In removing pins from crossheads and rods it was formerly the practice at the Cumberland, Maryland, locomotive repair shop of the Baltimore & Ohio Railroad to heat the parts and then extricate the pins. The use of a blowtorch was forbidden in doing this, as it tended to weaken the parts. A machinist contrived a pin-knocking device which did the work without the necessity of applying any heat. At Locust Point, Maryland, on the Baltimore & Ohio Railroad, a carman, belonging to a spot system unit, laid before the local coöperative committee his design for a simple appliance, consisting of a set of levers, to adjust pin lifters on train cars. So satisfactorily did this function that it was made a standard for the Maryland district by the master car builder.

Every so often a "buggy" or light truck burdened with from one to two tons of scrap metal was moved at the London, Ontario, car shop of the Canadian National Railway System, to the scrap bin for unloading. Two men were occupied for an hour getting the metal into the bin. It was advised in coöperative meeting that eyebolts should be affixed to the corners of the truck which might then be chain hoisted and dumped by means of a steam or electric crane. This operation, which has become the practice, took just one minute. At Leaside, Ontario, also on the Canadian National Railway System, a proposal of management was that a ring should be imbedded in concrete at the transfer table to facilitate the haulage of cars to and from the shop. In four months' time the company was reimbursed by savings for its outlay on this device.

At the bottom of each driving box on a locomotive is a receptacle known as a cellar, used to hold grease and waste. It was customary at East Clinton, Illinois, on the Chicago & North Western Railway, to knock these off with a wedge. A coöperative suggestion has led to a cheaply made appliance being used on the cellars, which operates by means of a bar attached to one wheel spoke and acts like a clamp on the axle. In conjunction with this a jack is employed to release the cellars without injury to the driving box. The fabrication of a jig to file into accurate divisions the sectional packing with which engine cylinders are sometimes equipped has been coöperatively proposed at Battle Creek, Michigan, on the Grand Trunk Western Lines. Experiments have shown that the savings to be realized from the use of this jig would be great. On the basis of a suggestion submitted by the machinists' committeeman at the Clinton, Iowa, shop of the Chicago & North Western Railway, a jig has been devised for drilling dowel holes in a specified make of crown brasses. At Miles City, Montana, on the Milwaukee System, a machinist pointed out that by making longer dogs the coach wheel lathe might possibly be changed over to turn locomotive tires. The necessary alterations to the lathe for this purpose have been completed and it has been shifted for service to another place in the shop.

*Shop-Made Equipment.*

CARRIERS as a rule have discovered that it is an economically sound policy to buy most of the standardized equipment required by the mechanical department. Tools and other equipment, however, adapted to special purposes can often be more advantageously produced at the repair point where they are needed. From one angle or another, coöperative meetings have been in the habit of dealing with the problems of shop-made equipment. Occasionally, too, they may launch into a discussion of particular forms of equipment that have proven valuable elsewhere. For example, at Boone, Iowa, on the Chicago & North Western Railway, in line with a toolmaker's suggestion a "home made" drill press cutter has been fashioned which will cut holes efficiently in the thin jacket iron covering locomotive boilers and cylinders. At the same station a boiler maker's suggestion has been accepted to the effect that wrenches should be made from old material to hold the die nut over the studs beneath the mud ring. Local administrators at the Clinton, Iowa, shop of the Chicago & North Western Railway have testified both to the amount of equipment of lighter caliber that has been manufactured in their plant and to the hints that they have received concerning equipment through the help of coöperation. The distance between center sills on box cars arriving at Clinton for repairs was fifteen inches. The shortest riveting gun at the station was seventeen inches in length and as a result the end of a car had to be torn out to splice the sills. It was pointed out in meeting, that an inverted handle, curving back under the gun, could be obtained which would reduce its length to fourteen inches and allow it to be inserted for action between the sills. Handles of this sort have been attached to guns and labor costs curtailed.

A carman's representative at the Dubuque, Iowa, shop of the Milwaukee System told his fellow committeemen that when he had been in service at another railroad point he had seen a simple but valuable tool known as a "crow foot" employed during the operation of turning a carriage bolt upon its nut. He advised that similar tools be made up for use at Dubuque. At the Galewood shop, Chicago, Illinois, of the Milwaukee System, in conformity with a boiler maker's suggestion a tool has been constructed for rolling small flues. All kinds of suggestions appear on coöperative minutes with reference to the building of ladders and scaffolding for use in motive power or train car repair operations. When coöperation was first introduced at Missouri Valley, Iowa, on the Chicago & North Western Railway, the shop forces were reconditioning refrigerator cars. An early item recorded as accepted on the minutes concerned the erection of eight-foot ladders which, if desired, might be set together in pairs and saddled with planks to form an excellent scaffold. On the suggestion of a boiler maker at the East Clinton, Illinois, shop of the Chicago & North Western Railway, wooden horses have been discarded, and angle irons with boards across employed instead to support the scaffolding at the front end of locomotives.

### Changes in Equipment Standards.

APTNESS has been shown by coöperative committees in indicating what they have regarded as profitable changes that might be effected in the mechanical standards applying especially to motive power and to an extent to train car equipment. Highly detailed specifications are followed in the construction of a locomotive or train car according to its type, and they are retained unaltered, as depicted in the blue prints, in making repairs unless orders to the contrary are received from headquarters. The chief mechanical officer, or officers of a carrier, ordinarily have the final voice with respect to equipment changes, but are guided, at least in important matters, by the opinions of the standards bureau or committee which is set up on most railroads. Ostensibly the best time to alter equipment parts, or arrange them according to a different standard, is when a locomotive or train car is undergoing repairs. As a matter of fact, the need for repairs is sometimes occasioned by a defective standard. As a rule, on American railroads, issues relating to changes in equipment standards have been thought to lie outside the province of shop workers, although casual remarks which they may make on the subject will often not go unnoticed by officers or supervisors. Under union-management coöperation, however, shop workers have in general become articulate on the question of standards. Suggestions recorded on this topic must necessarily be transmitted for consideration to the standards bureau or committee of the carrier, and may ultimately reach a chief staff officer of the mechanical department. While many suggestions respecting changes in standards have been accepted, a rather large proportion have always been turned back as impracticable. Frequently it has been found that, although the coöperative proposals are ingenious and seemingly good, they would, if made effective, entail a structural or mechanical weakness in another direction.

Technical language is usually required to describe suggestions bearing on standards and only two will be cited. In 1928, sixteen machinists, working in three shifts, were employed at Norfolk, Nebraska, on the Chicago & North Western Railway. These craftsmen had discussed among themselves the manner in which the equalizers on R-I locomotives, about three months after they had been cleaned and repaired, began to chafe the frame, a chargeable defect under the regulations for locomotive inspection. As a result, they instructed their representative on the coöperative committee to present the view that the bosses on the outside of the equalizers should be changed to the inside in order that more clearance might be allowed, and chafing of the frame avoided. This idea, registered as a suggestion, has been accepted as valuable by the standards committee, and the change involved designated in a blue print of July 2. The chief of motive power has sent out a circular letter making the alteration in the position of the bosses standard on all R-I locomotives. At Battle Creek, Michigan, on the Grand Trunk Western Lines, it was suggested that a hole be put through the center of the crosshead pins on locomotives, which should be filled with grease as a lubricant for the front-end brasses on the main rods. The flow of lubricant could then be controlled by an adjusting screw on the outside of the pins. This change has been sanctioned and adopted as a standard for all locomotives operated in the region.

## Chapter XII

## Suggestions Relating to Materials and the Betterment of Working Conditions

MONEY appropriated by the executive officers of a carrier to its maintenance of equipment stations is consumed for the most part in wage payments and expenditures for materials. Labor costs, of these two major forms of outlay, generally rank the higher, taking often from 60 to 70 per cent, and occasionally up to 80 per cent, of the combined total. In both sections of the mechanical department, the ratio between labor and material costs tends to fluctuate from month to month, depending either upon the character of the work done on locomotives or upon the type and condition of train cars brought in for repairs. Whatever the ratio may be, the outgo for materials is in any case significant, and steps taken to economize in their use are important. Methods of handling and controlling materials, if they are to be effective, should involve a purchase of the most serviceable of them for each repair operation, and in order to lessen delays, a retention of a carefully balanced stock at repair stations, so that the right volume of each article required will be kept on hand. Materials, too, should be protected against the elements or other sources of damage, and be used in such a manner that wastage will be reduced to a minimum. Furthermore, a lowering of labor costs may be expected wherever a well-governed system is introduced for the transfer of materials about the plant.

### *Proposals Relating to Shortages, Suitability, and Re-use of Materials.*

THE wisdom of putting the storekeeper as a representative of management on the local coöperative committee is readily seen from an examination of the character of suggestions presented with respect to materials. Many proposals relate to the question of material shortages which the stores department is expected to correct. Whenever a pressing need for a certain class, grade, or size of material occurs between meetings, it may be referred at once to the storekeeper, and then placed later on the coöperative minutes. Undoubtedly a proportion of suggestions regarding shortages is drummed up to make a showing, but the majority of them may be considered as sincere, and should assist the store-keeper in formulating plans and in drawing up his requisitions. Moreover, while attending coöperative meetings, he is able personally to explain delays and discrepancies in delivery. Minutes of specimen meetings at stations on the Baltimore & Ohio Railroad have recorded suggestions concerning shortages of material as follows: $3/4''$ globe valves, $3/4''$ bolts, in all sizes below $18''$, three different sizes of flat iron, Westinghouse yokes, and B. 4. water glasses at Willard, Ohio; $1/8''$ and $3/16''$ sheet steel and 5 ampere snap switches, at Lima, Ohio; and paint spray at Cleveland, Ohio, the delivery of which was asked as speedily as possible. At the London, Ontario, car shop of the Canadian National Railway System an employee's suggestion embodied information to the effect that the stores were "running too near a margin on bolts," of which there had been a shortage of six sizes during the preceding week. Meanwhile bolts were being supplied from the London shop to another station. The stores department has acknowledged that bolts had been shipped elsewhere, and has given assurance that the home shortage would be watched more carefully in the future.

The suitability of materials for work operations has often engaged the attention of coöperative committees. Notice, for example, was taken of the fact at Missouri Valley, Iowa, on the Chicago & North Western Railway, that the rivets specified for use in flooring certain freight-train cars were too long, and to be of any service must necessarily be bent over or shortened. A coöperative suggestion has led to shorter rivets being supplied, which has meant a saving in material costs, and better workmanship. Similarly a request of the committee at the Cumberland, Maryland, locomotive repair shop of the Baltimore & Ohio Railroad has been granted that 4″ brake rigging pins should be furnished instead of 4½″ pins, as the latter had to be cut off and redrilled for use, a waste of both materials and labor. At Boone, Iowa, on the Chicago & North Western Railway, the sheet metal workers' committeeman complained of the poor grade of pipe which was being received and secured an investigation by the master mechanic. Employees on the car department's committee at the Transcona shop of the Canadian National Railway System, near Winnipeg, Manitoba, have on various occasions referred to the unsatisfactory quality of lumber supplied to them for maintenance purposes. Both they and the representatives of management on the committee have also repeatedly asked that for the sake of economy, a cheaper kind of wood be substituted when it has been believed that it will be equally serviceable in certain repair operations. Under the American Railway Association's code of rules for the interchange of traffic, if wrong materials go into the repair of cars of other railroads, the owning carrier, to which the charges are remitted, may refuse payment. At Cone, East St. Louis, Illinois, on the Baltimore & Ohio Railroad, where much light repair work is done to "foreign cars," it is alleged that the coöperative committee has, by its advice on the use of proper materials, saved the company from considerable interchange of traffic losses.

Reiteration of the injunction to practice frugality under union-management coöperation has resulted in many interesting and valuable suggestions for the employment of materials to their fullest extent. Often these suggestions have pointed out how odds and ends of left-over material might be used advantageously. What may be called the acme of thrift was displayed by the carman's representative on the committee at Norfolk, Nebraska, on the Chicago & North Western Railway, who had noted the manner in which carpenters tossed aside the stub ends of pencils once they had become too short to use. He proposed that pencil holders be obtained and given to the carpenters in order that they might use their pencils to the last bit. This suggestion has been accepted and the necessary holders made by sheet metal workers in the local tin shop. When 2″ by 2″ lumber was cut at the Clinton, Iowa, shop of the Chicago & North Western Railway, a quantity of three-cornered pieces remained which were customarily discarded. It was suggested that these pieces be nailed around the inside of box cars as grain strips to block the seeping of grain kernels through cracks and holes. This has not only been done at Clinton, but the residue stock has been shipped to perform a similar function at other stations on the line. As the result of a cooperative suggestion at the London, Ontario, car shop of the Canadian National Railway System, short clippings of new pipe that formerly went to the scrap bin have been used, in place of nipples taken from the stores, to make drains for baggage cars.

## The Storage, Free Movement, and Protection of Materials.

THE location in, and transfer of materials about, the plant have also been topics thoroughly discussed in local joint coöperative meetings. While committeemen have generally acknowledged the value of keeping a careful check on all materials issued, they have been inclined to stress the importance of having materials so distributed that they may be readily accessible to those who would use them. Consequently they have favored the establishment of subordinate or petty shop stores, as well as the setting up of racks, boxes, and other receptacles at vantage points close to work. At the Minneapolis, Minnesota, shop of the Milwaukee System the supply of pipe had always been retained under the immediate supervision of the storekeeper; now, in answer to a coöperative suggestion, it is located near the men requiring it. Likewise a proposal accepted at Miles City, Montana, on the same railroad has led to a stock of tank shoes and driver brake shoes

being placed in a building known locally as the brick shed to re-
lieve workers of the necessity of going to the stores to fetch shoes.
Whenever standard studs were in demand at the Stratford, Ontario, locomotive repair shop of the Canadian National Railway
System they had to be procured from the general stores in the
main shop balcony. This matter has been taken up in coöperative
meeting, and authority obtained to have the studs kept in the
petty stores in the machine shop. Under another heading in chapter xi consideration has been given to the attitude of coöperative
committees on the subject of securing tractor systems to convey
materials, and building better driveways to facilitate their transfer. The storekeeper at Council Bluffs, Iowa, on the Chicago &
North Western Railway, requested through the local committee
and was granted a company telephone for the storeroom to assist
him in filling orders more promptly. At the Fort Rouge shop of
the Canadian National Railway System, Winnipeg, Manitoba,
the car department's committee sought a remedy for the cumber-
some method by which materials were issued from the petty stores
building in the coach yard. This difficulty has been solved by
cutting an extra doorway into the structure. A great economy in
the handling of materials has been effected at Port Huron, Michigan, on the Grand Trunk Western Lines, through the removal in
accordance with a coöperative suggestion of a post in the blacksmith shop. This post was so located in proximity to a large
machine, that it prevented long materials such as steel sills or
angle irons from being swung about unless they were taken outside the shop.

A variety of ideas has been brought before coöperative meetings with a view to protecting materials from harm. At Belle
Plaine, Iowa, on the Chicago & North Western Railway, where
the spot system is applied on outside tracks to the rebuilding of
gondolas and other freight-train cars, nuts and bolts tended to
become rusted through exposure. Due to a coöperative suggestion action has been taken whereby four wooden boxes with metal

lids have been built as containers for this material and distributed along the repair tracks. Cyanide was at one time stored in wooden kegs at the bolt and forge shop of the Baltimore & Ohio Railroad, Cumberland, Maryland. In answer to a suggestion the policy now is to keep the cyanide in an iron box as a safeguard against danger and for purposes of added economy. Discontinuance of the customary plan of spraying with an antirust solution the iron plates that were stored outside the shop buildings at London, Ontario, on the Canadian National Railway System was advised in coöperative meeting, because the oil still adhering to the surface of the plates caused them to slip when placed in the shears. Instead, after investigation by a subcommittee, it has been decided to protect each pile of plates with a light metal covering made from scrap by the sheet metal workers at the station.

### Salvaging and Reclamation.

THE fate awaiting worn-out or obsolete materials and shop equipment in the mechanical department of railroads is diversified. Articles may be destroyed by burning, if inflammable, or committed to the dump as worthless. Other lots of scrap, which have been salvaged and possibly sorted out, may be disposed of to the junk dealers for what they will bring. Still other portions may be reclaimed and used again in the same form as a residue of themselves, or for some different purpose by a process of re-formation. The approved maxim would appear to be that nothing should be destroyed which can, without too much labor, be salvaged, and that nothing should be sold for scrap which can be more economically reclaimed for further use. The collection at all repair stations on a carrier of even the tiniest fragments of scrap will have a favorable effect upon its financial balance. Sir Henry W. Thornton has always been a very persistent advocate of reclamation policies on the Canadian National Railway System. A story that has been told about him reflects this attitude. On one occasion, it is said, when he was being conducted around a western region shop by a local officer, he suddenly halted and began prodding at something with his cane. His eyes had searched out a discarded nut over which he pondered reflectively. The officer hastened to explain that the salvage man had been off duty that week, sick. "Oh!" replied Sir Henry, "I thought he was dead."

Witness is constantly borne to the fact both by local officers and supervisors, that coöperation gives them a splendid opportunity to instil a better understanding among their men of the advantages of salvaging and reclaiming materials. Conversely it may be inferred, that as the interest of the workers in these matters enlarges it will have a stimulating effect upon management. Thrift campaigns, such as have been waged in American industries within recent years, have unquestionably had beneficial results in effecting a conservation of materials, but their influence, once the campaigns have been over, has always gradually waned. Union-management coöperation, it may be argued, through giving regular attention to questions of salvaging and reclamation, allows for a greater continuity of policy. Coöperation has meant a great deal from this point of view to a maintenance of equipment station like Dubuque, Iowa, on the Milwaukee System. A leading reason, it has been estimated, why repair work formerly cost so much more at Dubuque, than at other stations on the Milwaukee System, was due to the inefficient methods practiced of saving materials. Coöperation, however, has brought a rigorous check up on the scrap pile at Dubuque which has materially lessened shop expenses. A typical reclamation proposal accepted at this point came from the blacksmith foreman who advised that old axles, valued for scrap at about sixty cents a hundredweight, should be made into driving spring hangers, the iron castings for which, when bought new, cost $7.50 a hundredweight.

In response to suggestions recorded at the Cumberland, Maryland, locomotive repair shop, of the Baltimore & Ohio Railroad, materials have been saved: by setting three drop pans of specified sizes under the oil lines in the power house to catch oil drippings that otherwise would be wasted; by constructing a rack out of discarded flues to hold boiler plates in the storeroom; and by removing the carbon sticks from dead dry cell batteries for the use of welders, in place of new pencils, in such operations as the electric carbon cutting of valve cage and cylinder bushings. A system of appraising the value of scrap before it has been hauled from the enginehouse has been devised through coöperation at East Clinton, Illinois, on the Chicago & North Western Railway. Also at this station the sills of condemned freight-train cars have been used to build narrow gauge service tracks upon which are run four-wheel trucks conveying materials. At the Clinton, Iowa, shop of the Chicago & North Western Railway, it was suggested that the worn-out braces taken from box cars might be of service in reconstructing the drop doors of gondolas. By shortening the braces it has been found that they may be economically employed to make the wooden part of these unloading doors which measure three feet square.

It was customary at the Missouri Valley, Iowa, shop of the Chicago & North Western Railway to reject every month many signal lamp glasses which had become scratched and pitted through the impact of flying sand. Now, thanks to a coöperative suggestion, these are repolished by sheet metal workers and put again into use at a nominal cost. Materials taken from the scrap yard have been used to complete a device, as suggested to the committee at the Battle Creek, Michigan, locomotive repair shop of the Grand Trunk Western Lines, whereby a much easier and more successful method has been introduced of turbining the scale from Wickes boilers in the power house. A representative of management in the car department at the Fort Rouge shop of the Canadian National Railway System, Winnipeg, Manitoba, suggested that heavy galvanized 1¼" pipe removed from the dismantled meat racks of refrigerator cars might be reclaimed and put to various uses. A committee was designated to inquire into this matter, and it has reported that the pipe in question was standard and should be quite serviceable.

*Ventilation, Heating, and Industrial Lighting.*

NORMALLY inside workers at maintenance of equipment points are not so densely crowded at their work as are the operatives in many nonrailroad industries. They are frequently employed in one-story buildings with reasonably high roofs and ceilings. Nevertheless the problem of ventilation may become more or less acute at railroad repair stations due to the smoke, fumes, and dust that are given off during work operations. Besides at engine-houses, smoke and steam vapor are incidental to the dispatching of motive power equipment. Railroad plants still in use that were constructed at an earlier period have been notably lacking in scientific methods of ventilation, and it has been accordingly at these that coöperative committees have had a greater opportunity to suggest betterments.

One of the most commendable achievements of a coöperative committee in relation to improving ventilation has occurred in the motive power department of the Milwaukee, Wisconsin, shop of the Milwaukee System. This shop is on low ground, from which the smoke, largely on account of atmospheric influences from Lake Michigan, oftentimes does not rise. Workers, particularly in the motive power department, suffered discomforts for something like forty years from these recurring leaden palls of smoke before the inauguration of the coöperative plan encouraged them to press for relief. Ventilating engineers, when consulted as to a solution, submitted plans to the company for an air-conditioning system, the cost of which, however, appeared prohibitive. Finally, a proposal for the installation of a home-made system of ventilation in the locomotive repair plant was advanced by a blacksmiths' representative on the coöperative committee which was adopted and forthwith given executive sanction. This called for the erection of eight new roof stacks, and a unique combination of the natural air movement in the plant with a power blast system by means of which the worst evils complained of have been removed. Though air purification has not been fully accomplished the men have expressed themselves as well satisfied with the change. The enginehouse at Washington, Indiana, on the Baltimore & Ohio Railroad, was built at a time when much smaller power was operated. The smokestacks of modern locomotives, when housed at Washington, were found to reach inconveniently near the exhaust stacks in the roof. Shortening of the roof stacks was attempted as a corrective, but this left insufficient draft, and the smoke simply rolled back into the enginehouse. As a result of a coöperative suggestion the stacks over thirty-two stalls in the enginehouse have been elevated in the roof to insure proper clearance. Then they have been built higher and wider above the roof in order to obtain enough air circulation to carry off the smoke. At Boone, Iowa, on the Chicago & North Western Railway, a wooden roof ventilator has been erected at the solicitation of the coöperative committee to free both supervision and workers from bad air conditions in the blacksmith shop. So too, after an investigation had been made in answer to a suggestion recorded at the Port Huron, Michigan, shop of the Grand Trunk Western Lines, four roof ventilators have been installed above its cabinet shop, where, on account of the location, the scanty air circulation in hot weather was very distressing to those at work.

At the Cumberland, Maryland, bolt and forge shop of the Baltimore & Ohio Railroad, fault was found in committee, with the way in which hot metal was thrown into buggies before they were cleansed of oil and chemicals acquired from use at the heat-treating furnace. Contact of the hot metal with the surface of the buggies generated offensive odors and smoke which spread through the shop. Not only has this practice been discontinued, but plans have been laid for the removal of the heat-treating furnace to another quarter. A decided improvement in working conditions has been reported from the car department of the

Transcona shop of the Canadian National Railway System, near Winnipeg, Manitoba, where, on the basis of a coöperative suggestion, a change was made in the Globe style of ventilators in the fume-infested paint shop. The same type of ventilator has been installed in other sections of the shop. Again, on the Baltimore & Ohio Railroad, coöperative proposals have led to repairs being made to the window ventilators in the machine shop at Storrs, Cincinnati, Ohio; and to increased ventilation being provided for the oil house at Lima, Ohio, where released steam was the cause of excessive humidity. In the motive power department's meeting at the Fort Rouge shop of the Canadian National Railway System, Winnipeg, Manitoba, a suggestion was made that in order to take away dust and fumes, a pipe be attached to the Peters cutting off machine in the toolroom.

Somewhat less imposing, though economically important, have been the list of suggestions dealing with problems of shop temperature and industrial lighting. A major issue raised in committee shortly after the inauguration of the coöperative plan at the Glenwood shop, Pittsburgh, Pennsylvania, on the Baltimore & Ohio Railroad, related to the unsatisfactory methods employed to heat the plant. As a result the heating system at this point has been completely remodeled. Another suggestion adopted at Glenwood has secured for the operator of the 100-ton crane a sheltering frame made of canvas that wards off a cold draft that otherwise would strike him during the winter months. At the Cleveland, Ohio, enginehouse of the Baltimore & Ohio Railroad, a request has been made that a steam coil pipe be applied on one side of the drop pit to make the situation more comfortable for men there at work. The carmen's representative on the committee at Belle Plaine, Iowa, on the Chicago & North Western Railway protested against the relative darkness in which his fellow craftsmen had to perform their tasks in the carpenter shop. Extra window space has been provided for the shop by the bridge and building crew. At Miles City, Montana, on the Milwaukee System, the sun's glare in the afternoon through the west side windows was very disturbing to workers in the machine shop. Following coöperative consideration this matter has been adjusted by sanding the windows.

### Mechanical Safeguarding.

ADVOCATES of union-management coöperation have never been unanimous with respect to the exact relationship which the plan should bear to safety work on the railroads. Though there exists a general understanding that coöperative effort is not to infringe upon the sphere of Safety First, this principle has been more strictly interpreted at one repair point than at another. Many local chairmen of coöperative meetings rule entirely from discussion any topic which they believe to be closely associated with the problems of safety. Others appear to think that while the educational program and issuance of rules connected with safety, and the investigation of work accidents should belong exclusively to Safety First committees, questions of mechanical safeguarding, and even shop and equipment inspection, should be open for discussion also by coöperative committees. It is evidently desirable that the functions of coöperative and Safety First committees should be more carefully distinguished than at present.

Several examples may be cited where in the advancement of coöperative suggestions mechanical safeguarding has been the principal object in view. In the operation of a double floor grinder at the Cumberland, Maryland, locomotive repair shop of the Baltimore & Ohio Railroad, particles of steel and emery tended to fly from the surface of the wheel in motion on one side into the face of the mechanic controlling the wheel on the other side. A light guard has been set up at the center of the grinder, as the result of a machinist's suggestion, to eliminate this hazard. At Cone, East St. Louis, Illinois, on the same carrier, to lessen the industrial risk, guards have been placed around the flywheels of the air compressors at the suggestion of the boiler makers' committeeman. Likewise, at the locomotive repair shop of the Canadian National Railway System, Stratford, Ontario, the question of obtaining protection from injurious particles for men employed on emery wheels was brought up in coöperative meeting. The difficulty has been overcome by attaching an extension to the side of the gear.

When some apprehension was felt at the Galewood shop, Chicago, Illinois, of the Milwaukee System, lest the traveling crane might be in an unsafe condition, a request was presented to the coöperative committee for its inspection. The machine shop foreman, however, having specially examined the crane pronounced it quite safe to operate. Issues relating to the protection of workers from fire hazards or to First Aid have sometimes come up in coöperative meetings. Attention of the committee at Chillicothe, Ohio, on the Baltimore & Ohio Railroad, was drawn to the fact that scrap wood was being burned very close to the stripping track where a worker-unit of carmen was employed under the spot system. This practice, regarded as both dangerous and inconvenient for the carmen, has been given up. A suggestion was entertained by the coöperative committee in the motive power department of the Fort Rouge shop, on the Canadian National Railway System, Winnipeg, Manitoba, that a safety wrapper be procured for the ambulance stretcher so that injured men might be lowered from high places. After a demonstration had been made of the serviceability of such a wrapper, the committee recommended it to the attention of those responsible for First Aid in the shop.

### Proposals Relating to Sanitation.

A RATHER complex array of coöperative suggestions is classifiable under the general heading of sanitation. Bad drainage, inside or outside buildings at a repair point, may involve more particularly an interference with work operations, or be essentially a matter of hygienic consequence. Of the latter character was the situation at Missouri Valley, Iowa, on the Chicago & North Western Railway giving rise to a general foreman's suggestion, upon which action was taken, that the drain from the sewer pump be attended to, as the polluted water had not proper clearance. At the Benwood, West Virginia, shop of the Baltimore & Ohio Railroad the blacksmiths' representative proposed that the ice box around the drinking fountain in the blacksmith shop and the drain leading from it be cleaned. This was referred for handling to the shop labor gang. The manner in which water may collect and remain undrained in and about enginehouse pits has been a common topic for discussion in coöperative meetings. At Ivorydale, Ohio, on the Baltimore & Ohio Railroad through coöperative intervention, repairs have been made to the floor around the edge of the pits where men often had to stand in water while applying crossheads, rods, and guides to locomotives. Again, other causes of unsanitary working conditions have been cited in meeting. A foreman on the committee, for instance, at East Clinton, Illinois, on the Chicago & North Western Railway sought action restraining caboose crews from sweeping refuse out of their cars which, he stated, was blown through the yard and among the workers in the enginehouse.

Proposals have frequently been introduced on the subject of obtaining an ample supply of good drinking water at a repair point, or of having it kept at a proper drinking temperature. Others have dealt with the provision of adequate toilet facilities or the matter of their location about the plant. Through coöperative effort a water bubbler has been installed near the large fire in the blacksmith shop, connected with the cooling tank, at Clinton, Iowa, on the Chicago & North Western Railway, and an old drinking fountain removed and a new one set up in a more convenient place in the enginehouse at Ivorydale, Ohio, on the Baltimore & Ohio Railroad. Necessary repairs have been made to the drinking fountain in the car department's locker room at Council Bluffs, Iowa, on the Chicago & North Western Railway after complaint had been made in committee of its lack of water pressure. When objections were raised in the car department's meeting at the Transcona shop, near Winnipeg, Manitoba, of the Canadian National Railway System, to the unsanitary condition of the freight car shop lavatory, it was decided to appoint a committee to investigate composed of a foreman, a worker, and an official of Division No. 4. In addition to the freight car shop lavatory, the committee also examined lavatories in the wood mill, coach yard, and coach shop, and brought in a general report which has been adopted. The report recommended that ventilators be installed in the lavatories as needed; that the floors and fixtures of lavatories be thoroughly cleaned once a day; that the men be requested by their locals to refrain from spitting on the floors; and that the foreman with jurisdiction should inspect each lavatory at periodic intervals. During the last few years the Baltimore & Ohio Railroad has received a considerable number of coöperative appeals from local points for locker rooms and additional toilet facilities, upon which action has been taken as the economic situation has warranted. Suggestions carried on the minutes of the committee at Dayton, Ohio, for example, embodied requests that wash and locker rooms be provided for the East Dayton shop and the Needmore repair track force, and that a new lavatory be constructed at East Dayton. A washroom was granted East Dayton after the question had gone to the system coöperative meeting.

*Miscellaneous Betterment Suggestions.*

A HODGEPODGE of other suggestions might be recited that in one form or another have attempted to better working conditions in the mechanical department. Though well-equipped quarters have been provided at a fair percentage of repair points on American railroads where workers may dispose of their lunch in comfort, at many they must still squat about to consume their meal in the most suitable place they can find. Coöperative requests for better lunching facilities have not always, of course, been acceded to by the companies, but in general they have endeavored to make the situation more pleasant for the men. As the result of a coöperative suggestion a new combination locker and lunchroom has been procured by the maintenance of equipment forces at Cone, East St. Louis, Illinois, on the Baltimore & Ohio Railroad. Yet, when the workers at Baileys, Maryland, on the same carrier asked that available space in one corner of the power plant be used for the construction of a dressing- and lunchroom the company demurred at making the necessary changes on account of the expense involved. However, an old coach was sent to Baileys which, adequately equipped with steam heat, proved a quite satisfactory place both to dress and eat. Following the receipt of coöperative petitions from various of its stations for the installation of kitchen equipment and the establishment of a *café* service which would allow for the purchase of hot meals, the Canadian National Railway Company agreed to set up a lunch counter at its Point St. Charles shop, Montreal, Quebec. The patronage accorded this service, nevertheless, has not been as large as the company desired, though food is sold at reasonable charges, and it has accordingly been loath to invest money in projects of like character at other stations.

Action has been withheld on a proposal submitted at Fremont, Nebraska, on the Chicago & North Western Railway that sheds be built for the housing of workers' automobiles at an estimated cost of $800, as the company feared that demands for such accommodations might become common on its lines. But at the Moncton, New Brunswick, locomotive repair shop of the Canadian National Railway System, in answer to a coöperative suggestion, plans were being drawn up in 1929 to erect a garage for its employees' cars on land just outside an entrance gate. Because the new concrete floor in the erecting shop was tiring to the workers' feet, the committee at the Stratford, Ontario, locomotive repair shop of the Canadian National Railway System, took occasion to ask officials of the road to hasten the laying of the mastic top with which it was intended that the floor should be covered. At Deer Lodge, Montana, on the Milwaukee System, a pipe fitter's protest, in coöperative meeting, has led to steps being taken to remedy the untidy condition in which he asserted that benches were allowed to stand around one of the engine pits. Through the agency of their coöperative committee, workers in the car department of the Fort Rouge shop, Winnipeg, Manitoba, of the Canadian National Railway System requested the company to sell its scrap wood by the wagonload instead of by the carload so that they might bid for it in that amount. In due course this matter was carried to the carrier's western regional committee and finally to its system coöperative committee for settlement. At the system meeting held in January, 1928, it was announced that, subject to arrangement between the stores and purchasing departments, employees would be permitted to bid on any scrap materials offered for sale, including wood, carpets, linoleum, and piping for use in building fences. Occasionally the question of work train accommodation has become a coöperative issue. Illustrative of this is the case of the blacksmiths' coöperative committeeman at the Galewood shop of the Milwaukee System, Chicago, Illinois, who secured an investigation by the master mechanic into the circumstance that as the work train running to and from the shop had only four coaches, it was so badly crowded both morning and night that some men had to ride on the platform and steps.

## Chapter XIII

## The Improvement of Morale through Coöperation

THE description of typical suggestions given in the three preceding chapters may be taken as indicative of the results of union-management coöperation on the railroads as they occur in direct and tangible form. The problem of the measurement of such results will be reserved for further study. Strong claims have also been advanced in behalf of union-management coöperation that it has been highly advantageous to the railroad industry in an indirect manner through the favorable changes it has wrought in morale. Primarily any change in morale may be considered to be a matter of individual concern. Still, morale has its social manifestations, that is, it may have important effects upon the conduct of human beings organized into groups, and it must be viewed from that standpoint as well. A prominent psychologist has at one moment referred to morale[1] as a "cult of condition" or "super-hygiene," and at another has termed it "the most imponderable, vital and fluctuating of all spiritual qualities." High morale undoubtedly indicates for the individual or group, the existence of a condition of mental well-being which stimulates them to undertake, to perform, and to complete. Against the future it sets up a new hope and an attainable goal. Low morale, on the contrary, is significant of mental cowardice, retarding effort, and removing the joy from work fulfilment; its horizon may be said to be close at hand.

In justification of the plan of coöperation on the railroads it has been asserted that it offers a new criterion of human values, and in so doing marks out an ascending path for morale. It starts from the premise that workers in industry, no matter what their

[1] See G. Stanley Hall, *Morale, the Supreme Standard of Life and Conduct,* especially pp. 1–21.

position may be, in general prefer to be active rather than idle, and to the extent that their mental condition is right, will have a "developmental urge" to exert themselves effectively. It recognizes, its defenders state, the mental resources and capacities of each individual irrespective of rank. It stresses the idea that those who administer in industry should follow their instinct for service, which, if the love of dominance is curbed, will give them pleasure, and that those whose business it is to accept authority should follow their instinct for workmanship, which if allowed to expand unhampered should bring them delight of mind. The technique of coöperation, they believe, provides the means by which these instincts may come to fruition, mental gratifications ensue, and morale as a result be greatly strengthened. In a doctrinal sense these claims are quite alluring, but the question naturally arises whether in its actual day-by-day functioning union-management coöperation has made the weighty contributions to the elevation of morale its advocates have contended. This issue will now be presented for review.

### Difficulties in Appraising Morale.

AT the outset it is freely admitted that to gauge with any precision the improvements in morale that may have taken place where coöperation has been in effect is for several reasons an impossible task. Morale has been appropriately referred to as a condition of mind, and only a limited number of thinkers would ever attempt to explain its manifestations on a purely rationalistic basis. It is too far within the realm of the spiritual to be subjected to mental testing, and accordingly is liable to all the restrictions imposed upon the measurement of a spiritual attribute. Although an interpretation of morale in a relative sense should be always illuminating, this can never be accomplished with any degree of mathematical accuracy. It is generally easy to state that the morale of a certain individual or social group is higher today than it was a year ago, or that it has sunk in the interval. But to specify to what extent it has risen or how far it has fallen is beyond the capacity of the investigator.

Prudence should be exercised, moreover, in accepting testimony on the advancement of morale under coöperation. Reliance in this instance must mainly be placed upon the judgment of those who have been closest to the situation. The officer in charge at a certain local point may speak with unqualified enthusiasm of the change in spirit that has animated his supervisory force and men since the beginning of coöperation. At another point an administrator with similar powers, either because he is constitutionally less emotional or because he sets less store on comparative values, may discuss the improvement in morale which he believes has taken place at his station in much more guarded terms. Actually, despite the impression conveyed, the up trend in morale in the latter case may have outdistanced that in the former. Likewise representatives of labor organizations in testifying to the laudable mutations of spirit which they consider have occurred among their membership, or within the ranks of management as a result of coöperation, are liable to the same subjective forms of appraisal. The investigator is compelled to balance the opinions obtained, trusting that overenthusiasm in one direction may be offset by conservatism in the other. Undoubtedly the greatest value should be set on views expressed spontaneously, and therefore with no premeditation as to their effect.

It has been often hinted that an element of propaganda lurks in statements made concerning improvements in morale through coöperation. Carriers committed to the plan, it may be assumed, will be eager to defend and vindicate their policy in having accepted it. The craft organizations on the other hand, pledged to its furtherance, have much at stake in connection with its ultimate success or failure. Each party to the movement accordingly has reason to depict its progress in roseate hue. How better can they represent to the public the industrial merits of coöperation than by expatiating upon its influence in heightening morale?

Even should the picture be considerably overdrawn, refutation must be difficult since morale is an incorporeal quantity exempt from regular standards of measurement. A temptation to uphold coöperation in such a manner is undeniably present, although the extent to which management and men have succumbed to it cannot be stated. To offset the possible effects of propaganda it may be regarded as a defensible policy to discount, in some measure at least, many claims of improvements in morale resulting from coöperation, especially when made by those who have been active in forwarding the movement. Concrete evidences will now be submitted to show how morale appears to have been benefited through the introduction of union-management coöperation.

### *Relation of Improved Morale to Plant Changes.*

PROLIFIC sources of ill will in any industrial plant are occasioned by the introduction of major alterations in work processes; departmental readjustments which may be incidental to such alterations; and the departmental readjustments effected for some other reason. Once workers, and even administrators, have become expert in the performance of their industrial functions at a certain place they seldom accept with equanimity changes that may be made in their work location or in their ordinary round of duties. The mechanical department of the average American railroad has during the past decade or so been casting aside many time-worn methods of work, and has been the scene of many plant reorganizations, and therefore has noticeably been a breeding ground of discontent. The leading change in processing, which has occurred in connection with train car maintenance, has been the inauguration of the spot system, described in chapter iii. The definite move toward specialization featuring the adoption of this system has been a sore trial to journeymen carmen, trained for general proficiency in their craft. Nor have local officers and supervisors always readily accommodated themselves to the new order of things, as the system has been developed. Yet repeated affirmations may be heard respecting the freedom from disquieting episodes with which the spot system, or modifications of it, have been introduced at stations on the carriers pledged to coöperation. When in 1926 the coöperative plan first began to function in the passenger coach department of the Milwaukee, Wisconsin, shop of the Chicago, Milwaukee, St. Paul & Pacific Railroad, unharmonious relations are said to have existed between supervisors and workers in the department, and supervisors to have been at odds with each other. In 1927, a scientific method of scheduling coaches through the shop was sanctioned, by which it was expected that repairs to from three to four cars would be completed in a day. Officers and labor officials alike at Milwaukee have signified their belief that the ease and simplicity with which this scheduling arrangement went into effect during the first six months after its adoption was mainly traceable to the coöperative spirit prevailing. Workers in the coach department were prepared to accept the specialization demanded by the scheduling system in the knowledge that, despite resultant economies in labor, they would be guaranteed regular employment. In passing it may be remarked that the crafts both in the coach and motive power departments at the Milwaukee shop are noted for their hostility to anything smacking of bureaucracy, and that their morale has been visibly strengthened by the fact that under coöperation they have been permitted a great deal of local autonomy.

Local management at the Clinton, Iowa, shop of the Chicago & North Western Railway, following the inception of coöperation, arrived at the conclusion that machine tools were too unmethodically dispersed about the machine shop, which meant the loss of many man hours in the needless trucking of materials. A redistribution of shop equipment was proposed which would line up shapers, lathes, and other machines according to type, a radical departure in view of the transfers of men and machines that would be involved. Officers at the station authorized the changes with some trepidation, being specially concerned about the reaction to the whole plan of one older key machinist who had been forty-four years in the shop. To their surprise the undertaking was completed with scarcely a hitch, owing, they agree, to the mutual understanding which had arisen through coöperation. The key machinist, whose new place in the shop was made particularly congenial, did not utter a complaint. Earnest endeavors have been made at the Dubuque, Iowa, shop of the Milwaukee System to advance both locomotive and train car repair sections of the shop to a position where they will be able to compete economically with other maintenance of equipment points on the carrier. To accomplish this, local officers and supervisors have frankly laid the situation before the men in a way that would have been unthinkable before the introduction of coöperation. Information has been disseminated on the costs of fuel, water, acetylene gas, and electricity, and the workers' help sought in reducing the outlay for these to the lowest possible basis commensurate with good workmanship. Formerly a miscellaneous array of smaller shops and offices were operated at Dubuque, entailing a proportionately high expenditure for steam heating. Reorganization plans have called for a greater centralization of work performance, consolidation of forces, and the shutting up of certain outlying structures. In consequence of this new policy, it was discovered that from November, 1927, to June, 1928, the power plant had consumed 1,973 tons less coal than during the same months of the preceding year. Water charges have also been brought down correspondingly by a husbanding of the supply in every direction. Some animosity to these changes was apparently evoked at first, before their meaning was clearly understood, which, however, under coöperative tutoring is said to have quickly disappeared.

### Effect upon Daily Work Performance.

A COMMON pronouncement in favor of union-management coöperation, has been the assertion that its influence in raising morale is well exemplified in the better work performance that regularly follows its introduction. The rightness of mind which coöperation begets, it is said, has its natural counterpart in rightness of action. So quickened, indeed, are the springs of action that indolence becomes an offense to right thinking. Accordingly motivation is afforded to get work done properly, which is reflected not only in the individual accomplishments of administrators and men, but also in their coördinated effort. There are two aspects, it is contended, from which these effects of the new morale upon work performance may be noted. In the first place they may be observed in the everyday routine of plant operations. Again they may be studied in their manifestations at a time when special services are requisitioned, or at a time when the mechanical department is faced with a real emergency.

Through the medium of strengthening morale, coöperation has led, it is believed, to a more conscientious application of the native abilities and industrial knowledge both of administrators and workers to the customary tasks in hand. As morale has improved, it has brought a greater concentration of mind on work operations, and this in turn has meant a more painstaking and patient control of shop equipment, and a more careful handling of materials. In administrators there has been stimulated a tolerance and tactful firmness which, though discountenancing sloth and indifference in the ranks of the employed, has been the cause of rough places being made smoother for those who require leading. Among workers, on the other hand, improved morale has fostered a fresh sense of loyalty and an amenability to discipline, each of which has unquestioned value to work performance. Actual proof of these contentions, however, is seldom adducible. While it is true that an officer or supervisor here, or a worker there, may be singled out as an example, and a tribute paid to his newly won forbearance, his added industry, and his greater mental concentration in relation to daily work, in so far as the majority of administrators and workers are concerned, the cultivation of qualities such as these can neither be readily discerned nor accurately predicated, and therefore can only be described in general terms. Possibly advocates of coöperation may take comfort in the fact that critics of the plan encounter similar difficulties in attempting to disprove their claims.

The effect of improved morale on work performance, if the above arguments are true, should be disclosed in the attitudes of management and men on the carriers indorsing coöperation toward the locomotive inspection, and safety appliance laws, and the regulations prescribed under them. In the case of locomotive inspection, it is of course a fact, that by the completion of a high standard of repairs to shopped locomotives, by the enforcement of strict rules of maintenance at its terminals, and by the retention at each local point of a sufficient and well-instructed group of company inspectors, any railroad may have a relatively low list of defects reported against its motive power stations. Even if the morale of its local forces is not particularly good, it may attain this end by implanting the fear of punishment in the minds of its personnel. When an individual administrator or worker knows that responsibility for defects reported may at any time be assessed against him, and that for lesser offenses he is open to censure, and for greater ones may be heavily penalized perhaps to the extent of losing his position, he is driven to exercise care in the performance of his duties. Punitive methods are employed by all railroads as a corrective for lapses, especially of a more serious nature, that make them chargeable under the locomotive inspection or safety appliance laws and the regulations prescribed under those laws, or that as a matter of domestic consequence alone, cause their moving units of equipment to fail while in service on the road. Carriers practicing coöperation do not ask that such methods should be abandoned. Nevertheless, they are convinced that through the functioning of the coöperative plan it should be possible to reduce the element of compulsion, and gain equally favorable or even better results. If, as is argued, management and men are properly infused with the spirit that should accompany coöperation, they will have the interests of their railroad at heart, and need no longer be constrained in the performance of their tasks.

The tendency, where union-management coöperation prevails, is for the railroads to depend increasingly upon the morale of their shop forces to assist them in maintaining good records under government forms of legal control and inspection. Through the agency of coöperative meetings and in other ways, information is spread at repair points, relating to the value of efficient work performance as a protection against the discovery by federal inspectors of too many defects in their motive power or train car equipment, and against the more grievous danger of having their locomotives removed from service. Instructions are given on the meaning for the carriers, of failures of their moving units of equipment after they have been dispatched on the line. Data are supplied concerning the financial loss entailed when engines are delayed on the road through running hot, breaking down, or failing to steam well. A bulletin board is sometimes set up at a motive power repair station on which is written a month-by-month record of engine failures in the territory served.

Figures may be quoted from the annual statistical summaries published by the Bureau of Locomotive Inspection, which show all the carriers committed to coöperation in a progressively favorable light since the beginning of the movement on their lines. However, as the motive power situation on one railroad is for a variety of reasons never the same as on any other, and as locomotive inspection can scarcely be regarded as uniform for all carriers, conclusions should not be too hastily drawn from comparisons made on the basis of the bureau's figures. During the twelve months ending June 30, 1925, the first normal inspection year after the shopmen's strike, 52 per cent of the steam locomotives examined on the Baltimore & Ohio Railroad were found to be defective. In the same year, 61 per cent were similarly assessed on the Pennsylvania Railroad, a leading competitor of the Baltimore & Ohio Railroad, while the average number charged with defects on all Class I carriers was 46 per cent. By 1929–30 the percentage reported as defective on the Baltimore & Ohio Railroad had dropped to 28, on the Pennsylvania Railroad to 25, and on all carriers to 16. An analysis of these figures will indicate that, in the interval, the Baltimore & Ohio Railroad had improved its position to better advantage than had either the Pennsylvania Railroad or the average carrier. During 1924–25, 4.0 per cent of the locomotives inspected on the Baltimore & Ohio Railroad were ordered from service, 8.4 per cent on the Pennsylvania Railroad, and 5.0 per cent on all Class I carriers. In 1929–30, .25 per cent were so dealt with on the Baltimore & Ohio Railroad, 1.45 per cent on the Pennsylvania Railroad, and 1.19 per cent on all roads. Here again the Baltimore & Ohio Railroad had comparatively the best record. Since the Chicago & North Western Railway embraced coöperation, there has occurred a notable reduction in the percentage of defects reported against its locomotives, viz., from 32 per cent in 1925–26 to 8 per cent in 1929–30. During the same period the percentage of defects charged against locomotives inspected on the Chicago, Milwaukee, St. Paul & Pacific Railroad fell from 21 to 6. In 1925–26, 57 per cent of the locomotives on the lines of the Canadian National Railway System in the United States were found defective; by 1929–30 the percentage had dropped to 26.

Depending upon local conditions and policies, committeemen for the crafts under union-management coöperation are held answerable for discipline as it affects the work performance of the men whom they represent. When a certain worker has become slack in performance and appears no longer amenable to discipline, a supervisor or general foreman often takes this matter up with the coöperative committeeman of his craft who, according to whatever methods he may think wise, will bring his remissness to the worker's attention. An effort is made to handle the situation calmly, discreetly, and as quietly as possible. The evidences in connection with most cases of this sort indicate that the difficulty has been cleared up by such methods unless the worker has been plainly lacking in aptitude for his trade. Sometimes, if he continues to be unreasonable, he is warned that his persistence will deprive him of the support of his craft organization, should he be accused of inefficiency or breach of discipline by his superiors. In coöperative meetings the presence of unproductive workers, or "drones," at a repair station has occasionally been a topic for discussion. Even supervisors have been criticized in the course of meetings, but this practice for obvious reasons has met with little encouragement. It is claimed that company rules, whether written or merely understood to exist, have generally been construed less rigorously under coöperation, having often been bent to meet the particular occasion. Sleeping by men during work hours, to cite an illustration, has always been regarded by officers of the mechanical department as a decidedly objectionable and punishable transgression. While in principle there has been no change in attitude on this subject among officers of the roads indorsing coöperation, they have tended to make it better for the offender by giving more attention to the grounds upon which he may have endeavored to explain his fault. For example, they have been inclined to weigh fairly the man's excuse that he fell asleep because of physical disability; the somnolent atmosphere or temperature experienced at work; the intermittent spacing of his work; or want of companionship on his work shift.

### Willingness to Render Special Services.

The personal dependability of administrators and craftsmen responsible for work performance has been increased, it is asserted, under coöperation. This has resulted in acts of self-denial for the company's economic welfare, which sometimes have been of peculiar value when a call has come for the rendering of extraordinary services. Workers, it is said, have been ready to conform to policies that will save the company the necessity of overtime payments, or outlays required for the hiring of additional labor. Two simple illustrations may be given of wage economies resulting from action taken by carmen at Cone, East St. Louis, Illinois, on the Baltimore & Ohio Railroad. At this station, where interline traffic is important, the carmen work in three shifts. If one man should be off work for any reason, the rest have been willing to assume his duties for the time being. This has released the company from the rule that it must provide a substitute, and to that extent has diminished the wage outlay. Individually the carmen have been ready to increase their burden on the understanding with management that no permanent reduction in force will ensue. Again, light repair carmen at Cone are often assigned for work at the end of the transportation yards. Generally they have been able to catch a ride to their destination on outbound locomotives. At one time they used to walk back, which took an hour and a half. Now, in answer to a joint request which they submitted, they are supplied with street car tokens and so can return in thirty minutes. Whereas working has been a trifle harder for the men than walking, the company has saved in the neighborhood of one hour's wages per trip for each man.

During the summer of 1928 a disturbing mishap occurred at the Galewood shop of the Milwaukee System, Chicago, Illinois, when the heavy centerpiece of the 400-ton wheel press broke clear across. This particular machine, which is employed to mount wheels on their axles and to dismount them, is required almost uninterruptedly in repair operations and an exigency was created in the shop. Should a new and expensive press be purchased, six weeks must elapse before it could be brought to the shop and set in position. In the face of this emergency, supervisors and men at once united their efforts to cope with the situation. A picked gang went steadily to work for a week on the centerpiece, using a ton of metal in and about the fissure, and at the end of that time declared the wheel press again fit for service.

Repairs had cost the company around $1,000, but a tie-up had been averted; the men had enjoyed the advantage of adding to the work done in the shop.

Officials of the Grand Trunk Western Lines have spoken with unfeigned approval of the special assistance rendered by the administrative and working forces at Battle Creek, Michigan, when preparations were under way for the introduction of a direct steaming system at the Elsdon enginehouse, Chicago, Illinois. It had been planned that the equipment for this system should be designed and largely fabricated at the Battle Creek shop, and then sent forward to the Elsdon terminal for installation. In order to meet the smoke nuisance regulations of the city of Chicago, the Elsdon enginehouse has been made practically fireless by the direct steaming method.[2] A locomotive on reaching the terminal now has its fire dumped at the inbound ash pit, enters its allotted stall, and by means of a flexible copper hose connection is fed steam continuously from high-pressure boilers in the power plant. Until again called for service its steam pressure is maintained uniformly at 150 pounds. Then, prior to dispatchment, a fuel bed is laid in its fire box which can be ignited in from five to six minutes while it stands at the water plug. As the locomotive runs to be coupled to its train, the fire is conditioned with little evidence of smoke. About $110,000 was spent by the Grand Trunk Western Lines on this unique direct steaming system which was thought a reasonable outlay in view of the results obtained. Already several other railroads have copied the plan. It is estimated that a saving in fuel amounting to $30 a day has been effected at the Elsdon terminal, while working conditions at the station have been made much pleasanter. As evidence of improved morale, it has been stated that in getting the equipment ready, the shop forces at Battle Creek entered busily and animatedly into the work assigned them in a manner that hardly would have been

[2] See "Grand Trunk Western Has Fireless Engine House in Chicago," *Railway Mechanical Engineer,* April, 1928, pp. 221–223.

dreamed of before the introduction of coöperation. According to
the statement of one officer, craftsmen were constantly approach-
ing those in charge of operations with the query: "Don't you
think that it would be a good thing if such and such were done?"

### Newer Attitudes Respecting Agreements.

IT may be argued that the facility with which the terms of a
joint system or individual craft agreement are carried out, on
any railroad, should afford some idea of the morale existing in
its mechanical department. Once union-management coöperation
has become firmly grounded on a carrier, a new note of modera-
tion, it is affirmed, has always entered into the interpretation of
any agreement it has with its shop workers. Indeed, a proportion of craft unionists seem apprehensive that their contractual
relations with the employing company should be so pacifically
interpreted under coöperation, that they may lose their ability
to fight. All disputes and grievances arising at a local point bear
some relationship either to a system, or to an individual craft
agreement, and must be settled in accordance with its terms. As
explained in chapter v, a definite routine is followed in endeavoring to adjust difficulties at local points which, if still unsettled,
may be taken for handling to conferences between higher executives of the company, and craft organization, or system federation officers. Finally cases may go to an adjustment board on the
carrier, or to other outside agencies authorized by the Railway
Labor Act of 1926.

On railroads where the mechanical unions are recognized, but
coöperation is not in effect, the local craft chairmen must frequently negotiate with management for a favorable interpretation of the terms of their agreement on the one hand and keep
their men "fixed in right condition" on the other. But where co-
operation functions to bring both parties closer in spirit, it is
said that craft chairmen are able to straighten out most difficulties by a word or two to an administrator or by a short talk

with a worker. As a result, a very significant diminution in the number of actual disputes and grievances arising at local points has occurred, and relatively few issues are now carried farther for settlement. This has made for better work performance and at the same time has meant a saving for the railroads in that, according to rule, all local disputes and grievances must be handled on "company time." Illustrations of the tempering effect that coöperation is believed to have had upon the interpretation of agreements could easily be multiplied. The master mechanic, for example, at Missouri Valley, Iowa, on the Chicago & North Western Railway has testified that whereas at one time he was called upon to deal with from one to three disputes and grievances a week, now months will go by without a single difficulty coming to his attention. John Howe, superintendent of the Cumberland, Maryland, locomotive repair shop on the Baltimore & Ohio Railroad, has intimated that for years only minor issues have cropped up for adjustment at his station. During a six months' period in 1928, but one case was taken on appeal to the head office of the carrier in Baltimore from the whole Cumberland division employing 2,000 shop workers. The records of the Baltimore & Ohio Railroad show that, while 261 disputes and grievances were referred to Baltimore for settlement in 1922, only 87 were submitted in 1926, and 33 in 1928. Since March 1, 1922, when a question relating to the differential rates paid to blacksmiths was carried to the Railroad Labor Board, the Baltimore & Ohio Railroad has adjusted all difficulties with its mechanical craftsmen without reference to any outside tribunal.

Still it must be remembered that as agreements grow older they become divested of various causes of friction, and normally disputes and grievances under them lessen in number. The agreements (*vide* chapter v) which apply on roads committed to coöperation were all drawn up originally in 1922 or 1923 and ought by this time to function much more smoothly. In order to discover what merit coöperation really has had in reducing contractual discord, it would be necessary to institute a thoroughgoing comparison between carriers that have adopted the plan and those having craft unions in their mechanical department that have not adopted it. The experiences of the Erie Railroad, if taken as a representative of the latter class, may shed some light on the problem. The existing system agreement on the Erie Railroad was negotiated with System Federation No. 100, on its lines, in the fall and winter of 1922–23. There are evidences that occasionally major and quite perplexing difficulties still come up for settlement on that carrier. The president of System Federation No. 100 has roughly estimated that by the beginning of 1929 disputes and grievances on the Erie Railroad had dropped to about one-third of their number in 1923. This record, though commendable, is plainly not as good as that given above for the Baltimore & Ohio Railroad. Since the Canadian National Railway Company and the Canadian Pacific Railway Company are bound by the same agreement covering their shop crafts in Canada, it might be thought that a worthwhile basis of comparison should be discoverable between them on the subject of disputes and grievances. To the credit of coöperation it may be pointed out that within recent years difficulties have fallen in number more rapidly on the Canadian National Railway System in Canada than on its great business rival. Yet apologists for the Canadian Pacific Railway in answer may refer to the circumstance that it has had contracts with its shop workers for over thirty years, and for that reason a more gradual paring down of its list of disputes and grievances need only be expected.

As management and men have learned to understand one another better through coöperation the latter, it is stated, have been disposed to hold less rigidly to the letter of certain rules in the joint agreements. The positive segregation of workers, according to trade jurisdiction, authorized by the shop crafts' national agreement was, as already noted, a leading cause of hostility to the mechanical unions on the part of many railroads before the 1922 strike. While the crafts on the carriers pledged to coöperation have not relinquished their faith in the value of carefully drawn trade lines, they have shown themselves willing to give flexibility to their rules, in the belief that the company will not use these concessions to their disadvantage. Trade barriers then have quite often been lowered to allow for a more economic work performance or for the more systematic scheduling of employment. Regulations affecting the allotment of work within a trade have also been interpreted more liberally. The writer, in visiting the Cumberland, Maryland, bolt and forge shop of the Baltimore & Ohio Railroad, observed a journeyman blacksmith handle material from the fire which only a helper should touch under a strict interpretation of the rules.

The direct interest taken by shop workers on the roads indorsing coöperation in the problem of increasing the volume of traffic moved over their company's lines may unquestionably be traced in large measure to a heightening of morale. However, as the action of the crafts in this instance is partly dictated by organized labor's policy of "fair listing" enterprises regarded as friendly to its aims, the actual contributions of morale toward quickening the workers' interest in the business done by their company is hard to discern. As early as 1924, System Federation No. 30 issued a formal appeal to American trade-unions asking their membership to patronize or otherwise lend their support to the Baltimore & Ohio Railroad, which, it said, was providing efficient transportation services and at the same time was eminently fair to its shop employees. Workers were urged to go by the lines of the Baltimore & Ohio Railroad when traveling, to make use of its services when shipping goods, and to solicit business for it by whatever means might lie within their power. Fair listing of the Baltimore & Ohio Railroad, as a result, became quite common among labor bodies, and has been extended to other carriers as they have adopted the coöperative plan. Signs are unmistakable that the practice of trade-unionists throughout the United States and Canada of "pulling for" these roads has brought them considerable additions in the way of freight, express, and passenger traffic. How far the roads may have lost business in other directions through antagonisms created by their close dealings with the unions it is impossible to state. Suggestions bearing on the problem of obtaining new business have not been plentiful in coöperative meetings, although this matter has often come up for general discussion toward the close of the proceedings. On the Canadian National Railway System an effort has been made to link up the coöperative movement with a program of mobilizing everyone in the company's employ to attract traffic to its lines. Officers on this carrier are eager to learn of the personal activities of workers in soliciting business. When it was reported to the car department's committee of its Fort Rouge shop, Winnipeg, Manitoba, that one worker had within a specified time secured forty-seven revenue passengers for the road, a letter concerning his achievement was drafted and sent to staff headquarters of the western region.

## Chapter XIV

## Problems Associated with the Measurement of Coöperative Gains

IF the data supplied in the last three chapters may be taken as a true index of the situation, there apparently is good reason to believe that the aim of union-management coöperation to forward the mutual interest of the employed and employing classes on the railroads has been rather abundantly fertile in an economic sense. By means of its particular technique, a diversified array of suggestions has been recorded and made effective. Through its influence upon morale, many other gains of consequence have undoubtedly been attained. What possibility is there, it may now be asked, that the economic results accruing from coöperation may be subjected to anything that approximates accurate measurement? The answer to the question should be based upon a survey of all the attendant circumstances, before an intelligent treatment of the important problem of distributing these gains between the parties to the movement will be in order.

In view of the idealism which pervades the doctrines of union-management coöperation, and of the standards it sets up, does not an introduction of the subjects of measuring and dividing its gains reduce discussion to a deplorably lower plane? A distribution of any increment in the business world is generally accomplished, it must be confessed, with an unemotional, matter-of-factness that might well occasion fears for the spirit of coöperation if thrust into a similar environment. Experience has already taught that, immediately the question of measuring and apportioning coöperative gains has arisen, the movement has always entered a danger zone. Still it is necessary that these issues should be squarely faced. Whenever a better quality of citizenship has appeared in the political state, it is fitting that the resulting benefits, to the extent that they are measurable, should be pro-rated among the inhabitants. By the same token it follows that, if coöperation has ushered in a better type of citizenship in industry, its gains should be divided among those who participate in it upon as just a basis as possible. Since the problems involved in the measurement and distribution of gains are complex, both management and men should be forewarned against unreasoning disputes in which cupidity may have an opportunity to triumph over coöperation.

### Bearing of Railroad Accounts on the Measurement of Gains.

PRELIMINARY to a consideration of the question of measuring the gains of coöperation it should be borne in mind that the mechanical department of a railroad is, in no sense, revenue-bearing. For the receipt of its gross income a carrier is mainly dependent upon the day-by-day intake of its traffic department which is secured from charges for its freight, passenger, express, and mail services. Yet returns to the traffic department would soon be entirely inadequate unless the carrier's roadway and moving units of equipment were kept in a proper state of repair, and effective transportation provided. This means that as money comes into the traffic department it is earmarked for various purposes, and then largely appropriated to a number of spending departments, of which the mechanical department is one. Direct appropriations are made to the mechanical department to cover the block of expenses necessary for the repair of train cars, locomotives, and other moving units of equipment. In these are included the outlay for wages and materials, and certain monthly charges which represent the depreciation on equipment. Repairs to machine tools, and other forms of shop equipment, are also paid for by means of direct appropriations. However, investments in new shops, engine-houses, and power plants, and for the purchase of new machine tools and other articles of shop equipment are listed, according to their character, either under an account for betterments and additions, or under an account for road and equipment. All plant repairs are charged to the group of expenses covered by appropriations to the department of maintenance of way and structures.

From the foregoing it would seem that the economic gains resulting from coöperation, in so far as they may be calculable, must be looked for in the columns of a carrier's disbursements. As a matter of fact, coöperative gains have been mainly of a negative sort, that is, they have emerged in the form of a curtailment of expenditures. Due to practices of economy any of these accounts from which money is spent for the mechanical department may be reduced and accordingly show gains, in case coöperation has been functioning successfully. Nevertheless the selfsame accounts, especially those that take care of the outlay for new structures and shop equipment, will have to be debited when used as a means of distributing the gains of coöperation back into the industry. The situation becomes even more complicated if it is remembered that the influence of coöperation quite often radiates beyond the boundaries of the mechanical department. Inasmuch as coöperative effort may lead to better work being done on train cars and locomotives, it may assist the transportation department in providing more effective service and be instrumental in whittling something from that department's heavy budget. Improved service in turn should increase the income of the traffic department, bringing a form of positive gain as the influence of coöperation widens. From what has been written it may be seen that the keeping of accounts as they affect the mechanical department, and the play of departmental interrelationships, both act to complicate further the problem of measuring coöperative gains.

## Results of Suggestions More Precisely Measurable.

UNDOUBTEDLY the benefits derived from a considerable proportion of suggestions adopted in coöperative meetings may be measured with a reasonably close degree of accuracy. This proportion varies according to the types of suggestions which predominate at local meetings, and the opportunities given to make an isolated test of their merits. As statistics on the matter are unprocurable, it may be roughly conjectured that from 20 to 35 per cent of all suggestions recorded at local points would fall within this measurable classification. Proposals referring to the introduction of shop-made appliances for instance, which speed up or otherwise assist production, are very often susceptible of measurement. If the increased output in relation to the employment of man power be studied, and account be taken of the cost of manufacturing the appliance, a determination of the actual financial gain accruing from its use should not be difficult. Many suggestions, too, which concern the modification of shop methods, the economy of materials, the re-use of worn materials, the salvaging and reclamation of scrap, and a percentage of those which deal with the relocating of equipment and the changing of standards of equipment should be capable of having their resultant gains measured with precision. The recital of a few illustrations where gains have been computed will give point to these assertions.

On the Chicago & North Western Railway, it has been customary to repair various classes of gondola cars at three stations, East Clinton, Illinois, South Pekin, Illinois, and Belle Plaine, Iowa. A coöperative suggestion registered and adopted at East Clinton advised that the channels which were taken from box cars dismantled at stations on the carrier might be used again in repairing gondolas. The standards committee of the railroad subjected this proposal to a preliminary investigation, and then asked the general foreman at Belle Plaine to test it out in actual practice. The general foreman obtained three discarded channels elsewhere on the line, and by timing work operations was able to calculate exactly what it would cost to re-use them on gondolas. The estimated expenditure for labor in converting each worn channel for service was $1.72½. To this was added its value if sold for scrap which was $1.41½, bringing the total cost of installing an old channel to $3.14. As the company had had to pay $6.50 each for new channels, it was decided that the net savings would amount to $3.36 in each instance of conversion. On the average, fifty gondolas a month could be fitted with formerly rejected channels at Belle Plaine, which should mean a reduction in expenses of $168 for that period. The economy at other points repairing gondolas would be proportioned to the number of channels required for re-use.

Under the plan of repolishing the damaged glass in signal lamps at Missouri Valley, Iowa, on the Chicago & North Western Railway, described in chapter xii, the outlay for reclamation was computed at about five cents a lens, whereas new lenses bought by the company cost sixty-five cents each. Since seventy-five lenses have been reclaimed by this method each month, $45, or approximately one-third the wages of a mechanic are saved, although it may be questioned whether the repolished glasses are as good as new. At Norfolk, Nebraska, on the same carrier, a worker, having noticed that the drain valves in the superheaters on oil-burning engines were rarely closed and were seemingly useless, proposed that they be removed and a hole bored in the plug to take care of the drainage. These valves, each costing seventy-eight cents new, were accordingly eliminated on 121 oil-burning engines on the division. After some time has elapsed it should be possible to discover what economy has resulted from this slight modification in standards. In answer to a coöperative request from carmen in the passenger car department of the Milwaukee, Wisconsin, shop on the Milwaukee System, new equipment in the form of air-operated jacks was purchased to lift coaches. An investigation disclosed that, due to the amount of labor involved, an average expenditure of $30 had previously been necessary whenever a car undergoing repairs was raised and lowered with hand jacks. Now with the new appliances it has cost $12 a car. As the shop handles three coaches a day, a saving of $54 is effected in that time, or in the neighborhood of $1,300 a month, less the interest and depreciation on the air jacks.

In the coöperative meeting at Port Huron, Michigan, on the Grand Trunk Western Lines, a complaint was registered against the quality of steel that was being provided with which to make up cold chisels in the shop. It was stated that owing to the use of inferior metal, the chisels tended to chip off during work operations, and too frequent delays were occasioned by the necessity of fetching new ones. After a better grade of steel had been ordered, it was found on examination that an average of $17.51 a month was being saved in material costs. Removal of the obstructing post in the blacksmith shop at Port Huron, Michigan, mentioned in chapter xii, led to an expenditure of $46.77. However, with the post gone, materials and repair parts could be handled more promptly in the shop, and as a result the labor charges have been lowered $35.36 a month. The transfer of a crane to the vicinity of the gear cases in the boiler shop at Deer Lodge, Montana, on the Milwaukee System, referred to in chapter x, was expected to reduce expenses $20 a month. The initial cost of imbedding a ring in the concrete to assist in hauling cars at the Leaside, Ontario, shop of the Canadian National Railway System, of which mention was made in chapter xi, was $35, but each month this innovation has given rise to an economy of $8.50.

On the other hand, the folly of putting suggestions into effect without measuring their results, when possible, has been amply demonstrated. In the car department of the Chicago, Illinois, shop of the Chicago & North Western Railway, it was proposed that the new frames required for motor cars sent in by section gangs for repairs should be built in the shop. Some of these were constructed by way of experiment, but the policy was quickly discontinued when it was found that they had cost around $115 as against the regular market price of $100. Again, it was suggested at the Minneapolis, Minnesota, shop of the Milwaukee System, that the method employed of sliding newly arrived wheels from the unloading platform down a chute into the wheel shop should be abandoned, and instead that the platform should be lowered to a level with the shop floor, and the wheels hoisted from the cars with an air jack. A study of the situation revealed the fact that the unloading of some 18,000 wheels each year with an air jack would cost $548 more than the existing method. Besides the lowering of the platform would entail an estimated initial expenditure of $628.

### Obstacles to Estimating the Benefits Derived from Most Suggestions.

FOR one reason or another the value of a majority of suggestions registered in coöperative meetings cannot be satisfactorily measured or is not measurable at all. The experiences of the Canadian National Railway Company, the only carrier which has so far attempted to deal specifically with problems of measurement, supply certain evidences on this score. In April, 1927, the superintendent of motive power of the carrier's Montreal, Quebec, district, and the assistant to the director of its bureau of economics, were named a committee with verbal instructions to ascertain, if possible, the money value of the benefits that had accrued from coöperation, by comparing the accounts of the maintenance of equipment department for 1926 with those of the preceding year. After a survey the committee announced in an interim report that, from the standpoint of unit costs of production, only 30 per cent of the maintenance work on train cars, and 46 per cent of the work on locomotives at the company's main shops were measurable in detail. These figures convey some idea of the restricted area within which efforts to estimate the gains that have resulted from suggestions bearing expressly on work performance must move. As it would cost $50,000 to analyze the data available, and as other factors would detract from the significance of the conclusions arrived at, the committee had decided to proceed no farther with the investigation. However, it incorporated in its report statistics relative to employment conditions on the carrier since the beginning of coöperation from which citations will be made elsewhere. In 1928, orders were transmitted to all repair points on the Canadian National Railway System where coöperation was in effect that, beginning with April 15, records should be kept of the disbursements, if any, necessary to take action on each suggestion accepted and of the monetary returns that had resulted or were expected to result from each. As yet no analysis of these records has been published. Officers of the company at repair points candidly admit that in only a limited number of instances have they been able accurately to show the net gains from suggestions on a financial basis.

Just what value, it may be asked, can be attached to most of the suggestions recorded that have had as their object a reconditioning of shop equipment? It is true that a real economy may be effected if a machine tool, or other form of equipment, is attended to at the time when its uses have become exhausted, and yet when it has not fallen into bad disrepair. Loss due to undermaintenance may be prevented when a coöperative suggestion insures repairs for the equipment at an opportune moment. Upon what basis, however, would it be possible to ascertain the loss thereby avoided? How far would the equipment have been allowed to go without adequate repairs had not the coöperative meeting called for action? While it is the earnest opinion of advocates of coöperation, that through its instrumentality the railroad companies have been protected from substantial losses of this character, they necessarily hesitate at attempting to estimate the economy realized. Such questions, in fact, are in the realm of supposition and hence must be left as incalculable. Almost the same circumstances apply when, in answer to coöperative suggestions, repairs have been made to structures and other plant facilities. In this case the funds required for repairs must come, as has been noted, from appropriations made to the department of maintenance of way and structures. A restoration of any portion of the plant, at the right time, may lessen the outlay demanded of this department in the future, or, again, may allow the company to wait longer before investing in betterments. Still, if a roof leak is stopped, a platform mended, a telephone system overhauled, a turntable repaired, or an air tank painted, who will be in a position to state what gains have accrued through loss prevention?

Less indefinite perhaps on the whole, but nevertheless often more or less vague, have been the economies resulting from coöperative suggestions with respect to methods of production control, such as plant layout, improved facilities of transfer as an aid to routing, or work scheduling. The reallotment of space in shops to departments, or the shifting of departments or shops to new locations, may in the opinion of company officials have been accompanied by distinct advantages, but to measure correctly those advantages is admittedly an involved matter or plainly impossible. Overlapping factors are liable to enter into the situation and prevent a segregation of the problem under consideration. Wherever improved or additional standard gauge or service tracks, crossings, driveways, etc., have been supplied, the gains arising above construction costs may generally be reckoned, if these facilities have been used for single or limited purposes, but if their use has been heterogeneous the question of measurement may become so complicated that nothing short of an expensive investigation would disclose the facts. Various suggestions that have occasioned a change in work scheduling may have brought benefits that in part at least should not be hard to estimate. When, as related in chapter xi, the carpenters' schedule on engine cabs at the Mount Clare shop of the Baltimore & Ohio Railroad, was set four hours ahead of the boiler makers' schedule to exclude interference between the crafts, by studying output in relation to time occupied, the gain in quantity of work done should be computable. Yet no very precise idea could be arrived at with respect to the effect which the elimination of friction might have had on quality of workmanship. A proposal, dealing with scheduling at any one point in a spot system of repairs, might be so correlated to the plan as a whole that to ferret out the gain would be scarcely feasible.

The continuous reporting of material shortages in coöperative meetings has seemed largely a perfunctory matter, but, as has been pointed out, may afford the storekeeper better opportunities to plan ahead, and occasionally may safeguard the industry against delay. Economies have undoubtedly emerged where more expert forecasting of material shortages has been permitted, although their measurement must ordinarily be quite elusive. In those instances, seldom occurring, in which it has been positively known what delay has been avoided through coöperative action, the savings might be figured out with some degree of accuracy. The securing of hand tools, charged out to work done, or of even lighter machine tools, through coöperative proposals has also been largely a routine affair, sometimes forestalling delay, but the gains are seldom determinable with certainty.

While the rôle assumed by local joint committees in connection with the purchase of more expensive types of machine tools and other shop equipment has been a decidedly interesting phase of coöperative development, its economic worth may be considered highly problematic. How much more effectively than heretofore has such equipment been bought under the influence of coöperative recommendations, committee discussions, and the establishment of investigatory subcommittees? It is clear that if the company's money has been invested more wisely in production goods as the result of coöperation than under methods formerly employed, gains have resulted, but to attempt to measure these would be idle since there is no telling what purchases would have been made, had there been no coöperation. It is conceivable that in the long run the deference paid to workers' opinions in the matter of equipment buying, which has unquestionably stimulated their morale, has been of greater industrial consequence than the suggestions they have advanced on the subject. In the same general class have been proposals dealing with the need for additions to and remodeling of structures, and other plant facilities. Coöperative committees, however, in this case have had more chance to display originality, and the gains from a percentage of their suggestions, as with those referring to transfer facilities already discussed, should be fairly measurable.

### Results of Improved Morale Seldom Measurable.

ARGUMENTS were submitted in chapter xiii to indicate why it would be next to impossible to gauge accurately the improvements in morale that it is believed have taken place under union-management coöperation. It would appear almost as hopeless a task to measure the economic gains that have resulted. Everyday work performance may have been bettered by changes in morale, yet in the majority of instances, who can tell to what extent? Illustrations have been given of the way in which under the tonic of strengthened morale, the staff at one railroad point rose to an emergency when their wheel press was broken, and at another rendered services of particular value in getting ready a direct steaming system for installation elsewhere. If, at the first station, it were definitely known that, except for coöperation, a new press would have been bought and the old one left unrepaired, an effort to compute the resulting gains might be successful. Otherwise data would be lacking as a basis for comparison, and any attempt at computation futile. Mechanical officers at the second station, although firmly of the opinion that the development of the direct steaming system in its preliminary stages was greatly assisted by coöperation, would assuredly be puzzled if asked to state exactly what coöperation contributed. Again, from an industrial standpoint there has been a significant gain when work processes, as has been claimed, have been altered or departmental adjustments effected more smoothly through coöperation. But here again economies cannot be interpreted in concrete form.

A comparative study of engine failures on any carrier indorsing coöperation should shed some light upon the advantages which may have been reaped from a heightening of morale. Railroad officials can generally figure rather closely the average loss incurred from an engine failure on their lines. Whenever a reduction in engine failures has been marked during a specified period, they should be able to determine approximately the company's savings from this source. Then by judiciously weighing the factors involved in making this result possible, they might at least conjecture the share to be accredited to improved morale. There should be nothing, also, to prevent a decision being reached on any carrier with respect to the amount forfeited on the average through time wasted, clerical expenses, etc., in contesting grievances and disputes. To the extent that a road practicing coöperation appears to have a better record on the score of grievances and disputes than others with which it might be properly compared, the effect of its improved morale should be measurable. At best, however, this would afford nothing but an exceedingly rough estimate of gains.

Suggestions which are regarded as mainly of advantage to the workers are seldom expected to bring a return commensurate with their outlay. Among these are to be grouped: proposals dealing with the subjects of ventilation, heating, industrial lighting, mechanical safeguarding, sanitation, and the provision of other facilities making for better working conditions, cited in chapter xii. The expenditures necessary for such purposes are actually intended for the most part to represent gains from coöperation that are turned again into the industry as a compensation for coöperative effort. They constitute more expressly, therefore, a problem relating to the distribution of gains, than one referring to their measurement. Nevertheless, the introduction of a new ventilating system or more adequate heating, lighting, or hygienic facilities at a repair point, though given as a reward for past coöperation, should spur craft workers especially to added endeavor and bring further economic gains.

*Summary with Respect to Measuring Gains.*

THE impossibility of arriving at anything like a true conception of the gains of coöperation by a method of integration has been definitely established in the foregoing paragraphs. No summation of the gains from individual suggestions and from improved morale can be made that will represent in plain financial terms the meaning of coöperation on the carrier indorsing it. A proportion of suggestions whose worth might be wholly or partly gauged with precision would simply be thrown together with a hodgepodge of those whose value, though real, must be based on little more than speculation. If to this an attempt were made to add the hypothetical gains from improved morale, no reliable total could be reached. Nor should it be forgotten that a summation of gains to be complete must include an estimate of the influence of coöperation as it radiates from the mechanical department to other departments of the carrier.

If gains cannot be determined by a method of integration, how then would it be possible to establish a ratio of value between the coöperative effort of management and men? At a given repair point 80 per cent of the suggestions may have been advanced by the workers and 20 per cent by management, and yet it would not necessarily follow that the contributions of the two should be rated proportionately at 4:1. For one thing the advice of representatives of management in meeting is likely to have had an important qualifying effect upon the ideas which the workers have presented. Again, the impracticability of trying to fix any exact relationship between management and men in connection with the results of improved morale will be quickly evident. Still, in no sense should inability to estimate total gains by a method of integration be regarded as prohibiting the introduction of a well-devised measurement plan on a railroad committed to coöperation. Confidence in the movement should necessarily be increased, if at least a fair proportion of the gains resulting from it are concretely and accurately measured. Information, moreover,

gathered in this way should be of service in correcting or cor-
roborating the data employed under any other system of com-
puting gains. The issues involved in the question of distributing
gains cannot be appropriately discussed until the achievements
of the roads pledged to coöperation in stabilizing employment for
their mechanical craftsmen have been taken up in detail. This,
therefore, will be the subject of the following chapter.

## Chapter XV

## The Stabilization of Employment

SURPASSED only by agriculture and the building trades in the number to whom it gives work, the railroad industry in the United States and Canada has long had an unenviable record for instability of employment. The seasonal fluctuation in employment among railroad workers on Class I railroads in the United States has been estimated to range about 10 per cent from a high point in the autumn to a low point in the spring.[1] Cyclical variations in employment are even more marked on the carriers, since they are gravely affected by business depressions, and correspondingly find their facilities heavily taxed in times of trade expansion. The department of maintenance of way and structures always heads the list for the proportion of men laid off or taken on each year, while the mechanical department in this regard comes uniformly next in order, and the transportation department third. As will be evidenced, one of the most disheartening features of railroad shop work in the past has been its lack of regularized employment.

### The Evils of Irregular Employment on the Railroads.

WORKERS have their names struck from the pay roll of a railroad company either by the expedient of furloughing or by dismissal. Furloughed employees understand that they have been laid off because of slackness in the work which they are fitted to perform, and will not be restored until the situation improves. Sometimes they may be idle so long that they give up hope of reëmployment, and drift to other occupations. An explanation was given in chapter v of the manner in which the forces on organized carriers are

[1] Cf. *Personnel Management on the Railroads,* published under authority of the Metropolitan Life Insurance Company, pp. 41–59.

governed by rules of seniority. When men are taken back to work by stages in the mechanical department, for example, furloughing will bear most acutely under rules of seniority upon those who are farthest down the list of a craft or division of a craft at a repair point. Under conditions where workers are released from service, a proportion with bad records may be let out singly, or in small groups, and generally they are never rehired. Larger quotas, however, may be released because a work "rush" has ended. As many of these as desire will probably be readmitted to service when business is again on the up trend.

Irregularity of employment on the common carriers, as in other industries, is chiefly thought of as detrimental to the workers, yet there are ways in which it may be prejudicial to the interests of the employing companies, and of the general public. From the point of view of the workers, furloughing has the very distasteful result of lowering their normal wage income. Men, for instance, in the mechanical trades dependent upon hourly rates of pay for their livelihood, are deprived, except on a shortened Saturday, of eight hours' wages for each day off work. Uncertain as to the length of a furlough, they either remain inactive, or can as a rule only take makeshift jobs at less pay to fill in the interval. Social disqualifications which tend to result from intermittent employment can merely be alluded to in this volume. They include: loss among workers of craft proficiency due to suspension of effort; weakening of their personal initiative and moral stamina because of economic insecurity; and the lapse of civic virtues among them, which so often accompanies reduced earning power. When employees are forced by long furloughs to seek other occupations, they may throw to the winds years of apprentice training and of valuable craft knowledge acquired as journeymen.

Unemployment may be the cause, on the other hand, of varied forms of economic loss to the railroad company. When men are on furlough or have been released after a period of activity, the railroad is bound to have plant and roadway equipment in excess of current needs. At such times machine tools and other types of equipment, representing a large fixed capital investment, will stand idle at local repair points, deteriorating from lack of use. Again, money may be tied up in stocks of materials that, in violation of principles of economy, must be carried over the dull period. Or, after the full force has been again put to work, the company may be compelled to buy materials in the market at high price levels. As almost the same supervisory staff must be retained when work is slack as when it is plentiful, funds are thereby wasted in salary outlay. Moreover, the railroads are confronted with a greater labor turnover on account of irregularity of employment, which means that more new appointees than otherwise would be necessary must be initiated into the ways of the company. Then the depreciation in skill, and, it may be, in moral fiber, that has occurred among workers laid off, will eventually operate to the economic disadvantage of the company restoring them to service. Reduced employment in the mechanical department will sometimes lead to deficiency of motive power and car shortages at a time when badly needed, thereby working a hardship to the public. Besides, the railroad pay roll is often depended upon to enliven local trade. Numerous repair points are situated near towns, or on the outskirts of cities where the expenditures of shop workers are the main element in the support of a business community. A local shutdown or curtailment of forces at such points not only decreases the dealers' sales but adds at the same time to their credit burden.

## *Fluctuations of Employment in the Mechanical Department.*

CERTAIN peculiarities in the business of transportation have encouraged the railroads to sanction irregular employment in their services. The value of a railroad's physical property, as well as its intangible assets, is always high in proportion to its income, and rarely is it blessed with a sizable working capital. On most carriers the policy in the past, indeed, has been to take in money and give it out from day to day with little attempt at forecasting the future. While more provident methods are constantly gaining favor among railroad executives, the older, hand-to-mouth way of doing things is still in evidence. Traffic returns, as already explained, constitute the bulk of a carrier's income. If these should decline, the funds available for current expenses—unless a modern budgeting system has been adopted—are at once restricted and all departments feel the pinch. There are directions, however, in which a carrier will pause before limiting outgo too rigorously. Attempts to economize in the transportation department, if carried beyond a certain point, will interfere with the efficient and safe running of trains, and the company will be put in an undesirable position when competition for business is keen. But expenditures for maintenance of way and structures may be curtailed for a time, and many workers furloughed or released from service. Another field for retrenchment is offered by the maintenance of equipment department, where furloughing and dismissal of workers are likely to begin soon after announcement has been made of a cut in appropriations. In the two last-named departments, a practice of deferring maintenance may be invoked by the carrier, which will often be continued until its train service has given warning signs of disorganization. Work in the meantime will have accumulated, so that when money again pours in from increased traffic, furloughed men can be called back and new employees hired.

Fluctuations in employment, it may be noted, do not affect in the same way all sections of the maintenance of equipment department. The running repair forces at enginehouses, and the light repair and inspection gangs in train car yards, can only be trimmed down slightly when traffic is on the wane. The more significant reductions in personnel always occur in the back shops, locomotive repair shops, and car repair shops of the carrier, where a postponement of maintenance is practicable. Within recent years, however, the introduction on many railroads of a system of assigning locomotives to longer runs has caused intervening enginehouses to lose their former status. As this change has been in progress, workers, as opportunity has allowed, have been transferred to other stations or have been furloughed never to return. Depending upon their territorial location, maintenance of equipment points tend to have peaks of seasonal employment on the occasion of a wheat, cotton, fruit, stock, coal, or other kind of "rush," when furloughs are unthought of, additional men are usually taken into service and overtime wages frequently paid. Repair points on some carriers pass through two or three seasons of special activity within the year. As soon as there are more normal traffic conditions, the extra force is dropped, and then, as business grows slacker, resort may be had to furloughing. On organized carriers, since the signing of the national agreement in 1919, the federated shop crafts have endeavored, in conducting their negotiations, to stipulate that the principles of seniority must govern when furloughing takes place. Nevertheless they may agree, as has Division No. 4 in Canada, and System Federation No. 76 on the Milwaukee System, that the working hours of the entire force may be cut to forty in the week before men are laid off on a seniority basis.

### The Carriers' Position Relative to Stabilization.

THE railroads now subscribing to the plan of union-management coöperation, previous to their indorsement of it, favored policies on furloughing and dismissal of employees, essentially similar to those approved by other carriers. But with coöperation they each have enunciated a new set of principles on the subject of employment, which, as their common objectives have been more clearly apprehended, have been held to be among the most distinguishing features of the coöperative movement. They each, in consequence, have authorized a regularization of employment in their maintenance of equipment department, and have made some headway also in extending similar principles to their department of maintenance of way and structures. In fairness it should, of course, be pointed out that other carriers, of which the Seaboard Air Line Railway is a notable example, have made commendable efforts to remedy irregular conditions of employment among their workers. Furthermore, industrial concerns outside the transportation field have been taking steps in the same direction. The contributions of union-management coöperation, however, to the stabilization of employment, because of the studied approach which the railroads have made to all the problems involved and the results so far achieved, may be regarded as possibly the most impressive yet appearing in the history of American industry.

There has been some misunderstanding of the obligations assumed by the several carriers on the question of stabilizing employment at the time when each entered the coöperative movement. It is apparent from the records, that one carrier only, the Chicago & North Western Railway, made a binding declaration on the subject, and this was merely in the form of a pledge that a minimum standard force would be established on its lines. The Chicago & North Western Railway's systematized coöperative program of 1925, after it had stated that regular employment would be of foremost advantage to the workers and also helpful to the company, since the continuous operation of its shop facilities was essential to an economic investment, went on to give assurance that an arrangement would be effected in the mechanical department, which would "ultimately and without delay permit work being performed by the minimum number of employees consistent with the various classes of work available." The Baltimore & Ohio Railroad, in drawing up its coöperative agreement with System Federation No. 30, in 1924, did not positively state that it would stabilize employment in its mechanical department. The coöperative plan, according to the text of the agreement between it and the federation, was merely "intended to help the stabilization of employment on the Baltimore & Ohio Railroad, thereby producing a situation of satisfied and contented personnel with improved morale, and consequently improvement in the service and production by greater efficiency and better quality of work." Definite guaranties on the subject of regularizing employment were likewise omitted in the memorandum of principles formulated between the Milwaukee System and its shop crafts in 1926, which, however, did propose "to devise means and adopt ways to put into effect such manufacturing practices" as would be of greatest assistance in lending security to employment, and in supplying materials and equipment to the railroad at lower costs. Nor has any covenant been entered into between the Canadian National Railway Company and its shop employees on this issue, although executive officers of the system at different times have asserted in writing that every effort would be made to stabilize employment conditions.

The almost complete absence of express agreements with reference to stabilization of employment has detracted little, if any, from the importance attached to it under the coöperative plan. In fact, the organized crafts, though lacking for the most part absolute guaranties in the matter, have entered coöperation on each railroad in the belief that the companies sincerely intended to put employment on a new foundation. "I have endeavored," said William H. Johnston in 1924, when speaking of the inceptive stages of the coöperative movement, "to impress upon management that before they can expect the man on the railroads to offer suggestions . . . it was essential that thought and study be given to the consideration of steady employment." In the meantime, so often has stabilization of employment been discussed in joint meetings between management and men, so numerous have been the communications between them on the subject, and so definitive and laudatory have been the public utterances of both railroad and craft officials in relation to it, that its enforcement, to the best of their ability, is now practically conceded to be an "unwritten" obligation of the carriers committed to coöperation. "We are trying to stabilize their work," asserted Daniel Willard

with respect to the shop crafts on the Baltimore & Ohio Railroad
in 1927, "we are trying to make their working condition as satisfactory as may be possible."[2] In an address to the system coöperative meeting of the Canadian National Railway System at
Montreal, Quebec, in January, 1928, Sir Henry W. Thornton
characterized insecurity of employment as a "great menace to the
employee," which to his mind created "an unhealthy condition"
both for the railroad and its personnel. He declared that the
establishment of regular employment, which was assuredly a
major problem of coöperation, should enable the railroad "to
attract and retain in its service the cream of the labor market."

### Coöperative Principles of Stabilization.

By degrees the principles involved in stabilization of employment
have coalesced into reasonably fixed form, and as a result have
approximately the same meaning on all the roads indorsing co-
operation. It is the aim under the accepted plan of coöperation
to have a regular working force at each maintenance of equipment point. This consists of an aggregation of the quotas that
in each given classification of work can be assigned to full-time
employment throughout the year, or as nearly as possible
throughout the year. The carrier is inclined to regard the normal
force as a minimum to which it holds its personnel after a careful
survey of work opportunities. To labor it appears rather to be a
maximum, that is, the highest total of workers to whom regular
employment can be granted. Men belonging to the normal force,
it is understood, shall not be furloughed unless the company, by
reason of a severe traffic slump, or other exigency, is able to claim
logically that layoffs are unpreventable. In this connection the
hope has been expressed, that with the evolution of scientific
methods of budgetary control on the carriers furloughing, even

[2] From an address delivered by Daniel Willard before the National Civic
Federation at New York City, February 17, 1927, reported in *Industrial Management*, May, 1927, p. 263.

when the business situation is distinctly unfavorable, should be practically abolished.

In conformity with the seasonal demands of each local station, the stabilization plan allows extra workers to be admitted to service above the level of the normal force. However, the seasonal peaks thus created must be kept low by coöperative vigilance, in fact, they should be eliminated, if at all practicable. Once the size of the regular force at any repair point has been determined, it is a first principle of stabilization that it be kept unaltered unless there are valid and convincing reasons for a change. Here arises the difficulty that mechanical progress in the railroad industry, toward the attainment of which it is expected that coöperative suggestions will lend their share of influence, is constantly tending to reduce the number of men required for service. An increase in business may suffice to counterbalance this effect of mechanical progress upon employment. Otherwise the company must grapple with the problem of providing additional work for the force, if it is to remain in undiminished strength. When the situation cannot be fully met in this way, it may not be considered a violation of the principles of stabilization if the force is gradually scaled down by such methods as checking the infiltration of apprentice-trained men into the trades, and by failing to hire new men as workers die, retire from the service, or for other cause separate themselves from employment. However, in order that normal forces may be preserved as nearly as possible intact, the shop crafts have stood firmly and insistently for the enlargement of work opportunities through development of the policy of manufacturing goods at repair points that ordinarily must be bought, and through a widening of the scope of maintenance and rebuilding operations. In large measure the carriers have acceded to these proposals, which have been more applicable at central, than at smaller, local stations. An account will now be given of the introduction and extension of stabilized employment on the carriers pledged to coöperation. This will be followed by a brief description of the manufacturing and other methods by which more work has been afforded in the mechanical department.

### Principles of Stabilization Put into Effect.

THE manner in which one situation of irregularity of employment was cleared up at the Glenwood shop, Pittsburgh, Pennsylvania, of the Baltimore & Ohio Railroad, in 1923, has been related in chapter vii. During the following three years staff and line officers of this carrier were concerned with the intricate and often disheartening problem of stabilizing employment at all its repair points to which the extension of the coöperative plan had been authorized. One difficulty encountered was that the introduction of many changes in production methods was causing railroads to trim down their forces at maintenance of equipment points. Besides, in keeping with policies current in those years, the Baltimore & Ohio Railroad was adding to the length of its locomotive runs, which necessitated a serious diminution of force at some repair stations, and the practical abandonment of others. Then an important traffic decline, which began on the carrier's lines in 1927, furnished a substantial argument for further reductions. Meanwhile arrangement of the details of a policy of stabilization was made harder for the carrier by certain employment conditions which had existed in its mechanical department since the shopmen's strike. While the strike was in progress, President Daniel Willard had bound the company, by specific verbal guaranties made to workers admitted to its service, in regard to their future seniority rights and permanence of employment. After the strike was over, many of these men remained with the railroad at various stations, where their presence often created a problem when the establishment of a full-time, minimum working force was attempted. In adherence to promises given, the officer in charge at a local point has never been permitted to cut farther into the list of any class of mechanics or helpers, in order to achieve a normal force, once the name has appeared of a man

accepted for service during the strike. By October, 1927, however, in spite of the fact that all the obstacles enumerated had
not been overcome, the carrier believed that the foundations of
its policy of stabilization had been laid. Since that date no furloughs worthy of mention have occurred in its mechanical department.

Unlike the other roads committed to coöperation the Baltimore
& Ohio Railroad, in dealing with problems of stabilization, has
found it necessary to give only limited attention to the question
of seasonal fluctuations in employment. As a result, its policy,
which gradually crystallized into final form between 1927 and
1929, is somewhat different. It has been decided that at any given
time management and workers employed in the mechanical department of the Baltimore & Ohio Railroad may be regarded as
consisting of two groups, its permanent and its temporary forces.
The permanent forces, aside from management, shall be made up
of workers who are assured of full-time employment; while
workers comprising the temporary forces shall only be given employment as business conditions allow, and therefore may be entirely eliminated in a period of depression. But the company
hopes that the permanent forces will always be retained intact
even when the traffic situation is at its worst. When vacancies
occur in the ranks of the permanent employees, temporary
workers shall preferably be advanced to fill them. At each repair
point a designated normal force shall be employed as a section
of the permanent forces. In July, 1929, this plan was virtually in
effect although not officially recognized as such, because at several stations the status of men taken on during the strike was
still an interfering factor. Management and men considered as
permanently employed in the mechanical department then numbered about 16,500; in the neighborhood of 1,000 men were rated
as belonging to the temporary forces. When a serious trade depression came in 1930, the railroad warned its shop employees
that curtailment of operating expenses would be necessary. Rep-

resentatives of System Federation No. 30 in convention then voted in favor of a reduction of hours worked in lieu of a reduction of forces. As a result the carrier signed an agreement with the federation's committee putting all its mechanical forces on a five-day-a-week basis.

Craft workers longer in the service of the Chicago & North Western Railway bear rather gloomy witness to the irregularities of employment at one time prevalent in its mechanical department. The earnings of this road, forming, as it does, a traffic network in a number of middle western agricultural states, have always mounted in periods of heavy crop and live stock loadings, and correspondingly slackened in other seasons. It was formerly the carrier's custom to sanction the occurrence of accentuated peaks and valleys of employment among its shop forces to match the rise and fall of its operating income. Now, under its plan of systematized coöperation, all sharp oscillations of employment in the mechanical department have been done away with. In accordance with its written promise, cited earlier in this chapter, it has scaled down the complement of workers at each of its repair points to a so-called authorized force, upon whom it has asserted a willingness to confer full-time employment.

The stabilization policies of the Chicago & North Western Railway may be illustrated by reference to the employment situation at its shop in Boone, Iowa. In 1928 the authorized force for the car repair and motive power departments combined at Boone was 416 men. "Rush" seasons ordinarily follow one another in succession between August 1 and November 1 at this point, when through shipments of California fruit are being carried eastward, and then as local grain crops are being hauled to their destination. In preparation for these months of increased activity, an effort is made to get equipment repaired in advance so that fewer extra men must necessarily be hired. Whereas, for example, the regular quota in the car department at Boone has been around 125 men, varying with the circumstances now only 25 to 40 more are taken on during the busy season. The authorized force for the back shop and enginehouse at Clinton, Iowa, on the Chicago & North Western Railway is in the neighborhood of 500 men. Here, in order to keep the force at work in dull seasons, locomotives are reconditioned, coated with white lead, and set on storage tracks, awaiting service when traffic becomes brisk. The manner in which stabilization operates for individual crafts on the Chicago & North Western Railway may be shown by quoting figures on employment from the records of its shop at Chicago, Illinois. In 1928, the passenger coach department of the Chicago shop was authorized to hire, among other craftsmen, 656 carmen, 110 sheet metal workers and pipe fitters, 73 blacksmiths, and 64 machinists. This company sought to keep its mechanical forces intact when depression hit the country in 1930, but was compelled to make certain reductions.

The consensus of opinion both among officers and men in the service of the Canadian National Railway Company appears to be that it has satisfactorily fulfilled all its undertakings with respect to stabilizing employment in its mechanical department. Still it should be borne in mind that this carrier performs much of its traffic functions in a rapidly expanding territory, and has suffered less than the average American railroad from the competition of the automobile. Since 1923, its first year of operation after the inclusion of the Grand Trunk Railway System, the Canadian National Railway Company's traffic (if 1929 be left out of consideration) returns have been steadily climbing. Operating revenues, which for the consolidated lines amounted to $254,-926,456 during the year ending on December 31, 1923, had risen to $304,591,268 for the fiscal year 1928. Passenger traffic, it is true, fell off slightly in this period, but the revenue tonnage for all commodities carried in freight traffic had meanwhile advanced from 57,248,338 tons in 1923 to 70,578,007 tons in 1928.

Although the employment situation on the Canadian National Railway System immediately showed signs of improvement after the appointment of Sir Henry W. Thornton as president in 1922, stabilization as a consistent policy has only been in effect in the mechanical department of the carrier's lines in Canada since the introduction of coöperation. Regular forces are now retained at all maintenance of equipment points in Canada, and although seasonal peaks of employment continue to recur, especially in the grain-growing areas of the carrier's western region, their significance has been largely minimized by planning work ahead. No shutdown, furloughs, nor reduction of hours worthy of mention, occurred anywhere in Canadian territory from June, 1925, until the summer of 1929. This splendid record, however, was marred when the scanty western crops of 1929 gave promise of a rapid decline in traffic returns. To meet the exigency until business should improve, the carrier was forced to furlough all its shop employees with less than six months' seniority, to lay off other workers at enginehouses and smaller car repair points two days in each month, and to shut down its main shops one week during the Christmas season. More drastic measures to curtail forces at this time were, nevertheless, taken by competing railroads.

Monthly outgo at local repair stations on the Canadian National Railway System is no longer regulated by current earnings as the general managers of each region budget for a year in advance. Upon the adoption of the coöperative plan, Sir Henry W. Thornton told the shop craft leaders in conference that an annual budgetary plan would be utilized in the mechanical department, under which, if possible, one year would be kept uniform with the other, although he could not prophesy what the company would do in a period of real depression. The Canadian Pacific Railway, it may be noted by way of contrast, has still been allowing appropriations to its mechanical department to fluctuate more or less with earnings, and occasionally lays off its workers for a week or ten days in a month. Labor officials in Canada, however, testify that this road has recently given clear indications of altering its employment policy to bring it into closer harmony with that of its government-owned competitor. Stabilization was already an actuality on the Grand Trunk Railway System, and on the mileage operated by the Canadian National Railway Company in New England, when steps were first taken to institute coöperation on these lines in 1926. Regular forces totaling about 2,000 men, of which the Battle Creek, Michigan, locomotive repair shop has 500 to 600, are now in service at the company's various maintenance of equipment points in the United States. To allow the carrier to retrench, as was required in 1929, the men decided that they would all work shorter hours. Because of the trade depression, this policy was continued in 1930, and the company's shops shut down a few days in each month.

As explained in chapter xiv, the interim report prepared by the special committee appointed on the Canadian National Railway System in 1927, to estimate the value of the gains of coöperation, embodied a comparative analysis of the accomplishments of stabilization of employment until the end of that year. Out of a possible 2,240 shop hours that might be worked in any year, the report estimated that, in 1927, employees in the mechanical department of the carrier had been in service 2,155 hours, which meant that they had lost only 85 hours on an average during that period. Whereas, in 1924, the percentage of idle time had been 11.9, since the introduction of coöperation it had been 8.0 in 1925, 6.1 in 1926, and 4.4 in 1927. Taking the average rate of wages as a basis, it was computed that shop workers had been able to earn $102 more in 1925, $139 more in 1926, and $150 more in 1927 than they had in 1924. Separations from the regular pay roll, due to action taken by the company, which had numbered 1722 in 1924, had dropped to 427 in 1927, a reduction of approximately 75 per cent. In view of the fact that total separations from the regular pay roll had amounted to 764 in 1927, and additions to it had numbered 669, the labor turnover in the mechanical department for that year had been only about 4 per

cent, while the net loss in the normal working force had been but
95 men.

The question of stabilizing employment on the Chicago, Milwaukee, St. Paul & Pacific Railroad has been linked with the
problem of establishing the carrier on a basis of operating efficiency during, and after its emergence from, a receivership. With
or without coöperation in effect, it was inescapable that the personnel of the road's mechanical department should be scaled down
considerably in order to bring about economies in production. As
many as 1,300 men were employed in the passenger coach department of the company's shop at Milwaukee, Wisconsin, in 1925,
but through the stringency of its financial position, and coöperative striving for stabilization, this number had been cut to a
regular force of 811 by 1928. Employment statistics for the
Tacoma, Washington, shop indicate that in February, 1926, 839
men were on the pay roll, whereas in June of the same year the
number in service had dropped to 502, only to rise again to 771 in
December. Such wide fluctuations had become impossible at Tacoma by 1928, where a regular working force of slightly over 400
men had been officially sanctioned. As on other railroads, normal
forces may be increased somewhat at points on the Milwaukee
System during "rush" seasons. This carrier has adopted a scientific budgetary plan for its maintenance of equipment department.
In 1930, it had to put all its shopmen on a five-day-a-week basis,
furlough some of them, and close its shops part-time.

### Methods of Providing Work as an Aid to Stabilization.

To implement the policy of stabilizing employment in the maintenance of equipment department, the carriers subscribing to
union-management coöperation have sought out ways of providing additional work opportunities for their mechanical crafts. In
this way it has been hoped that the normal forces established for
the department might be larger at the beginning, and later might
be protected in a measure at least against losses due to the con-

tinual mechanization of industry, developments in production control, and improving methods of transportation. The importance of expanding work opportunities in its shops as an aid to stabilization was recognized by the Baltimore & Ohio Railroad upon entering coöperation, and has been the subject of repeated discussions between it and the shop crafts since that time. It has been estimated that this carrier, in the period immediately following the 1922 strike, was in the habit of letting out to "contract" shops approximately 20 per cent of its maintenance work on train cars and 25 per cent of its work on locomotives. By 1925, however, it had entirely abandoned the farming out of repair work, all of which it henceforth did on its own property.

Manufacturing of the store order supplies needed in its mechanical department, though not a new policy, has been greatly extended by the Baltimore & Ohio Railroad within recent years. Heavier equipment parts are mainly manufactured at its Mount Clare shop, where one-quarter of the force is engaged in such operations, and at its Cumberland and Glenwood repair shops and Newark, Ohio, foundry. Here, according to the distribution of work, main and side rods are forged and finished, cylinders, superheaters, and other gray iron castings completed, springs of various types and sizes manufactured,[3] and bushings, bearings, etc., cast from brass. In 1924 a bolt and forge shop was opened at Cumberland, Maryland, to which were transferred certain manufacturing facilities from other stations. The output of this shop has been gradually increased until it now produces over a thousand articles, mostly of smaller size, that are used in motive power and train car repairs. From 60 to 70 per cent of the metal scrap collected on the road is retained for manufacturing purposes, being charged at its market value to the shop re-using it. Also, to help increase work opportunities, the task of modernizing locomotives on the Baltimore & Ohio Railroad has been assigned

[3] See "Spring Plant of the Baltimore & Ohio at Mt. Clare Shops," *Railway Mechanical Engineer*, July, 1928, pp. 109–113.

to the mechanical department. This policy was adopted as early as July, 1923, and its first results were hailed with enthusiasm when in September of the same year engine No. 1003, satisfactorily remodeled, was dispatched into service from the Glenwood shop.[4] Altogether, since coöperation was adopted on its lines, between 500 and 600 older locomotives have been similarly fitted out at points on the carrier to cope with modern traffic conditions. Besides, some half dozen new locomotives have been built entirely in the company's shops.

Owing to expanding traffic the provision of more work for its mechanical department has not been of such vital consequence to the Canadian National Railway Company's policy of stabilization, as to that of the Baltimore & Ohio Railroad. Nevertheless the shop craft representatives on the Canadian Government's lines have persistently set forth their claims on this issue before regional and system coöperative committees. At its 1926 meeting the carrier's joint system coöperative committee appointed a fact-finding subcommittee on manufacturing materials, which reported back to it at its 1927 session. During the discussion following the report, it was revealed that few equipment parts were being bought by the railroad in comparison to those which were being fabricated at its Montreal and Transcona iron foundries, its Moncton brass foundry, and at other important repair stations. The subcommittee, however, suggested that it would be economically advisable for the company to undertake, in addition, the manufacture of air brake cylinders and certain other castings, superheater headers, and engine driving and truck axles. At the system coöperative meeting of 1929, a statement was read showing that the labor cost of manufacturing materials on the carrier during the preceding twelve months had been nearly three-quarters of a million dollars, or about 10 per cent of the total pay roll at its

4 This episode is referred to in an article by Otto S. Beyer, Jr., entitled, "B. & O. Engine 1003," in the *Survey*, Graphic Number, January, 1924, pp. 311–317.

leading shops. Recurrently the company's program of modernizing and converting its equipment has been used to keep its shopmen busier. Then, too, a number of new switching engines and many new train cars have been built by its mechanical forces. Plans for 1929 called for the construction in shops of the Canadian National Railway System of 75 new caboose cars, the steel underframing of 22 passenger coaches, and the steel plating of 54 other train cars of different models.

More or less similar policies have been maintained on the Milwaukee System and on the Chicago & North Western Railway since their acceptance of coöperation. Whereas at one time on the former, a considerable proportion of the brake shoes needed for maintenance purposes was bought, now all are made at its central shop in Milwaukee, Wisconsin. Facilities have been provided at the Milwaukee shop for the heat-treating of springs, which has necessitated the services of eight more mechanics and seven more helpers in the blacksmith shop. In the passenger coach department of the shop, eighteen wooden sleeping cars have been converted into suburban coaches by the application of steel underframes and steel plate exteriors, five old observation cars have been turned into standard parlor cars, and various other cars changed in design or modernized. A large number of engines have been remodeled in the motive power department. Furthermore, as related in chapter xi, ten new, all-steel baggage cars have been built by the shop forces at Milwaukee. Plans have been formulated for the erection of an extensive plant at this station to be used entirely for the construction of freight-train cars. In the car department of the Chicago & North Western Railway's shop at Chicago, Illinois, a great amount of remodeling work has been done to passenger coaches and dining cars, that before the introduction of coöperation was sent out to contract. Converting of train cars to other than their original uses has also become a common practice at this point. In the motive power department of the company's Chicago shop, boiler makers are shifted to the manufacture of new boilers to stock, whenever their regular work grows slack.

It may be watched with interest how far the creation of additional work opportunities by these methods can be depended upon, in the future, to offset the effect of industrial advancement upon employment conditions on the roads committed to coöperation. No matter how keenly the carriers may desire to engage in the manufacture of shop order materials, it is clear that they will always have to buy a percentage of these in outside markets because of the highly specialized facilities required to make them. Besides, the test of economic value will always exercise a restraining influence on the practices of modernizing and converting equipment. It is true that carriers may at any time give more employment by building new train cars and locomotives in their shops, but should they erect a separate plant for that purpose, they may be considered to have actually set up an enterprise apart from the maintenance field. Fear of offending the supply and equipment-building companies with whom they have been accustomed to do business, lest in some way it should react to the disadvantage of their traffic returns, has impelled the railroads to halt before adopting a too liberal policy of increasing work opportunities in the mechanical department. As a government road, the Canadian National Railway Company has been hampered in this respect by pressure exerted through political channels.

# Chapter XVI

# The Fair Sharing of Gains

WHAT bearing may the question of stabilizing employment in the mechanical department of a railroad be considered to have upon the issue of dividing its coöperative gains? How far may its shop workers be said to have been repaid for their coöperative efforts by the award of regular employment? The opportunity to work full time, or approximately full time, without fear of layoff unless through exceptional circumstances, has undeniably been a boon to employees in the mechanical department. Each additional day they have worked as the result of stabilization, has meant just so many more dollars in their pay envelopes. While this has been of chief advantage to junior men on a seniority list who have been protected against a furloughing of part of the force, it has also helped those higher up on the list by avoiding entire shutdowns of the plant. Moreover, the workers have been freed from the oppressive anxiety which is a constant burden to the minds of those who are aware that their means of livelihood is insecure. Herein lies a benefit of stabilization that cannot be reckoned in terms of money.

Needless to state, if it could be shown that stabilization of employment were wholly or even mainly to the advantage of the shop workers, it might be treated as an important recompense to them for their participation in coöperation. Over a period of time, however, stabilization may be expected to bring very definite, economic contributions to the railroads which enforce it. Admittedly, the plan of establishing regular forces at maintenance of equipment stations has necessitated adjustments in work performance that have cost the railroads some money. But within a year or so, this initial liability should have been discharged, and the companies be in a position to realize a return from the new employment policy. Continuity of employment should always lead to increased efficiency; the carrier's investment should be husbanded by the utilization of their shops and equipment throughout the year; while savings must assuredly accrue from a diminution in labor turnover. For these reasons, instead of being in any sense a burden on the company adopting it, stabilization of employment as a permanent factor in industry should rather become for it a real source of profit. Viewed accordingly from a purely material aspect, each carrier's furtherance of stabilization may perhaps be justifiably interpreted as a distribution of coöperative gains, only to the extent that a slight loss has been borne at the time of its introduction. It may be best to think of stabilization of employment, then, as an industrial phenomenon accompanying coöperation which puts money into the pockets both of the workers and of the employing railroads.

Yet it is incumbent upon the workers to remember that the granting of regularized employment has come about as the result of a manifest expression of the coöperative spirit on the part of railroad management, and the company which that management represents. It is indicative of the fact that the workers' plight under conditions of unstable employment has been noted, and an effort made to satisfy their desire for greater permanency in the terms of their service, and for the additional earning power which stabilization will bring. Even if it be assumed that the carriers from the outset knew that they must ultimately benefit by discarding older, unsound methods of employment, there is reason to believe that in each instance they favored stabilization primarily to meet the needs of their workers rather than to increase profits. Besides, in taking action to enforce stabilization they have surrendered the "fear of unemployment" weapon which industrialists have used so often and so effectively to keep their workers in line. In a measure, too, as has been related in chapter xv, they have braved the ill will of outside business interests by manufacturing materials, etc., as an aid to stabilization. Shop workers, therefore, though they may rightfully ask that the results for them of stabilization be omitted from the estimate when

their share of coöperative gains is being computed, are morally
bound to give due credit to the railroad company for bestowing
the advantages of regularized employment upon them. It would
seem but fair that they should weigh the company's attitude in
this matter carefully, and under certain circumstances possibly
press their demands for an allotment of the gains less insistently
because of it.

### The Companies' Surplus Gains from Coöperation.

THE definite conclusion was reached in chapter xiv that the gains
of coöperation are impossible of measurement by a method of integration. It was also pointed out how equally futile it would be
to seek to establish a ratio of value between the coöperative contributions of management and men. No help of a positive character, then, can be expected from these sources in an endeavor to
find a basis upon which the gains of coöperation may be divided.
It is true that almost every suggestion registered in coöperative
meetings, of which illustrations were given in chapters x–xii,
benefits the company and workers in differing proportions according to its type. Likewise every improvement in morale brings
an advantage of varying degree to each of the participants in
coöperation. In the everyday procedure of business the gains
from suggestions presented, and from improved morale are auto-
matically apportioned to the company and to its employees. The
problem of distribution would be very simple if it could be demonstrated that in this self-regulative manner each party receives
approximately its fair share of gains. The workers, however, have
been thoroughly convinced, and railroad management has generally been ready to admit, that the companies receive more lu-
crative returns from practices of coöperation than do the men.
Whether this be true or not may be roughly estimated by
comparing the gains which one apparently receives, as business
proceeds on its ordinary course, with the gains received by the
other.

The workers have had more benefits conferred upon them by the types of suggestions, as set forth in chapter xii, which have dealt expressly with such questions as ventilation, industrial lighting, heating, mechanical safeguarding, sanitation, and locker and lunchrooms. In giving effect to suggestions of this character the railroads, whose greatest profit from them has been to secure an added measure of contentment among their employees, have undoubtedly spent sums of money considerably in excess of what would have been their ordinary outlay for the purposes involved. Furthermore, it may be asserted that the workers reap an advantage in varying degrees from nearly every other suggestion presented, because of these there are few that do not make toil lighter or otherwise better working conditions. On the other hand, to be listed as mainly of benefit to the companies, are the array of suggestions that in diverse ways have brought economies in labor, have added to the quality of repairs, have helped obtain the right equipment and the right materials, have saved structures and shop equipment from deterioration, have salvaged and reclaimed scrap, have changed motive power and train car standards, or have caused transportation to be safer and more efficient. To balance the advantages thus distributed between the parties on any road is, of course, precluded by inability to compute accurately more than a percentage of the gains. However, if the investigator makes a wide survey of the minutes of coöperative committees, attending certain of their meetings in person, and if he examines evidences gathered from a sufficient number of suggestions, the results of which can be measured, he will assuredly come to the opinion that the carriers' gains have outranked those of the workers. A surplus of gains from the suggestion-technique of coöperation has belonged to the companies, which always, it may be assumed, has increased where more alertness and originality have been shown by representatives of management and men in coöperative meetings.

Heightened morale due to coöperation, it would seem, has given most of its economic contributions to the railroads. The beneficial results of improvements in morale are seen in connection with regular work performance, including a lessening of engine failures and assessable defects under the locomotive inspection codes and safety appliance regulations; the rendering of special or emergency services; the effecting of departmental readjustments and changes in methods of work; the enforcement of discipline; and the reduction in the number and severity of grievances and disputes arising under agreements. These have been preponderantly in the companies' favor. The workers have obtained a personal satisfaction from the new spirit animating them which has tempered and shaped their actions, and which may mean something, it is true, from the standpoint of working conditions, but not much else. Consequently improved morale may be said to have brought clear and pronounced increments of advantage to the carriers, easily surpassing those that have accrued to the workers. The significance of this surplus of gain from morale would be more readily understood if its value could be translated into figures.

A brief summary of the situation may now be given, which will indicate the positions occupied by the companies and their employees, where the distribution of coöperative gains is left to the natural course of industry. In the case of the economic results flowing from the suggestion-technique of coöperation, the opinion has been set forth that the carriers have been recipients of the greater share of gains. In the case of the benefits arising from improved morale, it has been shown that whereas the companies have obtained much of tangible value, the workers have obtained comparatively little. Nevertheless, as has been previously stated, the obligation rests with the workers to give substantial recognition to the fact that they have been granted more stable employment through the good will of the companies. When these several factors are balanced in the scale it would appear that the companies, even if a judicious allowance be made for the effects of stabilization, have in the outworking of coöperation come into the possession of an undoubted surplus. It is merely repetitious to assert that, on account of the difficulties of measurement, there is no telling what might be the exact amount of this surplus on any carrier. Hence, leaving the distribution of gains to the natural course of industry fails to meet the essential requirement of union-management coöperation, that they be apportioned between the company and its workers on an equitable basis. It remains then, if the purposes of the movement are to be fulfilled, for the parties to coöperation on each railroad to seek ways and means of arriving at a decision, fallible though it may be, with respect to the size of the company's surplus, and to determine what portion of it should in fairness be turned back to the workers. Still, it may be argued, the policy to be followed by a railroad in sharing its surplus with the workers must largely hinge upon its economic condition at the time.

### Sharing Gains by an Addition to Wages.

THE problem which faces each carrier of taking action with reference to its coöperative surplus, under the principle of fair sharing of gains, may first be dealt with from the point of view of the shop crafts' wage schedules. Would it be advisable to allot to the workers what might be considered their just portion of the surplus in the form of an addition to their regular scale of wages? Actually there are only two leading methods open to the carriers by which they can requite their employees for coöperative effort, namely, by bettering their working conditions, which is already being done, or by awarding them some form of money return. If the latter method is tried, it must be accomplished either through increasing the workers' standard wage rates, or by granting them a recompense apart from and independent of wages. To increase wages is apparently under the circumstances the simpler expedient to adopt, but upon examination will be found to be beset by obstacles.

Wages are fixed for shop workers organized in the mechanical department, as explained in chapter v, by direct negotiations between representatives of the crafts and the individual carriers. The six federated shop crafts, bargaining together, have in each instance signed a joint system agreement, covering all their ranks, with the carriers committed to coöperation, while the other trades, which may or may not be under the plan, have their own agreements with them. The system agreements, all of which originated in 1922, are subject to amendment or revision in conference, whenever either party by written statement gives the other thirty days' notice of its desire for a change. Conferences are similarly held to deal with modifications of the separate agreements of other crafts. A supplementary wage payment, therefore, as a reward for workers' coöperation might be very opportunely determined on the occasion when the terms of an agreement were under consideration. In the same manner the supplementary payment might be altered periodically to correspond with the results of coöperation. It would be possible to make distribution uniform by adding so much to the hourly wage, or a proportionate amount to each rate in the schedule.

On the whole, however, the idea that they should receive a share of the carrier's surplus in the form of an addition to wages has not been attractive to the shop crafts. It has been realized that this would be more or less inconsistent with the staunch endeavor hitherto made, to keep the coöperative movement out of the arena of collective bargaining. Experience has shown that wage schedules are often set, and other craft issues adjusted, after lengthy and sometimes bitter debate. In fact, it may at any time occur that a question of wages will require for its settlement the aid of the United States Board of Mediation, or may go for determination to a board of arbitration before which evidence will be massed in truly legal fashion. At all events the atmosphere of collective bargaining, while not necessarily militant, is generally tense, and is liable to develop characteristics uncongenial to the coöperative spirit. Besides, the risk is involved that the coöperative recompense may be lost to view in the midst of wage parleys. Or it may be that the company, having given a coöperative award, will tend to show itself indifferent to claims for an advance in the standard wage rates.

Only once to date, during the history of the coöperative movement on the railroads, have steps been taken to repay the workers through additional wages. When, following the introduction of the plan, the bonus system of wage payment, to be described in detail in chapter xix, was given up on two regions of the Canadian National Railway System, it was decided that all the carrier's shopmen should be granted a supplementary wage rate of two cents an hour. This entailed an outlay approximately equaling the amount that it had formerly cost the railroad to enforce the bonus system. Sir Henry W. Thornton intimated that the company had introduced, and was prepared to continue this flat additional rate, as a reward to the shopmen for the whole-hearted manner in which they had given effect to the coöperative plan. But objections to such action were quickly raised by the Canadian Pacific Railway Company, which inferred that the Canadian National Railway Company, as a member of the Railway Association of Canada, having a working agreement with Division No. 4, had by its two-cent award broken faith with the rest of the association. Meanwhile a plea for higher wages was being urged by the federated shop crafts on Canadian roads, which eventuated in a four-cent increase in mechanics' wages when Division No. 4's agreement with the Railway Association of Canada was revised in January, 1927. During the negotiations preceding this settlement, the Canadian Pacific Railway Company vigorously contended that the two-cent addendum granted on the Canadian National Railway System should be incorporated as part of the four-cent advance, and finally won its point. In consequence the Canadian National Railway Company has been practically barred from giving its coöperating shop workers another supplementary wage award unless it should be willing to drop from the association and negotiate a separate agreement with the shop crafts. For reasons of its own the carrier has been disinclined to withdraw

from the association, and the workers have been loath to surrender what they believe to be the advantages of a national agreement in order to obtain their coöperative recompense by means of
a wage addendum. Accordingly as matters stand, a revival of interest in a supplement to wages need hardly be expected on the
Canadian National Railway System.

It has been freely predicted that under the influence of coöperation, wage negotiations should be conducted with much less
acerbity than formerly between the railroads and the organized
crafts. In verification of this forecast, it may be pointed out that
to date amicable relations have subsisted in all conferences on the
carriers where wage issues have been discussed since they accepted
the plan. Nor has resort been necessary on any railroad to an
outside authority for the settlement of a wage dispute. Whether
relatively higher wages should be hoped for on the carriers
pledged to coöperation than on other organized roads is open to
question. Doubtless when they think a wage advance is due, the
workers on the roads indorsing coöperation should find it easier
to bring management to their point of view. Yet, on the other
hand, their conference committee, having rather extensive knowledge of the carrier's financial condition, might at times be less inclined to press for a wage increase than the committee on another
carrier. Under the wage awards made in 1929 (*vide* chapter v),
the standard rates granted to shopmen on all the carriers practicing coöperation were set very close to the highest paid to the
same class of workers on any organized American railroad. It
appears to be a policy of wisdom for the crafts to be satisfied
with their position under these awards, lest they weaken their
claims for a wage addendum, or other form of money payment as
a recompense for coöperative effort.

### Bearing of Railroads' Economic Condition upon Distribution of Gains.

FAILURE on the part of a carrier, to apportion to the workers a
share of its coöperative surplus by means of a wage addendum,

leaves it the alternative of granting them an extra payment apart from wages. Such extra payment would have certain of the characteristics of a bonus or premium, but would be different in that it would have no direct concern with wage issues. For lack of a better word it might be termed a coöperative honorarium. Otto S. Beyer, Jr., has been consistently of the opinion that if the fair sharing of coöperative gains is to have the significance that should belong to it, the workers should receive a money award, and more recently he has advocated that they be given a payment unrelated to wages. Inability as yet to furnish a standard by which gains may be measured has been Otto S. Beyer, Jr.'s, handicap in advancing his claim, as it has been of other craft officials who have thought alike with him. One carrier only, the Canadian National Railway Company, has unequivocally acknowledged that a surplus has accrued to it through coöperative practice, a share of which, it believes, should fittingly go to its employees. A committee has been appointed under authority of the executive officers of the Baltimore & Ohio Railroad to inquire into the measurement and distribution of coöperative gains, and the report, when completed, will show that carrier's attitude on these issues. The other roads indorsing coöperation have for the most part kept their own counsel on the subject of a surplus, although by no means denying its existence. Before any conclusions are offered respecting an extra money payment to the workers as a reward for coöperation, it will be first essential to discuss briefly the traffic and financial situation of the carriers involved during the past few years.

The business experiences of the Baltimore & Ohio Railroad since 1924 have been mainly governed by the fact that about one-half its regular freight carriage is normally in coal, and that, along with its competitors in the territory which it serves, it has been hit by the decrease in short-distance passenger traffic. Nineteen twenty-six was a good year on this carrier when, consequent upon an enlarged production of bituminous coal, its revenue freight tonnage rose 9.1 per cent as compared with 1925. But in 1927 came the coal miners' strike, and at the same time rate changes to the detriment of the carrier, which, coupled with the effect of poor returns from passenger travel, brought a heavy traffic slump on its lines lasting until the middle of 1928. Revenue freight tonnage fell off 5 per cent in 1927, and for the whole twelve months of 1928 showed another drop of 4.4 per cent. Statistics of the number of passengers carried by the railroad indicate a total decline for the period, 1925–28, of 30.4 per cent. In the face of this adverse traffic situation, it cannot be wondered that the carrier strove to introduce economies in all its departments. That it was successful in its endeavor is reflected by the circumstance that, whereas its operating revenues decreased by approximately twenty million dollars in the years 1927 and 1928, it was able in the same interval to scale down its operating expenses to the extent of seventeen million dollars. The company's operating ratio mounted from 74.3 in 1926 to 75.6 in 1927, but was reduced to the low level of 72.9 in 1928. Regularly each year of the period in question, the road paid a common stock dividend of 5 to 6 per cent. A traffic up trend, which began on its lines in the latter half of 1928, continued during 1929, only to suffer a reverse as depression spread over the country in 1930.

The Chicago & North Western Railway and the Chicago, Milwaukee, St. Paul & Pacific Railroad have each been suffering for a number of years from what they contend is an inadequately remunerative rate structure, and simultaneously have each been losing business through the effects of motor car traffic. Because of difficulties peculiar to itself, the Milwaukee System stopped paying dividends in 1917, and then having gradually slipped to a position where it was unable to meet its current liabilities, was forced to apply for a receivership in 1925. This road's troubles developed when, soon after it had completed its Puget Sound extension to the Pacific Coast, the opening of the Panama Canal offered a competing coast-to-coast water route which hurt it severely as a new solicitor of transcontinental traffic. It found itself unprofitably hauling five loaded cars over its lines eastbound, for every three loaded cars which it moved in traffic westbound. The period of agricultural depression which followed the war so intensified its plight that bankruptcy was inevitable. The receivers placed in charge of the road agreed that its physical state was excellent, but that it was financially handicapped in having a funded debt which was more than twice the size of its capitalization. Remarkable economies introduced particularly in its operating department during the receivership, together with a plan of financial reorganization made effective when the receivership ended in January, 1928, seem to have insured the carrier's solvency in the future. Instead of the customary deficit, an operating surplus of over nine million dollars was recorded for 1928. Economically speaking, the Chicago & North Western Railway was in an almost stationary condition from 1925 to 1928. A slight rise in the amount of revenue freight tonnage carried on its lines during these years was practically offset by diminished returns from passenger traffic. By holding down its operating expenses, however, the carrier lowered its operating ratio from 78.1 in 1926 to 77.9 in 1927, and again to 76.7 in 1928. It has been paying a regular dividend of 4 per cent on its common stock and each year applying a certain sum to its profit and loss account.

Allusion was made in chapter xv to the progressive advances in operating results that have taken place on the Canadian National Railway System since 1923. Nevertheless, this seemingly favorable picture requires an explanation. Of the four units which were amalgamated to form the Canadian National Railway Company in the period, 1918–23, two were in bad financial straits, a third was in receivers' hands, and another, composed of certain government lines, had never paid its way. The system thus started with huge annual obligations, such as interest on its funded debt and on government advances, rentals, etc., which have not yet been met by operating income. In 1923, the first full year of operation, a net deficit of nearly fifty-two million dollars was charged to the people of Canada. Traffic expansion and good management on the system have meant in the intervening years only a reduction in the annual deficit, which by 1927 had been curtailed to the neighborhood of thirty-eight million dollars, stood at less than twenty-five million dollars in 1928 but increased again under bad crop conditions in 1929. With its present capital structure the carrier will remain a burden on the Canadian tax-payer until the annual deficit is wiped out, but before this can be accomplished there is a possibility that the Parliament of Canada may cancel its indebtedness to the Government.

By way of summary, then, it may be stated that during the period under review the position of the carriers pledged to coöperation has been: that the Baltimore & Ohio Railroad has passed through a traffic depression, in the midst of which, however, it never failed to pay its accustomed dividends; that the Milwaukee System has been in bankruptcy from which it has emerged rehabilitated, but with its earning capacity still undetermined; that the Chicago & North Western Railway has been marking time industrially, though never lacking an assured income; and that the Canadian National Railway System, in spite of expanding business, has been merely trimming down its deficits, and hoping for the day when, unless its capital structure be changed, it may discharge all its obligations without government aid. Until 1928, no road, it appears, was in an exactly prosperous condition, a fact which must be considered in deciding whether, since the introduction of coöperation, an attempt might have been made to divide surplus gains with the workers in some form of money payment. The depression of 1930 has again affected the situation.

Obviously it would be both unwise and unreasonable for the workers to ask for any form of money payment as a reward for coöperative effort when their company is in financial trouble. At such a time they must be content if it gives them all the employment possible, and should bend their energies toward helping it out of its predicament. Should they, however, withhold their claim for coöperative recompense in circumstances when the company may be experiencing a serious traffic slump, and yet still be able to declare its customary dividends? Here the principle to be followed is not so clear, although it may be urged that it should not prevent the workers from at least seeking a discussion of their claim. If a conference should result upon the issue, the policy of the company should then be to give the workers a detailed account of its financial condition, when a disposition of their claim should be possible on a basis of mutual understanding. But in a period when the carrier's business is in a generally healthy state and its outlook favorable, unless it should adopt some other satisfactory method of requiting them for their effort, the workers may justifiably expect that it will deal very explicitly with the problem of dividing an equitable portion of its coöperative surplus with them in the form of a money payment. An advantage would lie with the honorarium or extra wage payment, over an addition to wages, in the fact that its amount could be determined by coöperative representatives who would fully canvass the situation on the carrier, and thereafter modify it as circumstances might dictate. The wage addendum, as already noted, could scarcely be dissociated from collective bargaining, and, once paid, would, if necessity should arise, be given up with greater reluctance by the workers.

### *Proposed Method of Estimating the Company's Surplus.*

ALLOTMENT to labor of its fair proportion of the carrier's surplus, needless to state, must be dependent upon the discovery and acceptance of a method whereby the size of the surplus may at least be appraised, if not accurately measured. In this connection an interesting suggestion has been advanced by A. J. Thomas, Assistant to the General Supervisor of Shop Methods, on the Canadian National Railway System. Well aware from experience of the limitations set upon a compilation of coöperative gains by a method of integration, he has proposed that an evaluation of the carrier's surplus might be attempted through an observation of its statistics of operation. More particularly he believes that a basis of measuring possible economic improvements resulting from coöperation might be found in an examination of the year-by-year levels of the carrier's operating ratio. The significance of this proposal will be better understood if a study is made of the system that has been employed by the Southern Railway Company,[1] of awarding a bonus to certain classes of its employees, when the results of their operating efficiency in a given year have compared favorably to a predetermined test ratio. A carrier's operating ratio is the figure obtained by dividing all the expenses directly charged to operation in its accounts by the sum of its operating revenues. A ratio of 75, for example, would indicate that it has cost the railroad $75 to provide services that have brought in a revenue of $100. To make A. J. Thomas' proposal effective, it would be necessary to analyze the contributions toward establishing the operating ratio for each year, of the individual department or departments practicing coöperation.

The initial difficulty involved in employing this method would be to assign its proper weight to each of the various factors that in any given year might affect the level of the operating ratio. As a matter of fact, the ratio might rise from one year to the next, and yet during that time the carrier might have bettered its operating position. The ratio on the Canadian National Railway System for the year 1926 stood at 82.5. For 1927 it had mounted to 85.2 and then declined to 81.9 for 1928. The high figure for 1927 was chiefly traceable to wage increases, to the extension of stone ballasting and the use of heavier rails in road maintenance, and to added fuel costs. Expenditures in the mechanical department actually fell in relation to operating revenues during 1927. A thoroughgoing analysis of the operating ratios for two suc-

1 *Vide* chap. xx.

cessive years would always be essential before it would be possible to compare them properly and to arrive at a decision concerning the results of coöperation. Allowance would also have to be made for the fact, as noted in chapter xiv, that the influence of coöperative endeavor in one department often spreads to affect performance in another. Again, it would have to be borne in mind that many coöperative suggestions refer to the outlay for new structures and shop machinery, which is itemized in accounts that do not appear in the list of operating expenses.

### Vacations with Pay as a Reward for Coöperation.

BLOCKED, in the attempt which it made in 1926 to give its mechanical craftsmen a two cents an hour addition to wages, the Canadian National Railway Company has in the meantime sought to reward them in another way. Early in 1928, craft officers on the carrier advised Sir Henry W. Thornton that the shopmen in its employ would be greatly delighted if, in acknowledgment of their coöperative effort, it could be arranged that they should receive a holiday with pay. Advocacy of vacations with pay for wage-earners, it may be remarked, is by no means a novelty in American industry,[2] but as yet has borne somewhat meager results except in a few trades such as printing, fire fighting, and street railway transportation. If the Canadian National Railway Company should agree to its shop workers' plea in this matter, it would be the first among railroads in the United States or Canada to introduce the vacation with pay principle among any worker group. Sir Henry W. Thornton did not delay long in assenting to the proposition, although not all his staff at the outset were friendly to the idea. When permission was granted to craft officers to give out information that it would be the carrier's purpose to allow its shopmen in Canada a vacation with pay, they decided to postpone their announcement until the annual convention of

[2] Cf. "Vacations with Pay for Industrial Workers," *Monthly Labor Review,* September, 1927, p. 49.

Division No. 4 should meet at Winnipeg, Manitoba, in April. Because its lines in the United States were faced with a different form of competition from those in Canada and for other reasons, the carrier had come to the conclusion that it would not immediately apply the award on the Grand Trunk Railway System or elsewhere outside Canada. However, as the convention of Division No. 4 was on the eve of assembling, Sir Henry W. Thornton was summoned to a conference with the Dominion Cabinet, where, if the stories that were in circulation may be believed, he was forced to put up a grim struggle for the vacation with pay principle, which to certain cabinet ministers was too revolutionary from an industrial standpoint. Whereas Sir Henry had been ready to accord the workers a two weeks' holiday with pay, under cabinet pressure he had compromised and the vacation time was shortened to one week. By the terms of the award, all Canadian shopmen with two years' seniority, whose crafts were embraced under the coöperative plan, were to receive the holiday during the summer months of 1928. To lessen interference with production, different vacation dates were arranged for the shops throughout the country. The award was again made in 1929, and bids fair to become a permanent institution on the carrier.

Restoration to its federated shop crafts, by the Baltimore & Ohio Railroad, of the prized rule originally embodied in the national agreement respecting overtime rates for work done on Sundays and holidays, may also be cited as a special melioration of employment conditions under coöperation. This overtime rule, involving the payment of time and one-half wages for all regularly assigned work performed on Sundays and holidays, was excluded from the first agreement signed between the company and the federated crafts in 1921 following government control. In appreciation of benefits derived from the workers' active participation in coöperation, the company negotiated the reinclusion of the rule in its system agreement with them during a conference held in September, 1926. Whether the carriers might be able to recompense their workers fully for coöperative effort by various methods of bettering their employment conditions without resort to a money payment, opens an interesting field for discussion. The desideratum of the moment is a studied plan of effectively estimating the value of the surplus accruing to each railroad company. Once a more definite conception is gained of the size of the surplus, apportionment of the workers' share of it can easily be made in a manner acceptable to both workers and management.

# Chapter XVII

## Apprentice Training under Coöperation

SYSTEMATIZED training of young men for service on the American railroads by methods of apprenticeship applies only in the maintenance of equipment department. It is true that prospective train service or traffic department employees may be given special instruction in the classes of work they are to perform, and be examined in relation to them, but nowhere on the railroads are they indentured as apprentices. A wide range of difference exists between the methods of apprentice training authorized by carriers for their shop workers, some of which are still rather primitive in type, and others quite elaborate, though all are much alike with respect to a few basic principles. On carriers in the United States where the mechanical trades are organized, the joint system agreements drawn up have continued in the main the apprenticeship rules set forth in the shop crafts' national agreement of 1919. These system agreements stipulate that from the time they are indentured until they have attained the status of journeymen, regular apprentices shall have served a period of four years, and helper apprentices a period of three years in their trade, with a minimum of 290 days in each calendar year. The rules enforced on Canadian carriers also follow those of the shop crafts' national agreement, except that they require a term of service one year longer both for regular and helper apprentices.

A well-developed plan of apprentice training, it may be argued, should provide an incentive, rather than a deterrent, to the entrance of young men into the railroad shop trades. There are always some who will fear the rigors of systematized methods of instruction, but the great majority may be expected to appreciate the advantages which an all-round preparation for craftsmanship will give them. Generally speaking, carriers have had variable experiences in enlisting apprentices for the mechanical department. At certain stations, more often those located at larger urban centers, they have occasionally been compelled to make use of special instrumentalities to attract enough applicants for admission to the trades to satisfy their requirements. At other stations, more often where they have a shop with an accredited reputation in a smaller community, they may have a waiting list of aspiring applicants and can institute a policy of selection. When the shop workers at a station are chiefly "home guards," the crafts tend to be more or less self-perpetuating; that is, fathers bring their sons or other relatives into their own or an associated shop trade. Usually on American railroads, it is easiest to recruit apprentices for the crafts of machinists, electricians, and sheet metal workers. The boiler maker and blacksmith trades on the whole have not the same allurement for the average young man, partly because they are known to be physically more exacting, and partly because they have been thinned to such a degree by the mechanization of industry. Again the combination of circumstances that freight carmen receive lower wage rates than do other shop mechanics, and cannot shift as readily to industries outside the transportation field, makes entrance into this section of the carman's craft less desirable.

Problems of apprentice training on the organized carriers are dealt with by specific rules on the subject contained in joint system agreements. Yet on the roads subscribing to coöperation such problems have engaged the attention also of coöperative committees. In this instance it is not intended that a coöperative committee shall usurp any of the authority of the conference committee on the carrier, although its recommendations can hardly fail to influence the policies of the conference committee. In other words, the conference committee through the system agreement still establishes the basic regulations governing apprenticeship on the carrier, but may have its views on the matter shaped and modified by coöperative advice. Especially have coöperative

committees evinced an interest in the details of the plan of technical education employed in the carrier's mechanical department by
means of which apprentices may obtain an adequate knowledge
of their trade. As the apprentice training system on the Baltimore & Ohio Railroad has been largely molded into its present
form by coöperative agency, it will be examined at some length.
Note will also be made of certain expressions of opinion on questions of apprentice training that have been delivered in the coöperative meetings of other roads.

### Establishment of the Baltimore & Ohio Railroad's Training Plan.

PREVIOUS to the introduction of union-management coöperation
on its lines, the Baltimore & Ohio Railroad had for a period of
years, like many other American carriers, trained its apprentices
in shop schools.[1] Young men, started in a trade, received their
practical training under one supervisor after another at a repair
point, and in addition were given technical training in classes
presided over by apprentice instructors on the company's pay
roll. Classroom methods of training were in vogue at eleven of the
company's more important maintenance of equipment stations.
Apprentices were sent to school for two hours a day, twice a
week. The company provided the books, instruments, and classroom facilities necessary for technical instruction, and apportioned wages to the apprentices for the four hours a week spent
in school. However, the classroom method of imparting technical
knowledge, as employed on the Baltimore & Ohio Railroad, did not
give satisfaction, with the result that when the shop crafts' strike
occurred in 1922, the company took occasion to abandon it.
C. N. Fullerton, at present supervisor of apprentice training on
the Baltimore & Ohio, has stated that the carrier discovered as

[1] Many facts stated in this chapter with reference to apprentice training on
the Baltimore & Ohio Railroad have been taken from an article on that subject written by C. N. Fullerton which appeared in the year book of System
Federation No. 30 for 1927.

weaknesses in the classroom system: that coördinated effort was lacking between its eleven schools, each of which has its own individual method of training; that the apprentices located at smaller points were unable to participate in the advantages; that supervisors objected to school hours in the plant, since apprentices were often badly needed for work operations during the time set aside for instruction; that apprentices on the average did not take seriously the opportunities provided for their technical training; that classroom performance was not a matter of record; that only the more ambitious of the apprentices appeared to receive the real benefits of training; and lastly that, in proportion to the results attained, the system imposed too heavy a financial burden upon the company.

Following the strike, apprentice training was in abeyance on the Baltimore & Ohio Railroad for a period of more than three years. The federated shop crafts meanwhile kept importuning the company for a new and adequate system of technical training, a plea to which management gave ready ear, but neither it nor the workers had a plan to offer. Eventually during the progress of a joint system coöperative meeting, held on October 6, 1925, Otto S. Beyer, Jr., ventured the opinion that, after a full and careful investigation of the subject, it should be possible to resume apprentice training on the road upon an entirely different and more satisfactory basis. At the suggestion of Col. G. H. Emerson, chief of motive power and equipment, who presided, a committee of four, equally representative of management and the crafts, was selected to study intensively the problems of apprentice training, and to report in favor of a plan of technical instruction that would suit conditions in the carrier's mechanical department. The personnel of this committee was: A. G. Walther, assistant supervisor of shops, and J. E. Cromwell who has been an apprentice instructor under the classroom system, representing the management; and C. N. Fullerton, general chairman of the machinists' district lodge, and K. W. Green, general chairman of the electrical workers' system council, representing the men. Three months were spent by the committee in visiting shops on other railroads where systems of apprentice training were observed, and in consultation with institutions that furnished correspondence courses of technical instruction to industrial enterprises. Consequent upon its survey, the committee recommended that the Baltimore & Ohio Railroad ask the Railway Educational Bureau of Omaha, Nebraska, to prepare a systematic study plan for the training of apprentices on its lines, fitted to its own peculiar needs. This bureau which had originally been set up with the approval of E. H. Harriman, transportation magnate, to facilitate the educational policies of the Union Pacific Railway, had upon Harriman's death become a private agency under the direction of D. C. Buell. The committee's recommendation was presented to the shop crafts comprising System Federation No. 30, each of which indorsed it in turn, and was then given final ratification by staff officers of the carrier. The new apprentice training plan went into effect on the Baltimore & Ohio Railroad on September 1, 1926.

*How Apprentices Are Instructed along Technical Lines.*

ADMINISTRATION of the Baltimore & Ohio Railroad's apprentice training plan is centralized at the offices of its chief of motive power in Baltimore, Maryland, with A. G. Walther as the ranking staff officer in charge. C. N. Fullerton acts as general supervisor of the plan in operation. Apprentices in training are taught by traveling instructors who follow a regular itinerary in visiting repair points. A full-time resident instructor has been appointed for the large Mount Clare shop, while at the Glenwood and Cumberland shops the company's draftsmen give a portion of their time to apprentice training. Complete records of the educational performance of each apprentice are retained on file at Baltimore until he has reached the goal of journeymanship or has been dropped from service.

Like other carriers that have instituted progressive systems of apprentice education, the Baltimore & Ohio Railroad has aimed at establishing in its plan a reasonable balance between the practical and the technical sides of training. Questions relating to the form of practical instructions which apprentices shall receive in the shop, are subject exclusively to negotiation between the carrier and System Federation No. 30. Assignment of apprentices to different classes of work during their three or four years of service, in order that they may be well instructed in all branches of their trade, has been embodied as part of the special rules for each craft contained in the carrier's joint working agreement with the federation. On the other hand, though one particular rule, as will be seen, in the joint agreement has been devoted to the question of making technical instruction compulsory, the main details connected with this form of training have been left for handling by mutual consent of the company and federation to the administrators of the plan and to the management of the Railway Educational Bureau. These together have decided that if apprentices are to become efficient journeymen, they should have a substantial grounding in mathematics and mechanical drawing. No matter then what trade an apprentice on the Baltimore & Ohio Railroad may have as his objective, he is always scheduled to receive a great amount of preliminary training in both these subjects.

Whenever an apprentice has been accepted into service on the Baltimore & Ohio Railroad, the Railway Educational Bureau is notified, and begins to transmit lesson papers to him through the mail. The apprentice must study his lessons outside working hours, and is required to write out answers to a list of questions accompanying each, which he returns by mail to the bureau. In order to keep abreast of the schedule for his course he must complete and receive a passing grade on two lessons a month. The bureau, after it has corrected and graded a test, remits it to the apprentice, and at the same time sends a record of his standing to the station where he works and to Baltimore. The first lesson is of an introductory character, giving the apprentice an outline history of the transportation industry, and its relationship to other phases of economic life. In fact, lessons of more general import are interspersed here and there among those that are distinctly technical, for the purpose of relieving the student apprentice's mind and broadening his vision. The training in mathematics leads by gradual stages from the more elementary principles, until the mensuration of plane figures has been reached, and the apprentice next finds himself studying the basic principles of mechanics. Meanwhile, under the heading of mechanical drawing he has been taught to read blue prints, to make freehand sketches of shop work, to complete simple and more intricate mechanical drawings, and eventually to excel in primary forms of machine drawing. During his third and fourth years of service the apprentice is given technical instruction bearing definitely on the problems of the shop craft to which he hopes to gain admission as a journeyman. Throughout these years he will of necessity make use of the knowledge of mathematics and mechanical drawing acquired in the earlier training period.

It must be stressed, however, that the apprentice training plan on the Baltimore & Ohio Railroad is in no sense a mere combination of scheduled shop practice with a correspondence course of technical instruction. The traveling instructors, and at certain points the resident instructors, establish close contacts with the individual apprentices, assisting them to grapple with their difficulties and stimulating them to increased endeavor. With the latest performance records of apprentices in their possession, traveling instructors make an effort once a month, at least, to spend from one to several days at each station under their jurisdiction. On their arrival at a station, they single out for special attention the young men who are weaker in their studies or more careless in their attitude. The instructor goes over papers on which a low grade has been obtained with the student, pointing out reasons for failure, and explaining worrisome problems. When apprentices become delinquent with their lessons through carelessness or indifference, the instructor discusses with them the penalties that will be imposed, and tries to dissuade them from laxity. Students whose records have at first been most discouraging have sometimes shown relatively fine progress later on as a result of this personal help.

*Punitive Methods of Enforcing the Training Plan.*

NOTEWORTHY in connection with the system of apprentice training on the Baltimore & Ohio Railroad have been the means taken to render its technical features compulsory. With a view to the maintenance of rigid educational standards on the carrier which will simultaneously afford protection to craftsmanship, the shop trades have eagerly agreed to make technical training effective by punitive methods of enforcement. To effect this, Rule No. 38 was incorporated in the system agreement between the federated shop crafts and the carrier, negotiated in conference on September 1, 1926. A revision of the rule drawn up on February 28, 1927, gave its terms a somewhat more drastic form. The first clause of Rule No. 38 in true pedagogic manner specifies that "regular apprentices who show no aptitude to learn the trade or assimilate the technical instruction furnished by the company" shall be dropped from service. Helper apprentices, similarly deficient, shall be "set back to helping," with their seniority, however, unimpaired if they have not been in training longer than a calendar year.

Rule No. 38 then indicates that a minimum of two lessons a month, on which passing grades have been secured, shall be demanded of each apprentice, and that whoever does not keep up to that schedule shall be considered delinquent and accordingly not in good standing. Nothing in the rule prevents a student from submitting more than two lessons a month, although it is considered undesirable that he should get too far ahead of the schedule. An apprentice is allowed to become two months in arrears with his lessons before steps are taken to discipline him. Even when delinquent to that extent, it is possible for him to clear his record by forwarding to the bureau his uncompleted lessons in addition to those which are currently required. However, the rule provides that after an apprentice has been two months in arrears he shall be given a hearing before the officer in charge at the local point, where all the facts in his case will be reviewed.

The hearing which the apprentice receives is conducted under Rule No. 32 in the system agreement which was negotiated in 1924 particularly to govern the disciplining of employees. As the local officer is aware that the apprentices who come before him can still make up their lost ground, he generally uses these hearings as an opportunity to impart friendly advice and possibly warn them of the consequences of further delinquencies. When a young man, otherwise promising, is actually finding the technical work too hard, renewed efforts in his behalf, by the traveling or resident instructor, will follow a hearing. The accumulation of three months' uncleared delinquencies brings the penalty that the student is no longer retained on the company's apprentice rolls. Still if this is the first occasion on which he has fallen behind, the way is open for him to seek readmission to service by following a prescribed course of action. To save himself he must, within ten days after his removal from the rolls, pledge his willingness in the future to abide by all the company's training requirements, and send on whatever lessons he is short to the Railway Educational Bureau. Should he succeed in clearing his record, the bureau transmits information to that effect to the chief of motive power at Baltimore, with whom rests the final decision as to his reinstatement. If taken back, in case he should ever again accumulate three months' delinquencies he will be permanently removed from the service.

In support of the Baltimore & Ohio Railroad's plan of technical training, it is claimed that it gives to all apprentices similar opportunities for instruction, irrespective of the size or location of the maintenance of equipment point where they are employed. The Railway Educational Bureau, it is stated, treats each student alike, and the traveling instructors time their stay at repair stations to accord with the number of apprentices enrolled and their individual capacities. The lack of coördination which existed under former classroom methods on the Baltimore & Ohio Railroad has been obviated, and the carrier's apprentice force knit into a composite whole. Moreover, the objectionable features of the ordinary correspondence school system of training have been dispelled, it is said, through the regular visits of the company's staff of instructors. However, the training plan on the Baltimore & Ohio Railroad would lose its effectiveness, it is believed, unless strictly enforced by punitive regulations. The value of the compulsory principle in education has been long and amply demonstrated in America in the free, tax-maintained school systems. Why, then, it is contended, should not a carrier such as the Baltimore & Ohio Railroad, desirous of establishing a high standard of technical instruction among its trade learners, adopt compulsion within its province after the fashion of the state? Concurrence of opinion between management and shop workers with respect to enforcement is taken as a guarantee that there will be no mitigation of the penalties promised. Besides, owing to the fact that the apprentice is first checked by means of a fair hearing, and then given a chance for reinstatement when dropped from the roll, it is thought that the method of enforcement is not unduly harsh. Records of the carrier show that of a total of 650 to 700 apprentices on its rolls, only 11 were finally dropped from service because of arrearages in the first six months of 1929. Those on schedule with their lessons during the same period numbered a little better than 85 per cent. The Baltimore & Ohio Railroad declines to admit to training as a regular apprentice anyone who cannot pass a test that might be given to a sixth-grade grammar school student. Actually a large and increasing proportion of the young men employed on the carrier have attended a high school or polytechnic institution.

The shop crafts' agreement with the Baltimore & Ohio Railroad also provides by Rule No. 37 for the training, in addition to regular and helper apprentices, of a group known as special apprentices. This group, according to the rule, must never be more than 5 per cent of the total number of apprentices on the carrier. Special apprentices shall enter between the ages of eighteen and twenty-six, and must have an accredited standing from certain recognized technical schools in Baltimore, Pittsburgh, or Chicago, or have been college trained. They are required to serve three years at practical operations distributed among the various trades represented at a repair point, and then in their fourth year to attach themselves to the craft in which they choose to become journeymen. It is intended that special apprentices because of their grounding in technical subjects, and their widely diversified shop training, should develop into mechanics who are particularly eligible for advancement to supervisory or official positions. At present from 2 to 3 per cent only of all apprentices on the carrier are enrolled in this group.

### Coöperative Interest in Apprenticeship on Other Carriers.

In contradistinction to experiences on the Baltimore & Ohio Railroad, the Canadian National Railway System has been employing the classroom method of apprentice training with quite evident success. Accordingly, when issues relating to apprentice education have been considered by the latter within recent years, it has decided merely to revise and modernize its existing plan. In 1927, the carrier's executive board appointed a subcommittee to inquire into problems affecting the education of its workers and to present a report on the subject. The subcommittee felt duty-bound to carry its report, in so far as it bore upon the mechanical department, before the joint system coöperative committee of the railroad when it assembled at Montreal, Quebec, in January,

1928. The system committee voted approval of the findings embodied in the report, commenting especially upon the value of its proposal that an educational officer be appointed with jurisdiction over the instruction of apprentices on all the company's lines.

While it advised a continuance of the apprentice training plan already operative in the mechanical department of the Canadian National Railway System, the subcommittee stressed the importance of having uniform methods of instruction at all repair points. The educational officer whose appointment it recommended should, it believed, be responsible for the character of the textbooks authorized and for their revision, whenever desirable. He should also have charge of the preparation of examination papers to be submitted periodically to apprentices in training, and should supervise the marking and correction of them. The report asserted that care should be observed in working out the details of the plan in order that classroom instruction might be made to synchronize effectively with practical shop training. It would be well, however, if the policy of standardizing the apprentice training plan on the carrier should be undertaken gradually, lest the program of apprentices already indentured should be disrupted, and textbooks and classroom equipment needlessly scrapped that were still serviceable.

With the object of safeguarding the interests of apprentices enrolled at lesser repair points where classroom instruction is impossible, it has been the practice on the Canadian National Railway System to transfer them to larger points where they are given technical training for a period of two years. At the Stratford, Ontario, locomotive repair shop, a certain percentage of the 85 apprentices enrolled in 1928 came from nearby stations on the line. The Stratford shop is of the "home guard" type, in which 80 per cent of the workers are property owners. The railroad shop trades are in high repute among the young men of the city, and as a result the shop superintendent generally has a waiting list of 100 or more applicants. At intervals, from 8 to 10 of these are subjected to tests, on the basis of which 2 or 3 are accepted for indenture. The prize-winning mechanical drawings of the Stratford students have been greatly admired at the Canadian National Exhibition held in Toronto, Ontario.

A rather lengthy dissertation dealing more especially with the training opportunities of coach carmen apprentices was presented to the car department's coöperative committee at the Chicago, Illinois, shop of the Chicago & North Western Railway in 1927. Complaint was made that the coach carman apprentice received too little individual attention from supervisors who knew that he would be but a short time in their department before being shifted elsewhere and that, therefore, they gave him "any kind of a job, just to keep him busy." It was suggested that, wherever possible, the apprentice should be assigned to do practical work with a mechanic who would take an interest in his welfare, that he should be appointed to perform tasks of a productive character, and that he should be encouraged to use the tools of his craft. The local craft committee, it was urged, should watch carefully the progress of each apprentice, ascertaining from him periodically whether he thought that he was getting proper treatment. In this way, difficulties might be smoothed away before a real grievance would arise. The coöperative committee referred these criticisms and recommendations to the railroad's vice-president in charge of personnel.

## Chapter XVIII

## Methods of Incentive Wage Payment Related to Coöperation

FROM the point of view both of production control and material handling, it has been demonstrated that the mechanical craft unions indorsing coöperation have not only recognized, but to a rather noteworthy extent have given practical effect to the principles of scientific management at railroad repair stations. Will this mark the limit of the crafts' acceptance of the principles of scientific management, or is it conceivable that they may find other features of value in its general program? Will they, for example, continue to bargain for wage rates fixed on a strictly time basis, or is there a likelihood that they will modify their stand on this issue? If methods of remunerating workers in American industries be examined historically, it will be seen that during the last ten years or more a significant trend has occurred away from the time wage system of payment, and toward the establishment of piecework, task and bonus, or premium systems in its stead. Such changes, it is true, have mainly taken place in unorganized industries, but have made sufficient headway in organized territory to warrant attention in this volume.

### Methods of Wage Payment Favored.

SCIENTIFIC management does not advocate any particular method of wage payment. Its exponents express the opinion that wages should be allotted according to whatever plan may seem best suited to the operations of an industry at a given period in its development. Preference, however, has always been stated for some form either of piecework, task and bonus, or premium system functioning in conformity with an accurate technique of work measurement. An industrial engineer, asked to devise a wage plan for an enterprise, has customarily given it a system which to his way of thinking has appeared most advantageous for it at the time. In consequence a great variety of systems of wage payment have come into existence, having the imprimatur of scientific management and classifiable as to their leading purposes, but differing widely in detail. That piecework systems have been more freely applied than task and bonus or premium systems within recent years, may be gathered from the evidences.

American trade-unions, thinking to bind their membership more securely together by the establishment of uniform working conditions, have for the most part favored the payment to each worker of a minimum standard hourly wage rate, according to his status in a craft or subdivision of a craft. During the war and for a short period after, when in a position to enforce their demands, the unions fought for the extension of time work, and succeeded in eliminating many piecework and other systems which they considered objectionable. Still it should be borne in mind that an important minority of organized workers have for a long time been receiving piecework scales, notably in the coal mining, needlecraft, boot and shoe, pottery, and glassware industries and, to a degree, in the metal industry. Moreover, there are signs that labor has begun to turn its attention to the theoretical aspects of wages as a problem in distribution, and is growing less dogmatic in the enunciation of time wage doctrines. In its forty-seventh annual convention at Los Angeles, California, in 1927, the American Federation of Labor set forth its already famous social wage theory, in which it claimed that the workers should be allowed a proportionate share from the increasing effectiveness of industry. Only by this means, it was declared, would they be continuously able to buy back the products of industry and thereby give it stability. In formulating this theory the federation, according to its own announcement, was bent on raising labor's wage aims to the higher plane of social justice. Is it not probable that, as the federation attempts to enforce such a doctrine through collective bargaining, it may be led to a new definition of policy on the subject of methods of wage payment? Organized labor has always accepted wage differences between crafts or divisions of a craft, based on length of training and trade skill, irksomeness of toil, physical strain, or unusual hazards. Yet its majority opinion in America has been opposed to wage differences within a classification of work based on the personal fitness and application of the worker. Some idea of the reasons why organized labor has clung to time work will become manifest in the following discussion of methods of wage payment, in which a brief effort will be made to show how union-management coöperation might function under a piecework or other incentive wage plan.

### The Grand Trunk Railway System's Bonus Plan.

BY way of preface to such a discussion, and in order to supply material for argument, an account may first be given of the kind of task and bonus plan which was operative at repair points on two regions of the Canadian National Railway System, at the time when it officially accepted coöperation. This wage plan really had its origin in the mechanical department of the Grand Trunk Railway System, years before its inclusion as a part of the Canadian Government's lines. As early as 1903, J. C. Garden, now general superintendent of motive power and car equipment of the central region of the Canadian National Railway System, became interested in the incentive wage proposals of efficiency engineers in the United States, and decided to formulate a plan of payment that might be suitably introduced at the Grand Trunk Railway System's shop in Toronto, Ontario, where he was general foreman. Originally he had in mind the adoption of a modified premium plan and has preferred that it should be so entitled, but as his modification bears no close resemblance to any well-known premium plan, and as it has been regularly called a bonus plan or system in negotiations, the term, "bonus," has been applied to it throughout this volume. The plan evolved by J. C. Garden was still immature when next extended in 1907 to the carrier's shop at Stratford, Ontario. By 1911, however, when taken to the shop at Battle Creek, Michigan, with the help of other administrators it had already acquired a more scientific character, and in this form was soon established at the remaining maintenance of equipment stations on the system.

The principle of work measurement or job analysis by means of time study was definitely embodied in the Grand Trunk Railway System's bonus plan. A time was fixed by actual demonstration for nearly all operations performed in reconditioning train cars and locomotives on the carrier's lines. Altogether more than three thousand distinct operations were subjected to time study, and scheduled for reference in the determination of wages. Each worker in the mechanical department who came under the plan was guaranteed a basic hourly wage rate, whether he performed his operation in the allotted time or not. But should his production pace be faster than the schedule he might earn a bonus in addition to his wage as a reward for efficiency. When, for example, an operation was timed to be done in an hour, and the worker accomplished it in forty-eight minutes, a saving of twelve minutes in the hour was reckoned to his credit, and a bonus paid to him equal to 20 per cent of his regular wage.

As the output of each shop worker was checked in accordance with the time allowed for the operation which he performed, a large-sized staff had to be retained for this purpose as well as for making adjustments in the schedule. The administration of the plan, therefore, was rather expensive. It was the practice to time operations with the end in view that any mechanic possessed of average skill could keep up with the schedule for his type of work. In this way the plan, though it tended to weed out the unfit, did not overtax those who were satisfied with the hourly wage. As a matter of fact most workers whose operations were scheduled earned a bonus under the plan. In a given year at the Stratford, Ontario, shop, bonuses were accumulated which on the average amounted to from 17 to 18 per cent of the basic wages paid, and some workers were adding as much as 25 per cent to their regular

wage income. Because the Canadian Pacific Railway Company
at this time paid higher scales to its shop mechanics than did the
Grand Trunk Railway System, surprise was often expressed that
the latter could hold its men. The explanation lay, of course, in
the circumstance that the Grand Trunk workers were able
through their bonus earnings to make up all, or more than the
difference in the wages paid by the two roads.

In so far as difficulties beset the operation of the bonus plan on
the Grand Trunk Railway System they were due, it has been
claimed, rather to lack of capacity in administration than to
fraud or partiality. Mechanical officers, then on the railroad,
state that the checkers and adjusters employed were not properly
qualified for their duties, and as a result value was not received
for the money expended. For this reason local complaints were
often heard against the execution of the plan, although in general it apparently proved satisfactory both to management and
men. The company's train car and locomotive inspectors, and certain other shop workers, whose operations could not be properly
scheduled, were outside the plan and were remunerated on a time
basis. As described in chapter vii, after the Grand Trunk Railway System had become part of the Canadian National Railway
System the view was officially expressed that production might
be increased if the bonus plan were established generally in the
mechanical department of the consolidated lines. Time workers
employed in the Atlantic and western regions of the carrier, however, were in no mood to agree to this, and the alternate proposal
to enter the coöperative movement won the day in the councils of
both management and labor. The bonus plan and coöperation
functioned together in a few major shops of the system until the
bonus plan was definitely abandoned in 1926.

*Arguments For and Against Incentive Wage Systems.*

Most task and bonus or premium plans of wage payment are
more complex in character than the one existing for many years

on the Grand Trunk Railway System, but nevertheless all are much alike in the purposes which they serve. Each assures payment to the worker of a basic wage rate irrespective of whether or not he performs his task within the time specified, and each, according to its own appointed method, awards him a bonus or premium for production related in some way to his attainment of the standard set. A piece rate plan differs from these in that it does not guarantee to the least efficient workers any basic return. Still if the rates set for piecework have been adjusted according to a scientific method of time study, the average worker should, it is claimed, always be able to earn a standard wage. Under the piece rate system most commonly applied, a uniform rate is paid for each piece or unit of work, no matter what may be the worker's output. Under a differential piece rate system, once the worker attains or exceeds a certain standard of output, the rate for each unit immediately advances.

Task and bonus, premium and piece rate systems of wage payment have been attacked by organized labor on many counts.[1] The wage distinctions, it has been asserted, which these systems allow between men of the same occupational group introduces the "contest principle" among them, causing one to be suspicious and envious of the other, striking "at the root of work-shop ethics," and weakening the whole structure of collective bargaining. Overspeeding, it has been contended, is naturally induced among the workers with its accompanying evil, overfatigue, while employers are tempted to hire "rushers" who will set a fast pace and eventually cheapen labor costs. Men unable to maintain the pace, who often are skilled workers past the prime of life, are heartlessly dropped from employment. The emphasis laid upon quantity rather than quality of output tends, it has been said, to make work increasingly monotonous and to destroy the workers' initiative. Under a task and bonus system, the task may be made so difficult to attain that the bonus given in no sense rewards the

[1] Robert Franklin Hoxie, *Scientific Management and Labor,* pp. 15 ff.

workers for their pains, and the company reaps the main advantage. Under a piece rate system, on the other hand, rate cutting may be systematically practiced whenever the workers show a high record of efficiency which means that in the long run more work will be done for the same or less pay. No incentive wage system, the critics have affirmed, affords a progressive method of wage apportionment, justly recompensing the workers for their added effort.

The way in which piecework and other incentive wage systems were voted out of existence in the mechanical department of railroads in the United States during the period of government control has been described in chapter vi. It may be pointed out, however, that the declarations of organized labor against these systems had little to do with starting the move for their abolition at that time. It is very doubtful, indeed, if the question of their abolition would have been raised at all had it not been for a wage controversy that had already arisen over the interpretation of Supplement No. 4 to General Order No. 27, issued by the railroad administration. The wage determinations of Supplement No. 4 had been construed to apply almost entirely to time workers, only guaranteeing to pieceworkers that they would not receive less than the rates of pay fixed for mechanical craftsmen of their class. But many pieceworkers had previously earned up to these rates, and therefore were incensed because they had not been given increases proportionate to those received by time workers. To make the discrimination against them, as they considered it, more obnoxious, a retroactive clause in Supplement No. 4 had awarded time workers six months' back pay. The protests which poured in to the Director General of Railroads on these issues took the piecework and other incentive wage systems for granted, and were in no way concerned with the problem as to whether they should be abolished or retained. It was only when a campaign for their abolition was later inaugurated that all the evils said to belong to them were vigorously related.

No more than an abridged idea can be given of the counter-defense offered by advocates of scientific management for the systems of wage payment which they prefer. While they have admitted that hazards of overspeeding will be found where workers are stimulated to greater endeavor by incentive wages, this danger, they have contended, should be largely neutralized and a check put on self-driving and overfatigue by scientific management's policy of standardizing equipment and work performance. Rate-cutting, though it may occur, is not, they have stated, in accordance with the principles of scientific management unless it accompanies a real change in the instructions governing work and in the time set for performing it. Arbitrary and unfair methods of rate-cutting are strictly under the ban of scientific management, and must be regarded as signifying a lapse in business morality.[2] They have stressed the assertion that scientific management substitutes exact knowledge for guesswork in setting standards of performance, and for this reason they have argued that the worker will be remunerated under a piecework or other incentive wage system in direct proportion to his efficiency.[3] As a rule, they have frankly acknowledged that these systems of payment tend to displace the poorest class of workers in an industry, but they have expressed the belief that such workers are likely to drop out of their own accord rather than wait for dismissal. They have urged that if a policy of selection is followed when workers are hired, incompetents will not be let into the industry with the result that in the end few need be discharged.

### How Coöperation Might Be Related to an Incentive Wage System.

In spite of organized labor's past indictment of incentive wage systems, may not a reconciliation be possible between it and advocates of scientific management on this issue? Although or-

2 Robert Franklin Hoxie, *Scientific Management and Labor,* pp. 161–162.
3 *Ibid.,* pp. 141–142.

ganized labor has bewailed the "contest principle" which piece-work and other incentive wage systems have been charged with engendering, an examination will show that it has been centering its attack on the unjust and discriminatory rates and time allowances which allegedly have been fixed under these systems, rather than on the fact that they propose to award varying incomes in accordance with efficiency to men employed at the same class of work. Actually, then, it may be concluded that it has been the problem of rate adjustments and time allowances, which more than anything else has caused labor bodies to be hesitant about accepting incentive wage systems. Trade-unions have generally thought that in the negotiation of wage bargains they have been executing their main function. The time wage has had for them a certain definiteness that has made its negotiation peculiarly attractive. It has meant uniform earnings for each worker based upon the productivity of his group as a whole. Under incentive wage systems, as the mechanization of industry goes forward and production becomes easier, the employer naturally seeks a downward revision of rates or a shortening of time schedules for the operations affected. Here it is, the unions have argued, that wage earners are likely to find themselves bargaining at a serious disadvantage. Their personal skill and application tend to be discounted in the negotiations, whereas the contributions of new equipment and methods of operation stand at a premium. Furthermore, the rates or time allowances fixed for single operations, included under the same class of work, eventually become disproportionate, which leads to bickerings and animosities within each labor group.

To present-day exponents of scientific management, labor's fear that it will suffer when rates are being adjusted or time allowances modified seems to be greatly exaggerated. Fair rates and time schedules, they insist, can be set and maintained, no matter what changes in processing should occur, by adherence to a scientific plan of work measurement. Convictions gained over a period of years, however, incline a large section of organized labor to put little faith in such a statement. Apparently the only effective way to satisfy labor that judicious rates and time schedules can be fixed, is to allow for its collaboration when work is being measured. This does not merely imply that workers shall be privileged "to stand around and watch" operations as they are being studied, but that the representatives whom they have chosen shall be empowered to set forth their views on any phase of work measurement by the terms of the agreement signed with the employing company. The men's clothing industry in the United States, it may be pointed out, which, since the New York market has recently given up time work, is almost entirely on a piecework basis, exemplifies in a remarkable manner the utilization of worker opinion in the determination of piece rates. Wherever locals of the Amalgamated Clothing Workers of America, a strong organization in this field, have been established, joint action governed by well-defined rules is always taken by management and the employees' committee when rates are either being set or adjusted. The stop watch is never used in connection with time study in the clothing factories or shops except to settle points in dispute. A somewhat parallel illustration is afforded by the system of determining piecework rates in the pottery industry. In this instance the United States Pottery Association, comprising nearly all the manufacturers in the industry, has an agreement with the National Brotherhood of Operative Potters. The association has specifically acknowledged that together with itself the brotherhood shall have "equal right to a voice in wage adjustments." An interesting feature of the wage situation in the pottery industry is that while the brotherhood has stood four-square for the piecework system, the manufacturers have stated a desire that a time wage be introduced in certain departments of the trade because of the damage done to their wares by too speedy operation.

The problems that have been unfolded in this chapter with ref-

erence to incentive wage systems are not at the moment of any
particular interest to the railroads which have indorsed union-
management coöperation, as they pay their workers according to
a time wage plan. Yet owing to what the future may have in store
in connection with these problems a discussion of them has appeared advisable. Other railroads or enterprises outside the field
of rail transportation, employing incentive wage systems, may
decide to enter the coöperative movement, or a change of attitude
concerning wage payment may take place on the carriers already
committed to coöperation. In either case the principles and technique of coöperation would have to be related to the proposition
commonly enunciated by those who formulate incentive wage
systems, that the workers are to be fairly remunerated according
to their efficiency. To a large extent the responsibility under these
circumstances would be thrust upon the agencies of coöperation
of determining what standards might be set up in the arrangement of the wage plan.

As rate adjustments and time scheduling have been the leading
sources of conflict where incentive wage systems have prevailed,
the handling of these under a *régime* of coöperation should be a
good test of its ability to bring harmony in industrial relations.
In the furtherance of this test it would seem almost inevitable that
the procedure by which work operations would be measured, and
upon which rate adjustments and time scheduling depend, must
come extensively under the advisory influence of coöperative committees. Enforcement of the "equal voice" principle would doubtless be a coöperative demand at the outset. Methods of time
study would have to be introduced which, if possible, would arrive at scientific results without arousing the sensibilities of the
workers; in the establishment of these coöperative committees
might be expected to urge that psychological considerations
should have a place along with mechanical standards. How a
proper balance might be maintained between the piece rates or
time allowances set for various operations belonging to the same

class of work would also be a matter of coöperative concern.
Then to avoid difficulties in administration such as were experienced under the Grand Trunk Railway's bonus plan, an adequate
system of checking and of inspecting all work performed would
have to be devised and continued. Coöperative committees would
strongly object to interferences with the quality of work through
excessive speed. Moreover, the tendency of incentive wage systems
to displace workers would necessarily have to be tolerantly dealt
with in the stabilization of employment policy in the industry.
Special defenses would assuredly be raised through coöperative
intervention for older workmen of declining capacity with a long
record of service in the trade. Altogether, in these and in other
ways, coöperative committees would discover that they had aug-
mented duties to perform where incentive wages were paid.

## Chapter XIX

## Coöperation in Other Railroad Departments

EXTENSION of union-management coöperation to sections of its operating department other than the maintenance of equipment department was begun by the Baltimore & Ohio Railroad early in 1924. In agreement with union officials of the trades involved, the carrier had authorized the establishment of a coöperative committee for each of its operating divisions, to which should be summoned a combined representation from its department of maintenance of way and structures, and its transportation department. The setting up of divisional coöperative committees, rather than joint local committees as in the case of the mechanical department, was deemed essential because of the fact that a large percentage of administrators and workers in the department of maintenance of way and structures, and the transportation department, must travel over the road in the performance of their duties. As the new committees came into existence, representatives of the traffic department's personnel with headquarters in the division were customarily invited to the meetings, with the result that the traffic department on the railroad may be regarded as virtually under the coöperative plan.

### The Technique of Division Coöperative Committees.

NINE trade-unions, in addition to the seven shop crafts, have as a result been committed to coöperation on the Baltimore & Ohio Railroad through its extension beyond the mechanical department. These include the four train and engine service brotherhoods, independent bodies unaffiliated with the American Federation of Labor, as follows: the Grand International Brotherhood of Locomotive Engineers; the Brotherhood of Locomotive Firemen and Enginemen; the Order of Railway Conductors of America;

and the Brotherhood of Railroad Trainmen. The other five organizations, all of which are affiliated with the American Federation of Labor, are the American Train Dispatchers Association; the Order of Railroad Telegraphers; the Brotherhood of Railroad Signalmen of America; the Brotherhood of Railway and Steamship Clerks, Freight Handlers, Express and Station Employees; and the Brotherhood of Maintenance of Way Employees.

From 1924 to 1928 meetings of the division coöperative committees representing these departments were held on the railroad once a month. In the summer of 1928, when the carrier was still feeling the effects of a prolonged traffic slump, it was decided that henceforth the committees should assemble only once in every three months. The division meetings are conducted at a very much higher cost to the company than are those held in the mechanical department. Not only are the division committees as a rule considerably larger, but a portion of their members, some of whom must be absent a day or more from work, have to travel to attend. As the meetings are convened on "company time," and expense allowances are granted to members who submit them, the total cost to the railroad invariably mounts up. Most committees assemble regularly at the official headquarters of the division superintendent, which tends to systematize their work and adds to the continuity of their proceedings. Others are called to meet at varying points on the division, as in this way it is believed that the personnel of the departments concerned should have a more equal opportunity to enjoy the benefits of the coöperative movement, and the public along the carrier's lines should get a better understanding of the import of the plan. The committee on the Toledo division, for example, does not only meet at Dayton, Ohio, where the superintendent's office is located, but also at other Ohio points such as Toledo, Lima, and Hamilton. Two of these stations are 177 miles apart.

No central coöperative committee has as yet been instituted

for the various division organizations on the railroad. The general managers, however, of the eastern and western lines exercise supervision over the committees within their territory. Their policy has been to allow each committee to develop a technique suitable to operating conditions within the division. This has caused considerable differentiation between committees in the detail of technique, although on all of them coöperative principles work out in substantially the same way. No single method has been adopted of securing representation from the employees on division committees. Under a plan on the Toledo division, each workers' committeeman holds office for a period of six months, and has an alternate who attends meetings when he is absent, and succeeds to his position when he vacates it. An election of alternates is thereby required, which takes place in the committee, as a whole, a month before the committeemen relinquish office. This basis of representation allows for a rotation of committeemen from a trade, and is thought to encourage a wider diffusion of interest in coöperative matters. Alternates, too, should have gained some knowledge of the functioning of coöperation previous to their elevation to the rank of committeemen. The regular plan employed admits none but the local chairmen of the different crafts to the committee. This is patterned after the system of representation followed in the mechanical department of the carrier, and results in infrequent changes in the personnel of the workers' committeemen since local lodges are in the habit of reelecting their chairmen over extended periods.

Management, irrespective of the plan used by the workers, sends its representatives to the division meetings on the basis of departments or subdepartments. It is significant to note that, unlike the practice observed in the mechanical department, only officers of the company go to division meetings as representatives of management. Supervisors, of whom there are a large number in the department of maintenance of way and structures, though few in the transportation department, are here ranked with the workers. In this connection it may be pointed out that supervisors of track men, who comprise the bulk of employees in the department of maintenance of way and structures, have as a rule authority over a very small gang, and for purposes of coöperation are appropriately classified with the workers. Inclusion of supervisors with the workers has the advantage of establishing a more balanced representation of management and men. The list of officers eligible to be present at meetings usually increases with the extent of the division; for example, two or more train masters, road foremen, or road foremen of engines may attend from different sections of a larger division. Representation of management and men has been combined where a single committee only has been formed for the Pittsburgh and Pittsburgh terminal divisions, and in like manner for the Baltimore and Baltimore terminal divisions.

The division superintendent may be the permanent chairman of a committee, or the office may be held part time by, or allowed to rotate exclusively among, members of the workers' group of representatives. On the Toledo division the chairman is always an employee who is appointed vice-chairman when the alternates are chosen, and who then moves up to the chairmanship as they are advanced to the rank of committeemen. It may be customary to allow visitors to attend meetings who may include, besides officers, supervisors and men in the service of the company, industrial managers, and public officers. Ideas are received and registered as suggestions by division committees, in approximately the same way as by committees in the mechanical department, though no uniformity exists in their notation. Some committees have numbered suggestions consecutively since the time of their first meeting, under the heading of items or dockets, while others keep a tally of them by the month and year. The company requires that each committee shall maintain a statistical record of its proceedings which it issues with its minutes for local consideration and for the attention of staff officers of the carrier.

Twenty to forty members, as a rule, form the complement of a division coöperative committee. Among representatives of management at meetings, in addition to the superintendent and possibly an assistant superintendent, are always the division engineer, one or more train masters, and the master mechanic, divisional officers in the order named of the department of maintenance of way and structures, the transportation and the mechanical departments. Officers subordinate to the division engineer who may be present are the roadmaster and assistant roadmaster, the signal supervisor, the master carpenter, and the general foreman of the bridge and building gang. Typical transportation officers appearing at meetings are the road foreman of engines, the assistant road foreman of engines, the division operator, the inspector of fuel economy, the supervisor of locomotive operation, the smoke inspector, the car distributor, and the relief inspector. The master mechanic attends alone from the maintenance of equipment department, merely by virtue of the responsibility he has of providing effective equipment for transportation purposes. Other representatives of management may include the supervising agent, the division freight agent, the division passenger agent, the division accountant, the inspector of accounts, the division storekeeper, and the captain of police.

Employees' representatives, summoned to division coöperative meetings from the department of maintenance of way and structures, consist mainly of foremen and men belonging to the signal, track, and bridge and building forces. Train and engine service employees running on the road have one or more committeemen for each of the four groups of conductors, brakemen and switchmen, engineers, and firemen. Yard forces have representatives of the yardmasters and their clerks, and of the running and switching employees in yard service. Dispatchers, telegraph operators, station agents, depot masters, baggage agents, tallymen, platform clerks, delivery men, and station accountants are sent to represent station forces. Moreover, attendance as workers' committeemen may be allowed to freight and passenger agents, police patrolmen, and members of the physical division.

### Types of Suggestions Recorded by Division Committees.

To an extent the subjects brought up for treatment in division coöperative meetings run parallel to those discussed by committees in the mechanical department. The department of maintenance of way and structures, like the mechanical department, is a productive unit, employing a smaller and lighter assortment of machine tools than it, but proportionately more auxiliary and measuring tools. Work methods in relation to the use of tools and other equipment, therefore, should constitute an important issue in the department of maintenance of way and structures. Furthermore, practices of economy are desirable in connection with the great amount of materials needed by this department for track, roadway, and building purposes. The transportation department, on the contrary, moves persons and goods in traffic and has no productive problems. Yet it should be interested in the economic purchase of the supplies required to equip road and yard engines, revenue trains, and other forms of rolling stock for service. Then, of greater consequence for it perhaps than for the mechanical department should be questions respecting the standards for motive power and train car equipment. However, there are matters of peculiar and specific concern to the transportation department which have arisen for consideration at division coöperative meetings. These may be grouped under such headings as the economical movement of trains, including the problem of delays, fuel economy, the use of signals and lights, crossing regulations, the location of deadhead equipment, the smooth handling of trains, train orders, and communications between stations, and joint transportation arrangements with other carriers. Of particular importance to the traffic department have been questions referring to the methods of routing and billing freight shipments, the spotting of cars for industries, the reduction of freight claims, and the provision of adequate facilities for the handling of freight and the accommodation of passengers. A limited number of illustrations will now be given of the types of suggestions that have come before division coöperative meetings.

From the evidences it appears that representatives on division committees from the department of maintenance of way and structures have been slow in presenting suggestions aimed at increasing efficiency in work performance, although they sometimes have raised for discussion questions relating to tool needs and storage. Their record in introducing proposals for economy in the use of materials has on the whole been better. In answer to a very early suggestion, for example, laid before the Toledo division committee by a signal maintainer, lists have been compiled indicating the prices paid for new materials and received from the salvage of discarded materials, in order that the personnel of the department, having specific information at hand as to the value of materials, might be led to practice greater economy. Representatives of the department of maintenance of way and structures have often taken occasion in coöperative meetings to allude to the unnecessary work put on track gangs through the carelessness of workers in the transportation and traffic departments. A section gang foreman pointed out to the Indianapolis division committee, that enginemen were in the habit of cleaning their ash pans wherever they happened to stop, and that work engines, having their ash pan doors open, scattered cinders all over the switches. Similarly, complaints have been registered against the dumping of gravel and other materials in the yards as a result of the improper loading of cars, the sweeping out of refuse from cabooses and passenger coaches while crossing bridges, and derailments caused by the haste and incaution of switching crews.

Questions relating to supplies for the transportation department have been treated from a variety of angles at coöperative meetings. Attention of the committee on the Cincinnati terminal division was drawn to the fact that carbon oil was being ordered and hauled a distance of two hundred miles from the company's store at Washington, Indiana, although it was possible to secure it in the quantity desired from stores much closer at hand. When this matter had been corrected, shipments of oil became more certain, and costs of carriage were at the same time reduced. As the result of a suggestion presented to the committee of the Pittsburgh and Pittsburgh terminal divisions, a small box as a receptacle for fuses and caps has been placed over the left side of the cab arch of locomotives. Discussion arose at the coöperative meeting on the Indianapolis division concerning the manner in which supplies piled on the rear end of engine tanks were being shipped to outlying stations. At night these would sometimes form an obstruction, it was said, over which members of the engine crew were liable to fall, a chargeable defect under the rules of the Interstate Commerce Commission. In consequence, it has been decided to forward all supplies through the regular freight channels.

In the occupations of driving and manning locomotives it is natural that engineers and firemen should discover flaws in their structural standards. At the Chicago division coöperative meeting an engineer objected to the position in locomotive cabs of cylinder cock levers which interfered, he stated, with the right seat box. These levers are connected to a rod operating a small cock in the cylinder which allows accumulations of water to escape. The engineer proposed a relocation of the lever in the cab, which has been accepted as standard, and made effective on all locomotives when shopped for classified repairs. Likewise a firemen's representative on the Chicago division committee referred to the inconvenience of operating the valve which controlled the injector overflow pipe on a certain class of locomotives, as it was situated too high to the right. He advised a new position for the valve which has been adopted as a standard for this class of locomotives. An older passenger engineer on the Toledo division pointed in committee to the hazards involved in backing road engines at night without a tender light. He explained how a wire might be run from the engine cab to the rear of the tender and a serviceable light affixed to the water tank. On the basis of his suggestion experiments were later conducted at Baltimore, and a position on the tank found for a light of the proper intensity, which has become a standard for all road engines. Again, committees have sometimes asked the company to plan a change in standard where fault has been found with the mechanical performance of a locomotive or train car. Recently at a yard foreman's suggestion, the committee of the Baltimore and Baltimore terminal divisions has sought the redesign of a certain type of uncoupling lever because when cars were being cut apart the mechanism tended to bind and time was lost.

An illustration of avoiding train delay through coöperative suggestion may be furnished from the records of the Toledo division committee. The telegraph operator on the committee stated that express, mail, and baggage handlers were in the habit of putting trucks between the main tracks at the Hamilton, Ohio, station to meet a southbound passenger train when another fast northbound train was on the point of arrival. The congestion was sometimes so great that the latter train would be delayed for from five to ten minutes. This difficulty has been adjusted by explaining the result of their action to the express, mail, and baggage handlers, and by eliciting promises from the operators' staff that they would supply regular advance information concerning the arrival time of the trains in question. The Interstate Commerce Commission has published careful regulations on the watering of animals and poultry in transit on the railroads of the United States. To comply with these regulations, it was often necessary at the Brighton transportation yard, Cincinnati, Ohio, of the Baltimore & Ohio Railroad, to take these cars from the east to the west end of the yard where the water supply was located. As an efficiency measure, by laying two hundred feet of main in accordance with the suggestion of a train conductor on the division committee, a supply of water has been provided at the east end of the yard and the car haul eliminated.

Suggestions applying to lights and signals have usually had a distinctly local significance, and have often been so technical in character that only experienced railroad men could understand them. Interdepartmental difficulties concerned with problems of lights and signals have sometimes been brought for handling to division committees. An engineer on the Indianapolis division committee, for example, asked why distant signals giving information ahead of the condition of home signals were apparently not being operated by the lever man at different points on the line. This has led to an inquiry into the matter by the division engineer at which the lever men have been given an opportunity to state their case. The Baltimore and Baltimore terminal divisions' committee has recently recommended to the carrier, that in order to facilitate train movements it should adopt a standard sign which will indicate when trains leaving a siding are clear of the pull out switch.

Speakers at division coöperative meetings have frequently dealt with issues bearing on fuel economy and at times these have formed the basis of recorded suggestions. An engineer on the Chicago division committee proposed that a plate or gate chain should be applied to the bottom of tender doors to prevent coal dropping through to the floor and roadbed. Officials of the company acknowledged the merit of this suggestion but decided instead that they would instal a coal-saving device on the system which consists of a sort of hinge on each tender door with a knuckle to tighten it. When trains are being made up, the engineer must lean well from his cab window to see that the impact is not too hard against cars being coupled. Rough handling of equipment is detrimental to both freight and passenger business. Due to a coöperative suggestion presented to the committee of the Baltimore and Baltimore terminal divisions, the position of the independent brake lever has been changed in locomotives in order that the engineer may operate it, and at the same time keep a proper lookout.

The value of establishing adequate means of communication on the line, and of reporting traffic movements promptly has been reflected in many coöperative suggestions. Requests have poured in for new or additional telephone service from representatives of one department or another, but have only been granted by the company when the reasons have seemed ample. At the Toledo division meeting a committeeman representing the bridge and building force asked for the installation of a telephone at the water station repair shop so that information might be readily transmitted concerning their class of work. To satisfy these workers and to meet the situation economically arrangements have been completed by which messages for the bridge and building force shall be sent to the crew dispatcher's office and then relayed to the water station repair shop several hundred feet away. A representative of the dispatchers and operators on the Cincinnati terminal division committee explained why it would be of great advantage if two freight trains arriving from the St. Louis division were reported ahead in order that the yardmaster at Elmwood Place might have a clear track for each. He said that these trains were a long time on the road and frequently had been in danger of penalty for excess service under the terms of the federal sixteen-hour law. If the trains were placed quickly, it would be easier to escape the penalty of the law, and overtime payments would be lessened. The division superintendent has taken action to secure the economies resulting from this suggestion.

A particular problem, related to the billing of freight shipments, may be cited, which was handled by the Toledo division coöperative meeting for the freight claims prevention committee. It was customary on the division to bill through to the destination of a train all cars that were to be cut from it *en route*, but with a notation on the waybill indicating the point at which each was to be stopped off. Yard clerks or the conductor of the train, it was said, would often overlook this notation with the result that a back haul of the car would be necessary, or else its contents must be unloaded and reshipped to the stop-off point. Such errors were costly especially when *per diem* charges must be paid on "foreign cars." For several months the coöperative committee pressed for a solution of this matter, and finally officers of the company agreed to issue a form of sticker to be pasted in the upper left-hand corner of the waybill which would clearly designate that the car was to be stopped off. Attention has often been drawn in meetings to the lack of certain types of train car equipment which should be provided for shippers if their business were to be retained. Other suggestions have dealt with the stopping of trains to suit the convenience of passengers, the erection or extension of platforms for the loading and unloading of passengers, and the arrangement of proper markings and signs for their guidance. In consequence of a suggestion laid before the Baltimore and Baltimore terminal divisions' committee, protection has been given passengers crossing the platform between trailers on a local run where electricity affords the motive power. A great many suggestions recorded by division committees have also embodied requests for supplies of drinking water, toilet, locker, dressing- and lunchrooms, shelters from the weather, and other facilities of advantage to the workers.

### Should the Maintenance of Way Force Coöperate Separately?

ANY attempt to estimate the gains of coöperative effort among the managerial and worker groups represented at division meetings would encounter the same difficulties that have been described for the mechanical department. The gains, in fact, which might accrue from suggestions made by the personnel of the transportation section of the operating department and the traffic department, would be even less accurately measurable than are those from suggestions in the mechanical department, because neither of the first-named are production units. The only reward for the practice of coöperation that has been sought by the crafts whose representatives attend division meetings has been the betterment of their working conditions. Regularization of employment has never been a topic for discussion by division committees. If this question were raised, workers in the department of maintenance of way and structures would necessarily have to be placed in a different category from the train and engine service men, or traffic department employees, and accorded special treatment.

In combining the transportation department with the department of maintenance of way and structures for coöperative purposes, the Baltimore & Ohio Railroad has had in mind the close economic interdependence of these operating units. Transportation crews, it has been thought, should observe roadway needs as they travel the rails, while maintenance of way men should in turn be able to give worth-while advice on the handling of trains. When the management of the two departments also participate, real advantages should result from the exchange of views. However, the arrangement has not worked out with the measure of success hoped for, because of the paucity of suggestions presented by the maintenance of way committeemen. This has no doubt been traceable in part to the circumstance that the numerous contingent of track workers on a railroad are ordinarily drawn from the ranks of wageworkers who have had a limited opportunity for mental development. Again, the wage-earning disparity which exists between maintenance of way men as a class and the majority of workers in the transportation department has hindered whole-hearted coöperative relations. It seems probable that maintenance of way employees might be coöperatively much more active if they were to meet in separate committees with representatives of management from their own department. A wide scope would then be allowed, by the productive nature of the work done in that department, for the submission of coöperative ideas of value. Besides, its workers should have added zeal for the movement if assurances could be given them that an effort would be made to grant them more regularized employment, and that they would be awarded in some manner a fair share of coöperative gains.

The Canadian National Railway Company, which for some time had been considering the advisability of extending the coöperative movement beyond the mechanical department on its lines, decided in 1929, with the sanction of organized employees involved, to draw up a separate plan of coöperation for its department of maintenance of way and structures. This plan has not been long enough in operation to judge its value. It was formulated on the basis of a report presented by a committee, representative of the company's management and the Brotherhood of Maintenance of Way Employees, appointed to make a survey of the system. The plan provides for the erection of joint local committees on each division of the carrier, to meet once in every two months; regional committees, to meet semiannually; and a system committee, to meet once a year. Before the close of 1929, five divisional committees had been set up, and on January 28, 1930, a system committee meeting was held, at which arrangements were made to hasten the creation of regional committees and of local committees on the thirty-five remaining divisions of the road. The company and union expect a liberal submission of ideas in committee meetings with respect to economy of materials and supplies, mechanical improvements, and the betterment of working conditions. Unquestionably, too, the living conditions of track and other gangs in the department will receive a good deal of attention before committees. The company is prepared to deal with the issue of irregular employment among its maintenance of way forces, and is anxious to raise their educational standards. The problem of educating these workers is not significant in the older-established sections of Canada, but rather in the remoter parts where they are largely of alien blood and language and have an inadequate understanding of the ideals and traditions of the country.

Chapter XX

# Further Instances of Union-Management Coöperation and Its Significance on the Railroads

IN this chapter consideration will first be given to types of union-management coöperation that have already developed, or that in future may be developed, elsewhere in the transportation industry. Brief evidence will then be adduced to show the adoption of coöperative practices by various industries in America, aside from the field of transportation, to which trade-unions have been a party, and certain general conclusions will be formulated.

At the outset attention may be directed to an arrangement effective for three years in its more inclusive form on the Southern Railway System, whereby classes of workers in the carrier's transportation department received added compensation for efficiency reflected in its statistics of operation.[1] When, early in 1924, the Southern Railway Company advanced the wage scales paid to its train and engine service employees approximately 5 per cent, it contracted to grant them a bonus of 1½ per cent for 1924 and of 3 per cent for 1925 and 1926 respectively, if in each of these years the ratio of an enumerated list of operating accounts to gross revenues should not exceed the ratio established by the same accounts in 1923. In case the ratio thus ascertained should go beyond the test ratio in any year, the bonus would be reduced by the amount of the excess until it might possibly be eliminated.

The accounts, seventeen in all, prescribed for use by the Southern Railway Company in calculating the ratio, included, besides outlay for wages as increased, expenditures for purposes which efficiency might control, such as loss of and damage to freight

[1] See articles and notes in *Railway Age*, March 8, 1924, p. 554; March 14, 1925, p. 740; March 12, 1927, p. 908; and July 9, 1927, p. 73.

and baggage; fuel and supplies; clearing of wrecks; damage to live stock on the right of way; and injury to persons. The *Southern News Bulletin*, monthly organ of the company, gave information in each issue on fluctuations in the ratio in order that the workers might keep track of their achievement throughout the year. The bonus agreed upon for 1924 was easily earned as the ratio for the year stood at 20.24 which, compared with the test ratio of 21.42, showed a reduction of 1.18 per cent. Results equally good were obtained under the plan in 1925 and 1926. However, when in 1927, the Southern Railway Company like other carriers in the southeast, in consequence of a general wage movement, increased the rates paid to its conductors, trainmen, and firemen 7½ per cent, it was mutually decided by management and employees that the coöperative bonus arrangement as it affected these classes of workers should be allowed to lapse. The plan, however, is still successfully operating in the case of the locomotive engineers, who to the number of about 2,000 on the Southern Railway System are stated to have received nearly $800,000 in bonus payments during a five-year period ending in 1929.

### Terms of the Mitten-Mahon Agreement.

THE possibility that a well-known employee representation plan in the urban electric railway section of the American transportation industry may eventually develop into a form of union-management coöperation was greatly enhanced by the so-called Mitten-Mahon agreement of 1928.[2] Thomas Eugene Mitten, upon his appointment as chief executive officer of the Philadelphia Rapid Transit Company in 1911, introduced a plan of joint action for its management and men which, several times revised,

2 Cf. "Mitten-Mahon Understanding," Service Talks, Mitten Management, Inc., March 27, 1928; and *Proceedings* of the Twenty-first Convention, Amalgamated Association of Street and Electric Railway Employees of America; *The Motorman, Conductor and Motor Coach Operator*, October, 1929, pp. 29–32 and 67–68.

now applies both on that system and on the International Railway Company of Buffalo, properties owned and operated by Mitten Management, Inc. Originally Thomas E. Mitten had expected to consummate this plan with the Philadelphia local division of the Amalgamated Association of Street and Electric Railway Employees of America, but, on account of dissensions in the ranks of the division, was driven to establish it on a non-union basis. In the interval since 1911, nevertheless, stipulation has always been made that the union through its local organization might at any time be included as a party to the plan on a property under Mitten control, should two-thirds of the employees so elect by secret ballot. The plan was still non-union in character in 1928, when, owing to the fact that Mitten Management, Inc., seemed about to take over urban electric railway properties in other cities where the union was already organized, it was thought advisable that the company's purposes regarding future industrial relations on those properties should be clearly defined. Conferences were accordingly opened between Thomas E. Mitten and William D. Mahon, president of the union, which resulted in the signing of a union-management agreement on March 25. By the terms of this it was provided that the Mitten plan might be extended with but slight modifications to any newly acquired properties on which the union was organized. Then, as soon as it could be demonstrated that the plan was working just as well on the newly acquired systems as on those at Philadelphia and Buffalo, organization of the latter would become an appropriate matter for discussion. In the meantime the Mitten-Mahon agreement has remained inoperative since Mitten Management, Inc., has not added to its property holdings. Seemingly the death by accident of Thomas E. Mitten in October, 1929, has not resulted in any change in the company's attitude toward the union.

The Mitten Plan requires the formation in each department of operation on an urban electric railway system of a number of branch committees, composed of two company and two employees'

representatives, meeting whenever the occasion demands.[3] Once
in alternate months, committees for the departments are assembled, made up of all their branch committeemen. Then a general committee, selected to represent both parties on the entire
system, is convened monthly. Any question which bears on working conditions may be dealt with by a branch committee with the
right of appeal to committees higher up. Should the general committee not be able to decide an issue, it may be referred to a board
of arbitration, consisting of one representative each of the company and the employees, and one neutral member. The general
committee is empowered to fix a basic wage rate and certain wage
differentials for the system, subject to change in accordance with
fluctuations in the cost of living. A supplementary wage payment
is at present made to employees as a reward for improvements
that have occurred in the service of companies under Mitten Management, Inc., due to their coöperative effort. This is derived from
an apportionment to them of one-half of a management fee of
4 per cent taken from the gross revenues of each company after
fixed charges and a regular dividend has been paid. By the terms
of the Mitten-Mahon agreement it was arranged that, if the plan
went into effect on an organized system, all disability, old age,
and other benefits should be handled by the union, for the part
maintenance of which the employing company should pay one
dollar per month for each worker.

Under this same heading reference may be made to the fact that
since 1926 a works council with limited powers has functioned on
an organized urban electric railway property, the Pittsburgh
Railways.[4] Monthly, a large workers' delegation, members of
local division No. 85 of the Amalgamated Association of Street
and Electric Railway Employees of America, meet in joint session

[3] Cf. W. Jett Lauck, *Political and Industrial Democracy*, pp. 177–187.
[4] See P. J. McGrath, "Union-Management Co-operation on the Pittsburgh
Railways Company," *American Federationist*, December, 1927, pp. 1445–1447;
and *Electric Railway Journal*, July 2, 1927, pp. 37–38; April 21, 1928, pp.
678–679; and June 1, 1929, p. 645.

with officers and supervisors of the Pittsburgh Railways Company, and discuss with them all matters that pertain to the efficient operation of the system and their own immediate welfare. Methods of scientific research are favored by the company, and there have been many special instructions to the employees on work performance, which they evidently have been striving to carry out in token of their willingness to coöperate. Since the adoption of its coöperative policy the company's relations with the public appear to have benefited through the greater courtesy shown to passengers by its "platform men"; accidents affecting the public and employees have been lessened; important savings have been realized in consumption of electric power; and car failures have been very measurably reduced. Whereas the operating ratio of the company's electric railway services stood at 79.7 for 1926, it had dropped to 76.3 for 1927, and to 75.9 for 1928.

### Coöperation on a British Railroad.

No treatment of the subject of union-management coöperation on the railroads would appear complete unless reference were made to the particular scheme of industrial relations adopted for all its departments in the winter of 1927–28, by the London, Midland & Scottish Railway Company, the largest carrier in Great Britain.[5] The initiative in formulating a program which would allow for a degree of worker participation in the management of the London, Midland & Scottish Railway was taken by Sir Josiah Charles Stamp, its general manager and executive board chairman. This program was duly submitted to the three strong unions embracing all organized workers on British railroads: the National Union of Railwaymen; the Associated Society of Locomo-

---

[5] For an account of coöperation on this railroad see an address entitled, "Education for Responsibility," delivered by William Clower, its Chief Officer for Labour and Establishment, before the Association for Education in Industry and Commerce at University College, London, England, January 4, 1929.

tive Engineers and Firemen; and the Railway Clerks' Association, and it then crystallized into definite form after it had received their approval. About 270,000 employees of the carrier have been brought under the plan, which, though dissimilar in technique, in its main purposes resembles that in effect on American railroads. The London, Midland & Scottish Railway Company in subscribing to this coöperative arrangement believed that its workers would be bound through the medium of their joint effort with management, to acquire "a sense of increased responsibility" in the performance of their daily tasks, and "an elevated conception of the dignity of their calling." The opinion, indeed, has been officially expressed that they would have a "matured capacity" for service only when there was a "harnessing of mind and will as well as of muscle."

Preliminary to the institution of the carrier's plan for coöperative endeavor, twenty-two conferences, each representative of a different area on its lines, were held, attended by officers and supervisors of the company and the chairmen and secretaries of local union committees. At these the objects of the plan about to be introduced were expounded, and views elicited on all phases of the railroad business. It was not deemed necessary, however, to set up any new machinery of a permanent character in order to make the plan effective. Use was simply authorized of the local joint conferences, and the central conferences that had been accustomed to meet on the carrier since its incorporation and had previously met on the railroads which amalgamated to form the London, Midland & Scottish Railway Company. Nevertheless, as the plan has come into operation, the number of such conferences has been greatly increased, and their time, instead of being devoted for the most part to a consideration of grievances, is now chiefly occupied with problems relating to the more efficient handling of the company's transportation services, and the achievement of economies in the upkeep of its buildings and roadway and in the repair of train cars and locomotives in its workshops. During 1928, some 1,450 local conferences were held on the company's lines, which was three times the total assembled in the preceding year.

At the invitation of Sir Josiah C. Stamp, workers on the London, Midland & Scottish Railway have also personally been transmitting suggestions to their officers, which they have thought the company might adopt with advantage. A monetary reward has been given for suggestions that have been of real merit. The company has acknowledged a saving of many thousand pounds sterling through worth-while suggestions culled from more than eight thousand that were submitted by individual workers in 1928. Employment of the already existing conference machinery to attain the objects of the plan, notwithstanding the fact that it has involved a continuous interspersion of coöperative issues with those concerning working agreements, has borne quite satisfactory results according to the testimony of both company and trade-union officials.

It may be pointed out that the plan on the London, Midland & Scottish Railway is but one of the more important schemes for coöperative management that have been introduced in Great Britain, especially since the publication of the Whitley reports, to which reference was made in chapter i. Contrary to what was originally intended, however, the Whitley plan took from the first its firmest root among the less highly organized industries of Great Britain, largely because the trade-unions were prone to distrust the employers, and because they feared through participation a loss of bargaining power. But added impetus toward forms of union-management coöperation in Great Britain should be given by the successful outcome of the recent Mond-Turner conferences.[6] At its 1927 sessions in Edinburgh, Scotland, the

6 Cf. G. D. H. Cole, "The Trade Unions and the 'Mond' Report," *The New Statesman,* September 1, 1928, pp. 629–631; Major L. Urwick, "Rationalization, Europe's New Industrial Philosophy," *Factory and Industrial Management,* January, 1929, pp. 38–40; and Ben M. and Sylvia K. Selekman, *British Industry To-day,* pp. 213–263.

British Trades Union Congress, recognizing the woeful economic
effects of the general strike of 1926, favored a constructive interchange of views with employers to bring about, so far as possible,
an increase in industrial efficiency. Within a few months thereafter Sir Alfred Mond, since raised to the peerage as the first
Baron Melchett, heading a powerful group of twenty-four employers, opened negotiations with the general council of the congress, seeking the coöperative assistance of organized labor for
the advancement of the country's industries. The majority of the
general council approved of the employers' ideas on "rationalization," a word which, since it was first coined during the international economic conference at Geneva in 1927, has been used
to refer in general to any "application of the methods and standards of science" to the solution of industrial problems. The
Trades Union Congress, when it met at Swansea, England, in
September, 1928, ratified the stand taken by the majority of its
general council throughout the Mond-Turner negotiations.

### Coöperative Practices in the Clothing Trades.

PREËMINENTLY illustrative of the functioning of union-management coöperation among non-transportation industries in America have been the agencies for joint dealing set up in establishments devoted to the manufacture of men's and women's
clothing. Here coöperation has been combined with a highly
methodized form of collective bargaining with, particularly in
the men's clothing industry, a form of voluntary arbitration at
its apex. Conditions of work in the men's garment trade, in fact,
have tended to be determined according to well-defined systems
of judicial administration, which make ample provision for ap-
pellate jurisdiction and are developing a continuously enlarging
code of rules for practice based on precedent. In this trade, the
Amalgamated Clothing Workers of America, strongest numerically of the needle-craft unions, has for years been ambitious that
its membership should acquire an increasing share of managerial

responsibility, and has been led, it is admitted, by the trend of events to concern itself more and more with "the engineering of the industry."[7] So carefully has this union developed its facilities for observation within the industry, that its representatives are in a position to furnish an expert opinion on almost any problem that may arise affecting the production or sale of men's clothing. On the whole its coöperative relations with the manufacturers have borne most fruitful results in the Chicago, Rochester, and Cincinnati markets, although its policies in this regard have been reasonably uniform at all garment trade centers. Through lack of space details of coöperative activities in the men's clothing industry will be furnished only for the Chicago and Cincinnati markets.

Employment conditions in the men's clothing establishments of Chicago where labor is unionized are mainly fixed at present by two trade agreements.[8] One agreement, signed originally by Hart, Schaffner & Marx in 1911 with a local of the United Garment Workers of America was in 1913 continued, and subsequently at intervals has been renewed, by the company with representatives of the Amalgamated Clothing Workers of America, after that union had become dominant in its plant. The other agreement, varying little as to its terms, was drawn up with the Amalgamated's representatives in 1922 by an important employer group, the Chicago Industrial Federation of Clothing Manufacturers. Both agreements provide that for each shop or floor in a plant, an accredited chairman shall be appointed to represent the union who shall handle all disputes and organization matters in its name, and, together with the ranking officer of the company, take a lead in developing and maintaining a spirit of industrial amity. Matters that cannot be adjusted in the shop are taken to an informal committee of mediation, made up of one or more deputies from each side. If this committee after an investiga-

[7] *Advance*, May 13, 1927, p. 7.

[8] See *Documentary History of the Amalgamated Clothing Workers of America*, 1920–22, pp. 136–143.

tion is not able to arrive at a settlement, it then certifies the case
to a trade board with a detailed statement of the facts. The trade
board, though it may be increased in size should the occasion demand, regularly consists of but one person, an impartial chairman, who has been selected with the approval of both parties. It
is thought essential that this chairman shall be capable of passing
judgment on all questions of a technical nature affecting the industry. An appeal, however, may be carried from a decision of
the trade board by either party, within ten days, to a board of
arbitration which likewise is composed of an impartial chairman,
but may be enlarged to three members. The verdict rendered by
the board of arbitration is always final.

The judicial procedure by means of which issues are dealt with
in the Chicago market has, it is claimed, through the elimination
of much needless friction between management and workers, given
evidence of the existence of a real spirit of coöperation and
brought tangible economic advantages to the industry.[9] A large
percentage of difficulties has been quietly settled in the individual
shops; many decisions of scientific value have been handed down
by the trade boards; care has been taken to employ arbitration
only as a last resort; and the strike weapon has fallen entirely
into disuse. Production is highly diversified in the Chicago market, and the many changes in style, selling methods, and price
quotations that have occurred everywhere in the men's clothing
industry since 1920 have created for the Chicago manufacturers
especially serious problems of readjustment. In spite of the effect
of these changes and of occasional periods of depression in the
trade, a generally healthy state of business has been maintained
in the Chicago market, which, it is urged, has been in large
measure due to the coöperative assistance given to management
by the union, as readjustments have become necessary. Representatives of the union have helped in the reorganization of shops
and in the introduction of new machine processes; they have

[9] *Ibid.*, 1926–28, pp. 10–15.

pointed out ways by which shops might be more economically managed as a result of experiments conducted under union authority; they have supplied the manufacturers with data relating to the technically exact and salable construction of garments; they have suggested new "lines" of output to augment a company's total volume of business; and they have even ventured ideas on the prices at which garments might be most profitably sold.

Specific advantages have emerged for the workers in consequence of the participation in industrial control allowed them by the Chicago agreements. Piecework rates in the trade are fixed and adjusted by a price committee upon which management and employees have each a representative. The employees' representative on the committee is chosen from among a group of union members, who, through study and experience, have become adept in helping to set rates. If this committee cannot decide upon a rate, the issue is then carried to the trade board. Union members, besides, are accorded "preference" when new workers are being hired or the force reduced; safeguards against unreasonable discharge have been erected for them under the machinery of administration; and the clothing manufacturers have made regular use of the union's employment exchange in filling vacancies in their shops. In 1923, a voluntary unemployment insurance fund was established at Chicago, to the maintenance of which the workers now contribute 3 per cent of their earnings and the employers a like amount.[10] From this, benefits equal to 30 per cent of full-time wages, not to exceed the sum of $15 a week, are paid to workers laid off or on short time employment, for a maximum period of five weeks in the insurance year. At Rochester, where arbitral machinery is also very effective and coöperation thriving, an unemployment insurance fund on similar lines was inaugurated by agreement between the Clothiers' Exchange and the Joint Board of the union in 1928.[11]

10 See *Documentary History of the Amalgamated Clothing Workers of America*, 1926–28, pp. 21–24.
11 *Ibid.*, p. 19.

Although of only a few years' growth, union-management co-operation is already quite virile in the men's clothing industry at Cincinnati, especially in the factories of the A. Nash Company. Prior to 1926, the Cincinnati market was conceded to be mainly nonunion territory. In a leading position among the city's nonunion clothing establishments at this time was the A. Nash Company, between whose management and workers an informal type of coöperation had sprung up in answer to the appeal of its founder and president, the late Arthur Nash, that the Golden Rule should be observed in all industrial practices.[12] But, as his policies brought him publicity throughout the country as a successful "open shopper," Arthur Nash was displeased at the fact that the hostility of organized labor was therefore aroused against him. The manner in which, on December 8, 1925, he gathered together all employees of the A. Nash Company, and dramatically asked them to join the Amalgamated Clothing Workers of America was the subject of many widely read news items of the day. During the less than two years that then elapsed between the workers' acceptance of his plea and his death on October 30, 1927, Arthur Nash is recorded to have given the union increasing responsibility "for planning and administering improvements in his shops" and to have completed arrangements for the inclusion of a workers' representative on the company's board of management.[13] Under coöperation in the Nash factories the workers have taken joint action with management to determine the quality and construction of garments, to remove work from outside contract shops to inside shops belonging to the company, and to effect an entire reorganization of one of the company's subsidiary plants.

The only wide-reaching attempt to introduce machinery for

[12] Cf. Robert Littell, "Golden Rule Nash," *The New Republic,* March 10, 1926, pp. 63–65.

[13] See *Documentary History of the Amalgamated Clothing Workers of America,* 1926–28, pp. 47–48; also, Robert W. Bruère, "Golden Rule through Union Eyes," *Survey,* May 1, 1927, pp. 148–150.

coöperative control in the women's clothing industry is now a
matter of purely historic interest and may be treated briefly.
From 1910 to 1918 certain distinctive trade agreements, known
as protocols, aimed at establishing peace in the industry, were in
effect between joint boards of the International Ladies' Garment
Workers' Union and clothing manufacturers' associations, more
notably in New York, Philadelphia, and Boston.[14] One form of
these, exemplified by an agreement in the New York cloak and
suit trade, advocated the principle of joint responsibility and
control in industrial relations, and the use primarily of methods
of conciliation for the settlement of disputes. Apparently neither
management nor workers at the time, however, were ready for the
type of industrial democracy involved, as the former disliked
giving up the paternalistic attitude they had long maintained in
their plants, and too many of the latter regarded the agreements
as committing them to a hateful "class collaboration." Another
form of protocol, employed in the dress and waist trade, stressed
the value of standardizing working conditions and systems of
production, and of settling basic issues in dispute by means of
arbitration. But this did not suit employers in the trade who
considered strategy more useful in furthering their business success than science, or workers who trusted more to astute bargaining and force to attain their ends, than the fixing of standards.
Nevertheless, before their collapse in the war period, the protocols
had unquestionably bettered the workers' position in the women's
garment trades, since they had gained for them the respect of management in what had been "a despised immigrant industry," had
brought them up-to-date shop appliances to make work easier,
had resulted in carefully devised standards of safety and sanitation, and had established fairer methods of determining wage
scales. The employers had meantime been freed from the strike
menace and had seen the industry in which their interests lay, so

14 Cf. Louis Levine, *The Women's Garment Workers,* especially pp. 196–207,
218–232, and 292–319.

often formerly an object of censure, become an object of public approval.

During the years when the protocols flourished at various centers, organization of the women's garment trades was practically nonexistent in the Cleveland market. Prominent Cleveland manufacturers took occasion throughout this era to develop plans of employee representation for their establishments, seeking at the same time to give effect to the principles of scientific management in connection with shop operations, and to provide their forces with steadier work. This was the situation when events occurring toward the end of the war led the manufacturers to modify their attitude of opposition to the Ladies' Garment Workers' Union, and eventually on December 24, 1919, to sign with its local board a continuing agreement by the terms of which the so-called "Cleveland Plan"[15] of coöperative management came into being, the most advanced yet set up in the women's garment trades. The parties to the agreement signified their intention to apply the "principles of true efficiency" to their industrial practices, stating that "coöperation and mutual helpfulness" were essential to the existence of right relations between them. Under this plan, trade difficulties are first handled by conciliation, but may finally go for arbitral settlement to a board of referees of three members mutually chosen to represent the public interest. In 1921 scientific production standards were instituted in the Cleveland manufacturers' shops subject to the control of a joint committee which has an engineer as its chairman. The board of referees sets wage scales once a year which must, it is understood, "have due regard to the productive value of the individual worker based on fair and accurate standards." A significant feature of the plan has been the manufacturers' guaranty that each worker shall be given at least forty weeks' employment in the year, or else receive pay at the rate of 50 per cent of his minimum wages from a fund to which the manufacturers make regular contributions.

[15] *Ibid.*, pp. 360–381.

*Coöperation in Other Organized Trades.*

THE textile industry in the United States and Canada, which from the point of view of the aggregate number it employs is but scantily organized, provides certain good examples of coöperative endeavor. The chief labor organization in this industry is the United Textile Workers of America, with which in a position of semiautonomy is affiliated the American Federation of Full Fashioned Hosiery Workers. The latter body, embracing in its thirty-odd locals mostly youthful workers of American birth, has officially pledged itself "to encourage capacity production"[16] and to obligate its membership to render "quality service" in return for management's acknowledgment of it as a constructive force in the trade and the award of favorable working conditions. In collaborating with management it has stressed the importance of taking steps to eliminate waste, to remove imperfections in production, and to make whatever adjustments may be thought necessary to advance the economic welfare of the employing company under a competitive *régime*. In the cotton goods section of the textile industry highly beneficial results are stated to have accrued from a formal coöperative agreement drawn up with its three thousand workers in 1927 by the Naumkeag Steam Cotton Company, of Salem, Massachusetts.[17] Here, by joint arrangement between management and the employees enrolled as members of the United Textile Workers of America, a technical engineer with extensive supervisory powers has been appointed for the company's plant. On the understanding that they shall be regularly consulted in the setting up of standards, the workers have shown a readiness to help forward all improvements in processing methods. Particular care has been given to the scientific application in the company's plant of what is termed the "stretch out," that is, the limit to which workers may be assigned to tend

[16] Gustave Geiges, "Full Fashioned Hosiery Industry," *American Federationist,* June, 1927, pp. 668–675.

[17] Cf. "Naumkeag's Story," *The Survey,* January 15, 1930, p. 466.

machine units performing continuous operations. In the event of the outbreak of a major dispute, the employees have agreed never to interrupt production until a period of at least sixty days, during which conferences on the issue may be held, has elapsed. Management on its part has covenanted to pay relatively high wages and to grant as regular employment as trade conditions will allow.

Assumption of responsibility for productive efficiency on a basis of coöperation with employing companies is also a very definite policy of the Upholsterers' International Union of North America.[18] This organization with jurisdiction in the upholstered furniture, cushion, mattress, and allied trades, has declared it to be the duty of its members constantly to report and to propose remedies for deficiencies found in the operation of the company's machines and shop appliances, and to lend their aid in expelling all other hindrances to production. Management in establishments where the Upholsterers' International Union is organized, is accustomed to receiving suggestions from its local shop committees with reference to methods of plant operation, quantity of output and quality of workmanship, and the details of apprentice training. In some instances management has been willing to intrust the distribution of work throughout the shop to a union member.

Representative of a specialized form of union-management coöperation is the newspaper engineering service conducted for the mutual advantage of publishers and its own rank and file by the International Printing Pressmen and Assistants' Union.[19] Through the agency of this, coöperative arrangement is made between management in the mechanical sections of newspaper

[18] Cf. William Kohn, "Co-operation As We Practice It," *American Federationist,* December, 1926, pp. 1452–1456.

[19] Cf. George L. Berry, "Printing Pressmen's Engineering Department," *American Federationist,* August, 1925, pp. 658–659; and William H. McHugh, "Pressmen's Engineering Service," *American Federationist,* June, 1927, pp. 676–678.

plants and the union, whereby facilities are provided for locating defects in the workmanship and appearance of copies of newspapers. Issues of the same publication for a number of days in succession, as received at the union's head office, are examined for faults by skilled men in the employ of the union, and recommendations for their removal submitted to the mechanical chiefs of the newspaper company. It is claimed that the union seeks only to establish facts in discovering defects, and accordingly is impartial in blaming workers, supervision, machine processing, or printing materials for their occurrence. Furthermore, it systematically checks up on its members when faulty production or carelessness of any kind has been charged against them. On the average, copies of five hundred newspapers have reached the union's head office for examination each day. Besides, it offers to assist with expert opinion any publishing company that is opening a new plant, installing new equipment, or repairing or generally overhauling old equipment. Whenever plant changes are under way, its local membership is bound to give management every assistance in keeping publication at a normal level. In recognition of the value of its engineering service, the union expects the newspaper companies using it to accord the pressmen in their employ the best possible working conditions.

For more than forty years the lignite and other coal-producing areas of the state of Colorado have been the scene of intermittent, bitter strife between mine operators and their employees. Toward the close of a violent strike which raged in the Colorado fields from November, 1927, until early in 1928, the Rocky Mountain Fuel Company, largest operator in the northern section of the state, decided to seek the aid of its employees in an endeavor to place industrial relations at its various mines on a new and sounder footing.[20] The company's policy achieved definite form when, in March, 1928, a controlling interest in its stock was ob-

---

[20] Josephine Roche, "Miners and Men," *The Survey*, December 15, 1928, pp. 341–344.

tained by Josephine Roche, an experienced social worker, and shortly thereafter Merle D. Vincent was appointed as its president and general manager. Extended negotiations were opened with District No. 15 of the United Mine Workers of America, with which as a result a labor contract was signed on August 16, 1928, embodying in addition to a wage scale agreement certain provisions of coöperative import. Company and miners' representatives mutually undertook "to substitute reason for violence, confidence for misunderstanding, integrity and good faith for dishonest practices, and a union of effort for the chaos of the present economic welfare." A basic time wage rate of $7.00 per day was set for the company's men which was twenty-three cents a day above the rate paid by other operators. To insure improved working conditions, a department of medicine, health, and sanitation was soon erected, to be administered by a commission of one employees' representative from each mine and an equal number of company officials. According to the company's records quite impressive results were attained under its coöperative plan during 1929. As compared with 1928, production at its mines advanced in 1929 more than seven-tenths of a ton per man per day. Whereas on the average its working force had been given only 178 days' employment in 1928, they were active 216 days in 1929. Moreover the average amount paid to all its employees in 1929 was $2,104.30, which was $443.29 above the average earnings of the preceding year. In May, 1929, the Industrial Commission of Colorado after a hearing ordered that a similar plan might be established at the Centennial mine of the Boulder Valley Coal Company.[21]

Joint international industrial councils, equally representative of organized labor and management, and having in each case basic coöperative aims, exist today in two important groupings of American trades. One of these, the National Council on Industrial Relations for the Electrical Construction Industry of the United

[21] Cf. *Monthly Labor Review,* June, 1929, pp. 180–182.

States and Canada,[22] formed in 1919, and composed of five employers' representatives and five representatives of the International Brotherhood of Electrical Workers, has as its primary purpose the searching out and removal of causes of friction and dispute within the area under its jurisdiction. On the other hand, in so far as debatable issues are carried to it for settlement, it is guided by "knowledge founded on research" in arriving at its decisions, and apparently is erecting by stages a "body of organic law" for the electrical construction industry. It has drawn up and recommended for use by local companies and their employees, a standard form of trade agreement; has stood for the rigid inspection of electrical work in the public interest; and, as a spur to craftsmanship, has favored the payment of wage rates to electrical workers sufficient to afford them "the enjoyment of proper social conditions." Another body, the International Joint Conference Council, also set up in 1919, functions for employers' associations and all craft unions, except that of the photo-engravers and lithographers, in the closed shop division of the book, periodical, and job printing trades.[23] This council has sought at its bimonthly meetings, where the employed and employing groups have each four representatives, to deal with problems of vital concern to both parties and to encourage a spirit of mutual respect and good will between them. It has succeeded in standardizing apprenticeship regulations for the closed shop division of the trades involved, it has instituted a pattern agreement for local contractual relations, and has endeavored to obtain the acceptance of a scientifically devised cost accounting system by employing companies. As a court of voluntary arbitration, however, it has not proved as serviceable as was expected, largely

[22] See Louis K. Comstock, "Joint and National Counseling in the Electrical Construction Industry," *Proceedings of the Academy of Political Science,* IX (1920–22), 613–623; also, Charles P. Ford, "Arbitral Procedure for Electrical Builders," *American Federationist,* February, 1927, pp. 178–181.

[23] See F. A. Silcox, "Standardization and Co-operation in the Printing Industry," *Proceedings of the Academy of Political Science,* IX (1920–22), 584–598.

because of recurring manifestations of local independence quite characteristic of the printing industry. Did space allow, an account might be given of interesting forms of union-management coöperation that also have been instituted in the cloth hat and cap, tapestry, carpet weaving, and glass bottle industries,[24] and in the longshoremen's trade.[25]

### General Results of Coöperation on American Railroads.

EVEN though at this writing union-management coöperation has had an opportunity for seven years to demonstrate its effectiveness on American carriers, it can scarcely be claimed that the time has arrived when anything like a verdict on it may be given. The brief evaluation submitted, of certain mental and material results attributable to the movement, is intended to be merely provisional. Since coöperation of the type existing on American railroads has been shown to be dependent for its success upon the attainment of a right attitude of mind both by administrators and workers, due weight must necessarily be attached to the views of the psychologists in any appraisal of its non-material accomplishments. Psychological investigators insist that most human beings possess a "creative impulse," or, as it has otherwise been termed, a "contriving impulse" which, despite the fact that it may be submerged or undeveloped at the moment, will appear when circumstances permit. In a recently published book[26] on problems of industrial psychology three leading influences are mentioned as tending to hinder the development of this impulse among wage earners. In the first place it is stated that under modern systems of mass or large-scale production, the identifica-

24 See Florence E. Parker, "Beneficial Activities of American Trade-Unions," Bulletin No. 465, *United States Bureau of Labor Statistics,* pp. 163–164.

25 Cf. Simon P. O'Brien, "Longshoremen Stabilize Their Jobs," *American Federationist,* May, 1927, pp. 573–574.

26 Charles S. Myers, ed. *Industrial Psychology.* Refer particularly to chap. ii, written by J. Drever, entitled, "The Human Factor in Industrial Relations."

tion of the worker's self with the article which he helps to fabri-
cate is at best exceedingly difficult. In such circumstances, the
individual worker's impulse to create must lie more or less dormant unless a group spirit emerges at his place of employment
which allows him, as a member of the group, to feel a proprietor-
ship in the product. A second factor said to interfere with the
worker's impulse to create, is lack of security in the tenure of
employment. When employment is irregular, workers, it is contended, become dispirited, and the urge to have something grow
under their hands is weakened. Thirdly, any source of irritation
in working conditions, no matter what it may be, will generally
have a counteracting effect on the "contriving impulse."

It is the view of psychologists that the more freely industrial
workers are able to exercise their impulse to create, the greater
the degree of satisfaction and contentment they will have in the
performance of their tasks. Economists would naturally add that
this state of mind should increase the workers' capacity to produce. With respect to the two last-named factors affecting the
impulse to create, it is clear that the accomplishments of union-
management coöperation have been of real value to railroad
workers. Its policy of regularizing employment has given them a
sense of occupational security unknown before, and for that
reason, it may be believed, has afforded a new and important
stimulus to their contriving instincts. Again, enough concrete evidence has been furnished in preceding chapters to indicate that
much occasion for friction on the railroads has been removed
through coöperative agency. In this connection, it may logically
be argued that the impulse to create must have been quickened
among administrators as well as in the ranks of labor whenever
industrial relations have grown more harmonious.

It is problematical how far union-management coöperation
may be credited with having fostered a group spirit among administrators and workers on the railroads, viewed as separate or
combined units of the force engaged in a related series of opera-

tions. It is true that in a manufacturing department of the railroads such as the mechanical department, administrators and workers may still largely identify themselves with the product; yet to do this becomes increasingly harder as processes continue to be subdivided both at motive power and train car repair stations. Hence the need for developments of the group spirit in the mechanical department, if administrators and men are to have a consciousness of the worth of their individual contributions to production. Unless this consciousness exists, the "creative impulse" will languish. Undeniably, a good many examples might be cited of impressive manifestations of the group spirit in the mechanical or other departments of the carriers pledged to coöperation, which have had their influence in shaping creative desires. On the other hand, it is the writer's opinion that too often, at a local repair point or on a transportation division, coöperation has only succeeded in bestowing the group conception upon the limited few, whereas the remainder in their rôle of producers, or in their performance of transportation services, have been left with little thought beyond their immediate surroundings. More intensive inculcation of aims and methods both among administrators and workers participating in the movement seems to be essential if the potentialities of the group spirit are to be appropriately realized. All things considered, however, the belief may be expressed that on the important, psychological test of a stimulation of the impulse to create, union-management coöperation has shown progressively favorable results in the railroad industry. Judged by other psychological tests, its record would probably be found to be equally favorable.

In consequence of its functioning through the special suggestion-technique that it has set up, and in the daily procedure of business, union-management coöperation has admittedly brought material gains to the carrier properties indorsing it. The difficulties that confront the accurate measurement of these gains have been dealt with elsewhere. Indeed, until a yardstick to estimate co-

operative gains has been agreed upon, the question of their volume
on any railroad must remain almost entirely in the realm of
speculation. It is hoped that from a perusal of chapters x–xiii inclusive, and of chapter xix, the reader will have been able to
form an opinion of the economic significance of these gains. A
study of the array of typical suggestions given in chapters x–xii
will have indicated the fact that the most of them have been of
the commonplace order and only a few of exceptional value. Still
it may be argued that it is through the accumulation at regular
intervals of a mass of less noteworthy suggestions that the accomplishments of local coöperation may best be judged. The adding together of the many, smaller-sized gains resulting from suggestions of such a character generally brings a commendable
aggregate of savings which are always more meaningful if they
have been the outcome of a wide extension of coöperative effort.

An almost similar verdict may be arrived at with respect to
the gains which coöperation has provided in the everyday conduct of the business of transportation. While, as has been shown
in chapter xiv, management and men have sometimes been united
to perform extraordinary services for the company through the
creation of a high morale traceable to coöperation, it is rather
by the effect of that spirit in dispatching routine work according
to uniform and continuing standards of efficiency, that the benefits of coöperation may best be estimated. Often, as was pointed
out in chapter ix, the task of first introducing union-management
coöperation on the railroads was made onerous by the suspicions
and craft narrowness of the workers, and management's skepti-
cism and unwillingness to share authority. Once this period, however, has passed, the movement has usually flourished with unin-
terrupted success for several years. The newness of the appeal
has supplied incentives that have not quickly died down, and because at the outset many industrial adjustments have been found
necessary, suggestions have tended to flow into coöperative meetings. But, invariably on roads where the plan has been long

enough in effect, a time is reached when interest begins to flag, and the list of suggestions gradually diminishes. Faith in coöperation under these circumstances is bound to be subjected to a crucial test. A considerable proportion of repair stations and transportation divisions where coöperation is practiced are now in this trying stage of experience. Whenever the movement arrives at this point, the only antidote seems to be a steady reaffirmation of coöperative principles. At the same time interest in the movement should revive, if both management and workers keep in mind the fact that, even though suggestions grow fewer in number, their regular and thoughtful presentation should still net gains worthy of the effort, and the very essence of the coöperative spirit is reflected in the day-by-day performance of quality work.

Apparently no good reason exists why the technique of union-management coöperation on the railroads should not be tested out, and with some modification be found applicable in other sections of the field of transportation and in various non-transportation industries. Railroad shops with their productive equipment may be regarded as factories of a kind, so that the technique of coöperation which suits them might be fitted to almost any factory condition. Ostensibly the technique would have to be scaled down in those numerous industries in which only one or two unions would be involved in the movement. Yet as many as six organized crafts might associate with management to put it into effect in a printing trade establishment. In any case, meetings might be held and suggestions received and registered on basically the same lines as now obtain on the railroads. Where large-scale factories are common and departmental interests are strong as, for example, in the boot and shoe industry, it would perhaps be desirable that a committee should be chosen for each department and a central committee for the plant as a whole. Or, where production is stepped up from plant to plant under a system of unified management, each plant might have a committee of its own, and a central committee be established for the entire organization. It is hard to predict what reception would be accorded the technique of coöperation at present functioning on the railroads, if it were introduced in the coal-mining, metal-mining, or possibly other extractive industries. Any agency that would be capable of strengthening morale, improving methods of production, and grappling with a serious problem of intermittent employment in the bituminous section of the coal-mining industry would confer distinct advantages, not only on operating companies and their workers, but also on the coal-buying public. In 1927 the building industry was deprived of a certain specialized form of coöperation on a wide basis when, mainly as the result of an unending dispute between two unions, the National Board for Jurisdictional Awards in the Building Industry was dissolved. A clear field has since been offered for the introduction of a plan of union-management coöperation in this industry, where seasonal unemployment is every year the cause of a great waste of labor power. A comprehensive application to the building industry of the technique of coöperation followed on the railroads would require a close and detailed study of the situation, as the building industry is predominantly small scale in its operations and its workers are organized into from twenty to thirty different trade-unions. It is hoped that the data supplied and views expressed in these pages will be of some interpretive value to employing companies and employees who may desire to establish their industrial relations on a more effective and mutually helpful foundation.

# Index

Decision No. 1036, R. R. Labor Board, reduced shopmen's wages 5–9 cents an hour, 76.

Dennison, Henry S., 117.

Division No. 4., Railway Employees' Department. Created, 55; agreement with Railway Association of Canada, 55–56, 59, 240; indorsed principle of coöperation, 1924, 94–95; national status, 104–105; unions embraced under, 105; represented on system committee, C. N. Ry. System, 114; agreed to forty-hour week before force reduction, 217; told of vacations with pay at 1928 convention, 248–249.

Duluth, Winnipeg & Pacific Railway Co., 6.

Electrical Workers, International Brotherhood of, 48, 308.

Employee representation. Plans developed in America, 3; "company union" on G. T. Ry. System, 55; P. R. R. adopted "company union" idea, 74; "company unions" on roads where strike lost, 78, 90–91; welfare plan at Commonwealth Steel Works, 99; attitudes of management, 116–120; views of organized labor on "company unions," 122–123.

Erie Railroad, 81, 196.

Firemen, Oilers, Helpers, Roundhouse and Railroad Shop Laborers, International Brotherhood of, 48; negotiates apart from shop crafts, 48–49; jurisdiction in mechanical department, 58; joined federated crafts in 1922 strike, 76; extent under coöperation, 104–105.

Fullerton, C. N., 253 n, 253–254, 255.

Full Fashioned Hosiery Workers, American Federation of, 304.

Gains, fair sharing of coöperative; little affected by stabilization, 233–235; dependent on company's surplus returns from coöperation, 235–238; could take form of addition to wages, 238–241; must be related to carrier's financial position, 241–246; could take form of payment apart from wages, 242, 246; operating statistics as basis for, 246–248; application of vacations with pay on C. N. Ry. System, 248–249; and restored overtime rule on B. & O. R. R., 249.

Gains, measurement of coöperative; dangers involved, 199; chiefly based on economy in disbursements, 200–201; in cases where suggestion benefits calculable, 201–205; where benefits hard to estimate, 205–209; futile in cases of improvement in morale, 209–210; conclusions, 211–212.

Garden, J. C., 266.

General Order No. 8, R. R. Administration, 49–50, 68.

General Order No. 27, R. R. Administration; began wage up trend, 1918, 66. Supplement No. 4 thereto raised shopmen's wages, 66; legalized rules objectionable to executives, 71; and protested by pieceworkers, 270.

Gillick, J. T., 119.

Gompers, Samuel, 8.

Grand Trunk Pacific Railway Co., 92.

Grand Trunk Railway Co. Agreement with shop crafts, 1922, 54; had "company union," 55; reaffirmed 1922 agreement in 1923, 55; divided between two regions of C. N. Ry. System, 92; bonus plan, 93–94, 266–269, 275.

*Labor Management and Production,* 8.

Ladies' Garment Workers' Union, International, 302–303.

—Locomotive Engineers and Firemen, Associated Society of, 294–295.

Locomotive Engineers, Grand International Brotherhood of, 276.

—Locomotive Firemen and Enginemen, Brotherhood of, 276.

Locomotive Inspection. Act of Congress established, 1911, 15; amendment of 1915, 15; amendment of 1924, 15; administration of inspection, 15–16; inspection codes issued by I. C. Com., 16–17; regulations exemplified, 17–19, 20; statistics show decline of hazards, 21; results on roads indorsing coöperation, 189–190.

London, Midland & Scottish Railway Co., 294–296.

Machinists, International Association of, 48; nurturing ground of coöperation, 80; chief advocate of, 1920–22, 84; helped on B. & O. R. R., 87.

Mahon, William D., 292.

Maintenance of equipment department. Section of operating department, 4–5; its work an economic necessity, 10–12; effect of interchange of traffic rules, 13; legal compulsion to maintain equipment, 13, 14–24.

Train car repairs: running, 26–27; light, 27; heavy, 28; car shop facilities, 28–29; application of spot system, 31–34. Motive power repairs: classified and unclassified, 29; at enginehouses, 30; at back and locomotive repair shops, 30–31; application of spot system, 34–35.

Officers and supervisors: powers of staff officers, 36–37; control of industrial relations, 37–38; powers of line officers, 38–40; duties of supervisors, 40–41. Worker types: I. C. Com. worker-classification rules, 41–42; carmen and other workers on train cars, 42–44; machinists, 44–45; boiler makers, 45–46; blacksmiths, 46; sheet metal workers, 46; electricians, 46–47; other motive power workers, 47.

Labor organization: local lodge of mechanical crafts, 49; regular and helper apprentices, 50; craft "grievance" committee, 50–51; federated shop committee, 51; system craft organization, 51–52; system federation, 52–53; the system agreement, 53–55; Division No. 4's agreement, 55–56; trade jurisdiction, 56–58; rules of seniority, 58–60; standard wages and differentials, 60–61.

Maintenance of way and structures, department of, does structural work for maintenance department, 149.

Maintenance of Way Employees, Brotherhood of; jurisdiction in mechanical department, 58; indorsed coöperation on B. & O. R. R., 277; and on C. N. Ry. System, 289.

McAdoo, William G.; made Director General of Railroads, 49; advanced helpers to be mechanics, 49–50; issued General Order No. 27 and Supplement No. 4, 1918, 66; authorized discarding of piecework, 67; stipulated no discrimination against union members, 68; appointed committee to frame shop crafts' national agreement, 68; letter asking more effective transportation policies, 79; appointed Railroad Wage Commission, 79; noted betterment of morale in 1918, 80.

McClelland, J. A., 93–94.

Melchett, Baron; *see* Mond, Sir Alfred.

Mitten-Mahon agreement, 291–293.